ABOUT THE AUTHOR

BARBARA FINLAY is Professor of Sociology at Texas A&M University,
specializing in women's rights. She also directs the Women's Studies
Program at the University.

GEORGE W. BUSH AND THE WAR ON WOMEN

Turning Back the Clock on Women's Progress

BARBARA FINLAY

ZED BOOKS
London & New York

George W. Bush and the War on Women was published in 2006
by Zed Books Ltd, 7 Cynthia Street, London N1 9JF, UK,
and Room 400, 175 Fifth Avenue, New York, NY 10010, USA

www.zedbooks.co.uk

Designed and typeset in Monotype Garamond
by illuminati, Grosmont, www.illuminatibooks.co.uk
Cover designed by Andrew Corbett
Printed and bound in Malta by Gutenberg Press Ltd

Distributed in the USA exclusively by Palgrave Macmillan, a division of
St Martin's Press, LLC, 175 Fifth Avenue, New York, NY 10010

A catalogue record for this book is available from the British Library
Library of Congress Cataloging-in-Publication Data available

ISBN 1 84277 784 X Hb
ISBN 1 84277 785 8 Pb
ISBN 978 1 84277 784 8 Hb
ISBN 978 1 84277 785 5 Pb

#67392906

CONTENTS

To the women everywhere
who are seeking an alternative to war and violence,
who need to escape violent homes and communities,
and whose lives are all too often prevented from flourishing.

And to the children of the next generation,
especially Ariana and Gabriela,
may you live in a better world.

PREFACE

The idea for this project was born while I directed the Women's Studies program at Texas A&M University, as I began to collect articles and books about George W. Bush and his policies with respect to women's issues. A primary motivation for writing occurred in the fall of 2004, when I was invited to participate in a session on women's rights at the Oxford Round Table at Oxford University, UK. In preparing that paper, I realized that there was much more material than I could fit into one thirty-page document or a twenty-minute talk. The enthusiastic reception for the information in my presentation at the conference encouraged me to begin to think about expanding it into a book.

Subsequently, over several months, I spent many hours reading, collecting information, and huddling over my computer as I put together this book. At times, the subject matter was such that I had to lay it aside in anger and near despair over the political situation in the United States: over my government's shameful actions in dark secret places where international law and human rights are ignored; over the disgracefully inadequate response to the suffering of the victims of Hurricane Katrina; over the fact that in the richest nation in the world we have growing economic distress at the bottom of the economic ladder while wealth expands exponentially at the top;

over the almost daily reports of environmental degradation; and over the arrogance of a dangerous group of fundamentalist far-right conservatives, who trumpet the pro-life line while sending thousands of young people to kill and to die in faraway lands. How is it that this country has elected leaders who promote such policies? The problems seemed overwhelming. But, in the end, the anger and despair were strong motivators to keep working and to bring this book to a conclusion in a timely manner.

Among those who were most encouraging in this project were Professor Joe Feagin, fellow sociologist at Texas A&M, who was very supportive of the idea, even giving me hints as to the organization of the proposal. I also need to thank Drs Jane Sell and Mark Fossett of the Sociology Department at Texas A&M, and Dean of Faculties Karan Watson, for finding a creative way to allow me to continue work while recovering from an injury. The time away from classes actually worked to my advantage by giving me time to complete this work.

Anna Hardman of Zed Books convinced me that this was a worthy project. Her enthusiastic support for my proposal, and the nature of Zed Books as a politically conscious enterprise, led me to choose this outlet as the best vehicle for publication. And I must mention my daughter, Dr Ginger Bloomer, whose constant support during difficult times was always there.

My main motivation in writing this book was a desire to resist in some small way the dangerous policies of the Bush administration and the conservative movement it represents, but also to add to the discussion a focus on women. Among the many recently published books critical of Bush, most have ignored women's issues. I therefore saw a need to take a gendered look at the Bush presidency, as I believed his policies to be unusually retrograde in that regard.

While the women's angle has been neglected by most critics, there are some notable exceptions in the work of certain research organizations, activist groups, and organizations that provide services to women, all of whom have been keenly aware of the problems for women with this administration. Much of the information in this book would have been impossible to uncover had it not been for the basic work of these organizations. Of special importance were the report by the National Council for Research on Women, *Missing* (NCRW 2004a), which was an early motivator to learn more about Bush's anti-woman actions. The National Women's Law Center, likewise, has been an extremely valuable resource – their *Slip-Sliding Away* report (NWLC 2004b) was similarly helpful as an early inspiration. The excellent work of the Institute for Women's Policy Research in Washington has for years been an important resource for me, and it proved to be invaluable in this research as well. The long References section and the Resource list in the Appendix attest to the fact that my research depended heavily on the work of many, many others who have helped to document the shortcomings and negative actions of the Bush administration. In the final analysis, of course, whatever problems exist in the present analysis are my own responsibility.

I

GEORGE W. BUSH'S
RADICAL AMERICAN REVOLUTION

Eternal vigilance is the price of liberty.
Wendell Phillips

On 12 December 2000, the Supreme Court of the United States handed down one of the most momentous decisions in its history: by a narrowly split 5 : 4 decision, the Court halted the vote count in the state of Florida in the November 2000 presidential election, thereby handing the presidency to the Republican candidate, George W. Bush. The decision was widely condemned and highly criticized, most notably by the dissenting members of the court: Stevens, Souter, Ginsberg, and Breyer.

Nevertheless, even though Bush lost the popular vote and later studies found that Al Gore would have won if the full Florida count had gone ahead (as it should have by law), and in spite of major irregularities in the vote, George Walker Bush became the 43rd president of the United States. The country had been traumatized by the emotion-wrenching divisions raised in the election campaigns and the post-election events. In the end, political circumstances (the president's brother was governor of Florida; the state's attorney general, who certified the vote, had been chair of the Bush campaign in the state; and the Supreme Court justices who voted to stop the count were all Republican appointees) determined the outcome. And yet, as of January 2001, except for the strongest activists, much of the public seemed relieved that at last the election conflict was over and the presidential election had reached closure. Most reporters and commentators believed that Bush would govern 'from the center,' in deference to his narrowest of margins and based on his campaign promises of moderation, bipartisanship, and 'compassionate conservatism.'

In fact, Bush's election led to the most right-wing government in the country's recent history, contrary to his rhetoric. His policies have favored wealthy elites while undermining supports and protections for the most vulnerable members of society; he has set back environmental protections and ignored international treaties; he has started wars on false premises, giving out billion-dollar contracts to corporations with ties to his family, his administration, or the Republican party; and he has done all these things and much more while maintaining a rhetoric that misleads much of the public as to his real actions and policies. Given Bush's relatively moderate campaign rhetoric and the circumstances of his ascendance to office, he surprised many by his hard-right turn once safely in office. It soon became clear that Bush II was not a New England conservative in the mould of his father. Indeed Bush brought with him a strident hostility to settled policies, a cavalier disregard for fiscal responsibility, and an ideological inflexibility that would shock many old-line conservatives.

> Observers were struck almost immediately by the assertiveness of the Bush II administration. After a few gracious comments about the need to recognize the implications of the closeness of the election, the Bush administration put forth an [agenda that aggressively sought to change decades of domestic and foreign policies]. Tax cuts, Social Security reform, energy policy, and defence were all areas in which the administration set out to make major changes.... This was, in short, not going to be the administration of an 'old fashioned conservative' ..., but a more radical administration that rattled some settled cages and made some major changes. (Campbell and Rockman 2004: 64)

The Bush record on the environment, energy policy, the military and foreign affairs, health care, and the economy; and his management style of delegation, secrecy, intolerance of dissent, dishonesty, and cronyism have been widely criticized and analysed by an ever-growing list of books, editorials, and articles. His popularity and support might have receded quickly had it not been for the '9/11' attacks on the World Trade Center and the Pentagon, a circumstance that the Bush–Cheney White House deftly exploited to promote their radical foreign and domestic policies at a time when many Americans were in shock and looking for 'strong leadership' to provide them security. In place of real security, however, it is now widely recognized that Bush brought greater insecurity to the nation and the world, squandering world sympathy and plunging the nation into unnecessary and unwise military ventures, extremes of deficit spending, violations of civil and human rights, and regressive budgetary and tax policies that increased economic inequality while enriching the few at the top. One can readily find a long list of anti-Bush book titles, editorials, opinion columns, and reports from a wide variety of sources. Unfortunately, the mainstream media generally went along with the Bush jingoism for the first years following the 9/11 attacks, failing to analyse his actions critically and ignoring contradictory evidence in a seeming loss of direction and purpose. It took the disgrace of the mishandling of Hurricane Katrina and the mounting casualties and chaos in Iraq to finally awaken some of the media commentators, but by then the second Bush term was well under way. It is ironic that only a few months after Bush won the election of 2004, his popularity rating had plunged to the lowest levels of any president at that point in his presidency (around 38 per cent approval overall), with the sole exception of Richard Nixon at the height of the Watergate scandal.

Yet, in spite of the many voices of criticism raised against the misjudgments, cronyism, and failings of the Bush administration, there has been much less consideration of his actions and policies with respect to women, people of color, and the poor. This may be partly because political parties in recent years have focused on the 'center' and middle-class issues, aiming as well to appeal to 'angry white men,' who left the Democratic Party for the Republicans in a backlash against feminist and civil rights gains in the 1970s. It also reflects a seeming 'blindness' to issues of continuing gender and racial oppression and discrimination, the majority of middle-class Americans and opinion leaders apparently believing that such problems were a thing of the past. By the 1990s, it was no longer common to hear the word 'feminist' with a positive connotation, and indeed it tended to disappear from the lexicon of most journalists except in negative caricature. The backlash, as described so cogently by Susan Faludi (1991), had been successful. At the same time, and especially during the Bush years, women's voices were heard less and less, as they were almost never considered as relevant 'experts' to discuss such issues as war, foreign policy, or the 'tough' issues facing the country. In spite of this public silence, as I hope to demonstrate in this book, the policies and actions of the Bush regime have been injurious in many ways to women's interests. The need for sound critical and feminist analyses of the Bush years is more important now than ever, in order to raise awareness and provide evidence to support efforts to reverse the trends set in motion by the administration.

In fairness, there have been some valuable analyses of Bush policies with respect to women,[1] but most of these have not received the attention they deserve. The most well-known and widely publicized criticisms have focused on Bush's anti-abortion policies and their implications. On the other hand, few in-depth discussions have appeared of Bush's impact on women's status and their rights in a broader sense, with the important exception of the work of a few research organizations whose work is accessible online.[2] In fact, because of the lack of media discussion of these issues, Bush's campaign slogan 'W stands for Women,' his claim that his wars in Afghanistan and Iraq were fought in part to liberate women, and his appointment of a number of highly visible women to Cabinet and other policy positions seem effectively to have undercut most attention to these issues. In contrast to the general impression, I will argue that George W. Bush and his administration have clearly set back the clock on women's progress both in the United States and abroad, in ways not often recognized by political observers. Just as poor people and minorities have been somewhat 'off the radar screen' in the past few years, women's issues have similarly been ignored or largely dismissed as being unimportant or insignificant by mainstream opinion leaders.

PRESIDENTIAL POWERS AND WOMEN'S RIGHTS

While women's legal rights in the United States are theoretically protected by a number of key laws passed in the 1960s and 1970s, there has been variation in how these laws have been interpreted and enforced over the subsequent decades.[3] Such laws can be defined narrowly or broadly, enforced vigorously or half-heartedly, taken seriously or largely ignored, depending in large part on the occupant of the presidency. Thus, while Nixon, Ford, and Carter were more or less supportive of women's equity laws, the Reagan and George H.W. Bush years saw attempts to redefine, weaken, or push back on some of the rights gained by women in the previous decades. Under these administrations, abortion access was restricted, family-planning funds were reduced, a 'gag rule' was issued prohibiting the discussion of abortion by clinic personnel, affirmative-action enforcement and definitions were weakened, and anti-discrimination laws were not enforced as vigorously as had been the case in the 1970s (Tobias 1997: 111–33). These trends were reversed again during the Clinton presidency. Thus, presidents have the power to influence women's status and resources even where no change has occurred in their legal standing, by the use of the 'bully pulpit,' by executive order, by budgetary measures, and by commitment to enforcement actions. George W. Bush has used all of these means to work against many of the gains women had made over the past three decades, along with pushing back on civil rights advances in general.

Because women in recent years have tended to favor Democratic candidates for their more liberal social policies, Bush and his handlers went out of their way in the two presidential campaigns to counter the negative Republican image among women. His 'compassionate conservative' slogan attempted to project a more centrist and 'soft' image of his harsh social policies, and his campaign recruited a number of conservative women to work for him, including his mother, his wife Laura, and Dick Cheney's wife Lynne. Bush's appointment of highly visible women was used as 'evidence' of his support for women's needs; his campaign rhetoric focused on how his economic policies would help American women and how his foreign wars had 'liberated' Afghan and Iraqi women. His claims to have supported the global human rights of women were largely left unchallenged by Democrats and the mainstream media.

In reality, though, Bush has never made women's issues a priority in any public sense, preferring to work behind the scenes to undermine many of the gains of recent decades so as to avoid controversy. If one looks for pronouncements by the current President Bush or his representatives about women's issues, they are few and far between except during election campaigns. Certainly there are no calls for attacking gender-based wage inequality or opposing discrimination, problems this White House denies even exist. The White House website that touts its major programs and priorities has no link to women, women's rights or women's concerns. Instead, if one executes a search on that website for 'women' or 'women's issues,' almost all the hits have to do with First Lady Laura Bush and her speeches about women's rights in Afghanistan or Iraq, or her speeches in support of breast cancer awareness. There is no recognition that women's issues might be important for the actual office-holders or the president; nor is there any recognition of women's equity issues, for example. The fact that women's issues are listed within the sphere of concerns of Mrs Bush – unelected, without power, holding only a symbolic position – indicates their lack of importance to the real powers within the Bush administration, in spite of his pronouncements about 'respect for women' in foreign policy. One searches in vain for some indication that George Bush or his administration might be aware of American women's domestic issues, which range from poverty to discrimination in the workplace to family violence and many other concerns. Indeed, most of Bush's efforts have been in the opposite direction: to deny gender discrimination, to weaken enforcement of women's protections, to reduce the resources that government provides to help women.

Bush's approach to racial and ethnic concerns is similar. Even though the problems of women in the United States are multiplied for most women of color, their needs are disregarded by this White House. Although Bush had sought to improve the Republican appeal among minorities, his actual race-conscious actions were almost all purely symbolic, not substantive. While he did appoint an ethnically diverse group of men and women to his Cabinet, for example, the opinions and attitudes of the women and minority appointees were far different from those of the great majority of the groups they came from. In numerous speeches and pronouncements, Bush gives frequent nods to African Americans, Hispanics, Asians, Muslims, and other ethnic minorities, but when one looks for serious policy initiatives about racial issues, they simply are not to be found. Instead, we find a number of symbolic measures, such as proclamations of 'Black History Month,' 'Women's History Month,' 'Black Music Month,' 'Breast Cancer Awareness Month,' and so forth.

CONSERVATIVE MOVEMENTS AND REPUBLICAN POLITICS

The Bush administration is much more conservative on many issues than even traditional Republican administrations, including that of his father. Ideological conservatives have been able to take over the party and bring people like Bush into power through the cobbling together of a loose and tenuous coalition of two key constituencies. The first are the traditional economic conservatives, those who generally represent the wealthier portion of the population and business interests, although many are moderate on issues of personal liberties such as reproductive rights. These are the more traditional Republicans who favor lower taxes, free-trade policies, and little regulation of business practice. They tend to be anti-union and oppose most equity initiatives as interference in business (e.g. they tend to oppose such worker or consumer protections as minimum wage laws, mandatory health insurance for workers, strict labor practice standards, environmental regulations, and affirmative-action requirements that might increase business costs). They also tend to be stingy on social welfare programs and favor the privatization of public functions. In most ways, George W. Bush's economic policies please this group, especially his tax cuts that favor the wealthy and his pro-business policies. Although his fiscal irresponsibility (runaway deficit spending) bothers this group, the benefits they gain from his other policies have kept them in his camp. Bush's personal politics are probably closer to this group than to the second key constituency, the religious conservatives.

Religious conservatives are a much more recent addition to the Republican family of supporters. Consisting mostly of fundamentalist Protestant Christians, but also including many conservative Catholics, this group promotes a fairly radical and antifeminist social agenda. Presenting themselves as supporters of 'family values,' 'traditional values,' and 'morality,' these groups oppose abortion, sex outside of (heterosexual) marriage, gay rights, and the many cultural signs of rampant 'immorality' they see in American culture. They frequently even oppose all forms of 'artificial' contraception, and certainly they dislike informing young students about such things. Many of these conservatives believe that the separation of church and state has gone too far in the country, supported by a 'liberal' media and so-called 'activist' judges. The Christian right supports mandatory school prayer, government funding of religious schools and institutions, and the teaching of creationism in science classes (while questioning Darwinian evolution). Many of these groups even teach the appropriateness of wifely submission to husbands, the sinfulness of sex before marriage, and the dangers of feminism to family and society.

George W. Bush in his personal beliefs is probably not as extreme as many of his supporters in this camp, but he has taken many actions to maintain their support, often in highly symbolic ways, including speeches and public statements of solidarity with their organizations. Beginning with his work with evangelicals in his father's campaigns in the 1980s, Bush, with the help of his long-term political adviser Karl Rove, has been very successful at attracting votes from this segment of American society. Although they represent a minority of Americans – no more than 30 per cent – they are highly motivated, well organized through their churches, and subject to rapid mobilization around such emotional issues as abortion and homosexuality. Bush has repaid religious conservatives generously through nominations to the court system and through restrictive regulations on foreign family-planning assistance.

The two groups of conservatives do not always agree, as traditional laissez-faire Republicans view the religious right as socially unsophisticated and extreme on many issues. But the patrician leaders know that they will not be able to win support for their wealth-friendly, pro-business agenda without the support of the religious conservatives. And so they have forged an uneasy, mutually beneficial alliance over the past decade that has proven very successful in winning elections, from the local level all the way to the presidency.

SIGNIFICANCE FOR WOMEN OF CONSERVATIVE SUCCESS

For women, the stridently antifeminist religious conservatives may seem more dangerous on the surface, given their loud insistence on rolling back reproductive rights and resources and their rhetoric about traditional gender roles. It is true: they do aim to reverse many of the gains women have made over the past thirty years. In fact, however, the economic conservatives support policies that are at least as harmful to a majority of women as workers, mothers of children, caretakers of disabled and sick family members, consumers, and retirees. The majority of women do not occupy the top echelon of the wealth structure that benefits from skewed tax cuts, stringent bankruptcy rules, relaxed environmental regulation, and fewer worker and consumer protections. As I will argue in this book, the welfare of many women has been placed at risk by fiscally irresponsible, corporation-friendly Bush policies – women who were already more vulnerable economically than men. On both the cultural and economic fronts, then, the George W. Bush administration has declared war on women.

In later chapters I take a close look at Bush's policies and actions in terms of their impact on women, examining at times related consequences for racial minorities and other disadvantaged groups. Perhaps no president has been as controversial among women's activists as has this one – an Internet search for 'Bush and women' turns up multiple sites with titles such as 'the Bush assault on women,' 'Bush's war on women,' 'Bush steps up attack on women's rights,' and 'Bush's Stealth Misogyny.'[4] On the other hand, George W. Bush's claims to support women's rights (and his skillful concealment of many behind-the-scenes actions) have seemingly convinced most of the public that there is nothing to worry about on these issues. Even though Bush's popularity declined precipitously in the first year of his second term, very few people blamed their disaffection on his policies regarding women. In explaining this contradiction between the view of the general public and that of women's advocates, observers have often noted that Bush knows how to use moderate – even feminist – rhetoric as a smokescreen behind which to hide regressive policies. The general public seems too distracted by the struggle for everyday survival and by the docile, entertainment-oriented media to examine critically the gap between White House word and deed. Here I will attempt to look beyond the rhetoric to focus primarily on the record of actions with respect to women, with some attention given to the manner in which the White House has managed its impression in the public mind so as to undercut criticism. I will not give much attention to the lost opportunities for progress caused by Bush's inaction on issues that cry for solution, although that topic could well fill another volume.

It is my contention that Bush's actions have consistently undercut feminist goals of gender equity and human rights, even though he presents himself as a supporter of women. Here, as with other progressive issues, Bush publicly promotes a relatively mild egalitarianism ('respect for women') while using his executive powers to undermine a wide variety of progressive achievements of the past few decades. In examining the record of the 43rd president of the United States, we should all take the words of Nixon's Attorney General John Mitchell to heart when assessing the George W. Bush era: 'Watch what we do, not what we say.'

PLAN OF THE BOOK

In order to examine the Bush record on women, I use primarily reliable and respected news sources, research reports, and scholarly studies to address these questions. While much of the public attention on the general topic of Bush and women has focused on issues of reproductive rights[5] – especially abortion-related issues – I will look at a variety of other ways that Bush's tenure in office has influenced women's progress and opportunities. At times policies not widely recognized as being 'women's issues' are found to have a disproportionate impact on women, and these are especially important to document and recognize.

In the next chapter, I present an overview of Bush's initial and continuing actions that undercut, reversed, or halted programs that supported women's progress in the past. In this chapter I briefly describe a variety of actions that reduced women's influence in the government and restricted resources and programs that had been available under recent administrations. In Chapter 3, I look at some of the networks of conservative think-tanks and lobby groups from whom Bush draws many of his appointees to executive policymaking positions. I then describe a selection of some of his controversial appointees in terms of issues of importance to women. Chapter 4 takes up the issue of their information management, showing how Bush has overseen an administration that manipulates, distorts, and suppresses useful information and science in the interest of ideological, political aims.

In the next two chapters I look at Bush policies with respect to sexuality and reproductive rights issues, both in the United States and abroad. I follow this with a re-examination of Bush's approach to women's human rights around the globe, especially in terms of his rejection of international structures and treaties that promote women's advancement. Next I look at Bush's record of extremist nominations to the courts and his Justice Department's failure to prosecute cases of discrimination against women and racial minorities. In Chapter 9 I examine the Bush record on education and health, including his attempts to weaken Title IX protections, his opposition to university attempts to promote diversity in student recruitment, and budget cuts to programs that help women gain access to higher education. Here I also examine the increased health risks to women incurred by Bush policies, along with reduced research funding for diseases that affect women. I also look at how Bush used a women's hospital renovation in Afghanistan for public relations purposes without properly outfitting it.

Chapter 10 analyses the Bush economic program in the context of his costly military invasions. Here I take up tax cuts, Social Security proposals, bankruptcy legislation, Medicaid, and growing poverty and welfare responses, all in terms of their differential impact on women. In Chapter 11 I look at the disgraceful and incompetent response to the devastation of Hurricane Katrina, which displaced many women and left them homeless and jobless, with little hope for assistance from the administration. By focusing on the Katrina disaster, a number of lessons can be drawn about the Bush presidency in general, including his pro-business, anti-worker bias.

Finally, in Chapter 12, I take up Bush's military ventures in Afghanistan and Iraq. Both wars were justified in part on the basis that they would prove liberating to the women of those countries. The evidence I present strongly contradicts this claim in both countries. I consider a variety of impacts that increased militarism and these particular wars are having on women in those countries, in the United States, and around the world. Of all the misadventures of the Bush administration, the unnecessary Iraq invasion has been by far the worst, having resulted in horrible suffering, disruption, and death to countless civilians, the majority of whom are women and children. The consequences of these actions are severe and far-reaching for women in Iraq and elsewhere. I attempt to analyse some of the most critical problems for women created by these disastrous actions.

In all of these chapters I describe and analyse the impacts of Bush's policies and actions on women and their hopes for progress, looking especially at his behind-the-scenes executive decisions that are often hidden from public view. The gap between Bush's rhetoric and his actions, evident throughout his presidency, is a constant theme of this book. I conclude with some thoughts for developing sustainable and nonviolent counter-movements in a world threatened by the presidency of George W. Bush and the conservative movement he represents.

2

IN THE CHINA SHOP: CLOSING AGENCIES, ELIMINATING INITIATIVES, CHANGING PROCEDURES

Once in office, Bush began to move forward on his conservative agenda, in spite of the circumstances of his ascendance to the presidency and in contrast to his moderate-sounding campaign promises. Observers who were paying attention were surprised by a number of early actions with respect to women's concerns. Bush began quickly to use his executive power to make numerous administrative changes, restructuring units whose missions affect women, changing enforcement of policies that protect women, appointing conservatives to policy positions, and redefining missions of women's programs. These changes were often done with little fanfare or explanation, covered only minimally by the press. The overall result has been to reduce government attention to women's equity issues and to change the goals of policy radically on these issues. This chapter briefly outlines some of the actions Bush took, mainly early in his presidency, to restrict women's programs and influence.

Percentage of women in executive positions reduced

President Bush has often been lauded for his appointment of women to highly visible and powerful positions, including to four Cabinet positions and some important White House staff posts. These appointments included Secretary of Labor Elaine Chao, Secretary of Agriculture Ann Veneman, and Secretary of the Interior Gale Norton. Christine Todd Whitman, a pro-choice moderate Republican, was named director of the Environmental Protection Agency, and Karen Hughes was brought along from her long career as Bush's handler and public relations adviser to be communications director in the White House.

Beyond this highly visible level, the percentage of Bush appointments of women to key policymaking positions in the executive branch has been less than that of the Clinton White House. Of 402 nominees requiring Senate confirmation put forward in the first year, 102 were women – about 25 per cent compared to Clinton's 37 per cent. Bush's percentage is similar to those of his father and Reagan in the late 1980s (Tessier 2001, 2002). According to a Brookings Institution study, women of color fared even worse under Bush: of the 24 African Americans of the first 264 appointees, only about a fifth were women.

Women's input excluded from appointments process

Bush disappointed members of women's organizations, who had for twenty-five years been consulted by new presidents in making appointments. Since 1976, women's groups such as the bipartisan National Women's Political Caucus (NWPC) had developed and maintained lists of highly qualified women to recommend for various appointive offices, a service that other administrations had welcomed. These organizations succeeded over the years in increasing the number of women with access to executive appointments. In a blunt rejection of this tradition, Bush turned a cold shoulder to these groups, creating early frustration and concern among advocates for women. Roselyn O'Connell, at the time president of the NWPC and chair of the 2001 Women's Appointments Project (herself a Republican), expressed disappointment about the lack of access women had to this White House. O'Connell was reportedly dismayed by being 'shut out' of the appointments process, lamenting 'It's a signal that we're just not that important' (Tessier 2001). Thus, in spite of Bush's campaign theme, there were troubling signs for women very early in his presidency.

Over time, the results of Bush's selection process became clear: the women he placed in influential policy-relevant positions did not represent the range of views of the NWPC or most women's advocacy groups. Instead, both his male and female appointees represent a relatively narrow (and well out of the mainstream) range of opinions about women, race, and social welfare issues (as will be seen throughout this book). Bush appointments tend to be supporters of 'family values' or 'traditional values,' codewords for anti-feminism and patriarchal values.

President's Interagency Council on Women eliminated

President Clinton formed the President's Interagency Council on Women in response to the 1995 Beijing World Conference on Women, with the charge of proposing ways to implement the Beijing Platform for Action (UNESCO 1995) within the United States. The Platform urged governments to implement policies to eliminate gender-based discrimination and to improve the lives of women in a serious and accountable manner. Clinton's highly placed Council was headed at first by Donna Shalala (then Secretary of Health and Human Services) and later by Secretary of State Madeleine Albright. Two reports came out of their work, *America's Commitment: Women* 1997 (2000), in which various federal initiatives and programs for women were reviewed for progress toward the Beijing goals. In an interview soon after the Supreme Court decision handing Bush the presidency, Ritu Sharma of the advocacy group Women's EDGE expressed hope that the Council would be continued.

> During the Clinton administration this agency has been quite effective in terms of consulting with women's groups and in pressuring various departments within the government to take women's equality seriously in their policies. It is hoped that although the function of the Council may change slightly, the actual structure will stay intact. (AWID 2000)

Such hopes were in vain, however, as the Council was eliminated soon after Bush's inauguration, along with most attention to the Beijing agreements (NCRW 2004a).

White House Office on Women's Initiatives and Outreach closed

In 1995, President Clinton opened an office in the White House as an advisory unit to examine the impact on women of new legislation and proposed initiatives, and to maintain communication with a variety of women's organizations. This allowed various women's groups to have some input into policymaking and to voice concerns at the highest level. Soon after George W. Bush was inaugurated, he closed this office without explanation, further signifying a lowering of priority given to women's issues. In a response to this decision, Betsy Myers, first director of the office, wrote in the *Boston Globe*:

> The White House Office for Women's Initiatives and Outreach gave women a seat at the president's table, allowing them to make important contributions on issues that have an impact in people's daily lives.... The benefits of collaboration made a significant difference in several areas for women that included equal pay, women's business development, domestic violence prevention, and breast cancer research. The closing of the office may appear small to some, but it is very symbolic. The decision for women, along with the reversal of important executive orders and policies, will be quite significant over the next four years. (Myers 2001)

Even women's business groups were upset by this action. Barbara Stanbridge, president of the nonpartisan National Association of Women Business Owners, a group that had been in frequent contact with the Clinton White House, issued a statement expressing her organization's dismay:

> Women will forgive the president for not winning their vote, but we will not forgive the president for eliminating our voice in the creation of public policy that impacts our interests. With each suc-ceeding day, the administration makes it clear that compassionate conservatism equates with rolling back progress. (Berry 2000)

White House access granted to right-wing groups

If traditional women's groups were shut out of the White House, conservative antifeminist groups were welcomed. Ultraconservative Tim Goeglein was appointed deputy director of the White House Office of Public Liaison to serve as a conduit to the president for conservative GOP activists. According to Jim VandeHei of the

Washington Post, Goeglein 'operates as a virtual middleman between the White House and conservatives of all stripes seeking to shape its policies' (VandeHei 2004). Overseen by political strategist Karl Rove, the office is 'central to how this president operates' to keep his antifeminist conservative base involved and supportive.

> It is Goeglein's job to make sure conservatives are happy, in the loop and getting their best ideas before the president and turned into laws. With Goeglein's assistance, Christian conservatives, for instance, were successful in lobbying Bush to push for abstinence-first funding to combat AIDS. (VandeHei 2004)

Because of Goeglein's close ties with Bush's political right-hand man Rove, his office has a very strong influence on policy, conveying conservative activists' desires to Bush.

Equal Pay Matters Initiative eliminated

In 1999, the Clinton administration instituted the Equal Pay Matters Initiative, providing extra funds to the Department of Labor's Women's Bureau to educate employers about equal pay issues, to improve the enforcement of Title VII pay-discrimination laws, and to provide women workers with relevant information and resources. The program had recovered over $15 million in back pay to women and minorities since its inception in 1999, focusing its efforts on ending pay discrimination, eliminating occupational segregation and promoting pension equity (Tierney 2002). This program was completely eliminated by the Bush administration, again without announcement or explanation. At the same time, all materials on reducing the wage gap were removed from the Department of Labor website (NWLC 2004b: 12–13).

Bush tries to eliminate regional offices of the Women's Bureau

The Women's Bureau of the Department of Labor was created in 1920 to 'promote the welfare of working women' and to work to enlarge their opportunities in the workforce. The Bureau maintains ten regional offices that act somewhat independently, focusing on local issues and reaching out to the region by providing resources, workshops, conferences, and advice to workers and employers. In

2001 the Bush administration attempted to shut down all ten regional offices of the Bureau. The plan to eliminate these offices, once made public (by critics of the administration), was abandoned due to vociferous protest from congressional members, newspaper editorials, and women's organizations (Taylor 2001). However, changes were made to the mission of the Bureau, with significant changes in its activities and the types of information it provides (see discussion later, in Chapter 4).

Bush tries to eliminate federal workers' contraceptive coverage

In another early sign that Bush was more interested in pleasing his ultraconservative base than in serving the needs of women, he shocked many by inserting a small paragraph in his 1,296-page FY 2002 Budget Appendix that would eliminate contraceptive coverage in federal employees' health insurance plans. There are 1.2 million female federal employees of reproductive age, many of whom rely on contraceptives purchased through their health plans. Bush's plan would continue to cover most other prescription drugs, but it singled out this one type of drug, which is used almost exclusively by women. Outraged women's groups and congressional representatives pointed out the irony that Viagra would still be covered for men, but oral contraceptives would not be covered for women. Although voters had been aware of Bush's anti-abortion attitudes, most had no idea that he also would not support contraception, which can prevent abortions. Although the Congress eliminated this part of the budget proposal, the attempt raised serious questions in the minds of many as to where Bush stands on women's reproductive health issues (Nakashima 2001).

Bush tries to eliminate Women's Educational Equity Act programs

The Women's Educational Equity Act promotes educational equity for women and girls through grants to organizations and individuals and helps educational institutions meet the requirements of Title IX. This program has received no new funding since FY 2002, when six projects were funded. Bush tried to eliminate the program completely in FY 2005, but women members of Congress spoke out and it received further funding. A new notice announcing competitions was released in March 2005, but the budget proposal for FY 2006 released about the same time again proposes its elimination (NWLC 2004b: 16; Women's Policy 2005).

Bush tries to eliminate Women's Military Advisory Committee

In 2002 there was concern among supporters of women in the military that Secretary Rumsfeld planned to eliminate the major women's advisory committee in the US military, the Defense Advisory Committee on Women in the Services (DACOWITS). His plan was to allow the committee's charter to expire without renewal. The committee was instituted in 1949 for the purpose of advising the Pentagon on women's issues in the military services. A number of conservative groups had criticized DACOWITS for being too 'feminist,' as the committee's recommendations often dealt with issues of gender discrimination and promoted further integration of all-male military positions. After the intervention of a woman member of Congress, herself a veteran, Rumsfeld retained the committee but he allowed its charter to expire so that he could revise it and replace the committee's membership. The new mission places more emphasis on family issues for military women and recruitment of qualified women, instead of expanding women's roles and vigorously pursuing anti-discrimination issues. The reconstituted committee was still deemed too 'feminist' for some conservative groups, who would have preferred to have it eliminated altogether, although critics say it has been 'left toothless' by the changes (NWLC 2004b: 49–50; Enloe 2004a).

Bush raises challenges to Title IX protections

In 2003, Bush set up a commission to consider changes to Title IX, the law that established equal educational opportunity for women in schools and universities that receive federal funds. The law has been extremely important in opening up opportunities for women where they had been shut out before, in areas such as science education, sports participation, occupational training, academic counseling, and other aspects of education. The commission made recommendations that would have seriously weakened Title IX protections, but, because of the outcry from universities and women's supporters, the recommendations were not implemented. However, two years later the Department of Education quietly issued new rules through administrative action that put in place some of the commission's recommendations, thus undermining some of the policies that had led to increased opportunities for women college athletes over the past three decades. Details of this assault on Title IX are discussed further in Chapter 9.

Bush weakens enforcement of anti-discrimination laws

According to the National Women's Law Center (NWLC), the Department of Justice has 'weakened enforcement of the laws against discrimination in the workplace,' significantly reducing the number of cases pursued compared to previous administrations and dropping cases that were already being prosecuted. During the Reagan, George H.W. Bush, and Clinton administrations, an average of thirteen cases per year were brought, and most impacted large numbers of workers. By contrast, in the first three years of the George W. Bush administration, only twelve cases (averaging four per year) were initiated, and the way they were framed guaranteed that they would be much more limited in impact, focusing more narrowly on individual grievances instead of patterns of practice that affect large numbers of workers (NWLC 2004b: 13). More recently, in 2005 the *Washington Post* reported that prosecutions by the Justice Department's Civil Rights Division for racial and gender discrimination had declined by 40 per cent between 2000 and 2005 and the cases pursued had focused on matters other than bias against women and minority workers. The change in focus led to major disaffection among many career civil-rights attorneys within Justice, a large number of whom had left the agency, according to the report (Eggen 2005b).

Bush cancels regulations on ergonomics in the workplace

In March of 2001 President Bush signed into law a repeal of the ergonomic workplace standards that President Clinton had established the previous year. These new regulations would have established new ergonomic rules to help prevent repetitive stress injuries, injuries that are especially common among women clerical and assembly workers.

The rules would have required employers to provide safe workspaces and to compensate work-injured employees. The Occupational Safety and Health Administration (OSHA) had estimated that the standards would have prevented over 450,000 musculoskeletal disorders annually and would have 'generated benefits of $9.1 billion a year' during the first decade of implementation (CNN.com 2001).

Bush cancels paid family leave plan

The Family and Medical Leave Act of 1993 mandated that American workers be given at least six weeks' unpaid leave at the birth of a new child or to care for a sick family member. While this was an advance over the previous situation, it still left the United States far behind other industrialized countries, most of whom provide at least twelve weeks of *paid* medical leave after childbirth and in other situations (Sapiro 2003: 47). In 2000, President Clinton had established a new policy under the Birth and Adoption Unemployment Compensation regulations, which allowed states to use surplus unemployment insurance funds to develop paid leave programs for workers who were new parents. As of 2003 some sixteen states were developing unemployment-funded paid family leave programs, although none of these had been fully implemented. In that year, however, the Bush administration's Department of Labor squashed those plans by restoring earlier regulations, thereby eliminating states' flexibility to use those funds to pay for family leave. Since parental leave is primarily used by women workers, this was a blow to women's hopes for better assistance in solving some of their most important work–family conflicts. As of now, the United States still stands out as one of the very few developed countries with no paid maternity or parental leave (Sherman 2003).

The actions described above are just a sampling of the types of policy decision taken by the Bush administration with respect to women's issues, most of which have not been widely reported by the press. In the following chapters, I take up some of these and other Bush actions and consider them in terms of their effects on women in the USA and abroad. Most of the actions described in this chapter had to do with closing down previous programs or initiatives or failing to act in behalf of women's progress and equality; in later chapters we will see evidence of a many-pronged assault on women's rights and advancement. When we bring all of these actions together in one analysis, it becomes clear that an antifeminist current runs deeply through much of Bush's policy.

3

POWER THROUGH APPOINTMENTS:
REWARDING IDEOLOGUES AND FRIENDS

The ability of presidents to staff positions, committees, and other posts can hardly be overestimated in its capacity to consolidate power, establish policy, and set priorities. The Bush administration has been unique in the degree to which ideology and party loyalty have influenced appointments, even to committees whose missions are to provide independent review of policy and proposals. In many cases, Bush has appointed to committees individuals who are on record as opposing the very mission of the committee, who lack appropriate qualifications, or who have serious conflicts of interest. These problematic placements have especially been seen on committees of relevance to women, such as those dealing with violence against women, reproductive health, AIDS policy, global human rights, and similar gender-related issues.

Appointments to Bush's Cabinet and other policy-related positions have generally had strong corporate connections and are very conservative on issues such as civil rights, labor rights, women's rights, gay rights, and social welfare programs. Although Bush has named a number of women to these positions, he has often chosen women who are far to the right of most women (and men) in the United States, and to the right of where he claimed to be during his campaigns and in public speeches. The networks of power from which Bush's appointees are recruited include such right-wing groups as the Independent Women's Forum, the Federalist Society, the Heritage Foundation, and the American Enterprise Institute, with serious consequences for women's policy. In general, Bush's appointments have consolidated the power of opponents of previous progressive gains throughout the federal government.

RIGHT-WING ORGANIZATIONS AND
THE BUSH ADMINISTRATION

Many Bush appointees have ties to very conservative, often openly antifeminist, organizations; both women and men are heavily drawn from a relatively small number of right-wing think-tanks or legal organizations. These organizations have greatly increased their numbers and influence in Washington over the past thirty years, especially in Republican administrations. Among the most important affiliations of Bush appointees are the ones I describe in the following pages.

Independent Women's Forum

Many women in the Bush administration have served as leaders in the antifeminist organization Independent Women's Forum. This women's organization was formed in response to feminist criticisms of Clarence Thomas in 1991, in order to counter charges of sexual harassment against Thomas and defend his nomination to the Court (PFAW 2005c). The IWF can be seen as a secular counterpart to conservative Christian women's groups such as Eagle Forum and Concerned Women for America, but these groups often work together. IWF is on record as opposing affirmative action, gender equity programs like Title IX, the Violence Against Women Act, and Women's Studies programs in universities. It consistently downplays the importance of sexual harassment and discrimination against women, claiming that these problems have been largely solved and are exaggerated by feminists. The IWF even denies, for example, that a discriminatory pay gap exists between women and men. The organization's website describes its mission as combating the 'women-as-victim, pro-big-government ideology of radical feminism.'[1] The

IWF promotes free-market, non-governmental solutions to most problems. Far from being a large-membership grassroots organization, IWF membership consists mainly of professional and highly placed conservative women who help to legitimate the Republican antifeminist agenda by providing a 'feminine' voice of support. Many of its members are the wives of powerful conservative Republican men. Major contributors to IWF include the Sarah Scaife Foundation, the Olin Foundation, the Bradley Foundation, Castle Rock Foundation, and the Carthage Foundation, all supporters of very conservative political efforts (PFAW 2005c).

Among the prominent Independent Women's Forum leaders or members named by President Bush to key positions in his administration are Elaine Chao as Secretary of Labor; Diana Furchgott-Roth as Chief of Staff of the president's Council of Economic Advisors, later moved to the Department of Labor; Anita Blair as Deputy Assistant Secretary of the Navy; Jessica Gavora, Senior Policy Advisor in the Department of Justice Office of Legal Policy; Nancy Pfotenhauer and Margot Hill to the Advisory Committee on Violence Against Women; Paula Dobriansky, Undersecretary of State for Global Affairs, and Kate O'Bierne as US Representative to the UN Commission on the Status of Women (NWLC 2004b: 60). Bush's first nominee for Secretary of Labor, conservative activist Linda Chavez, was also a board member of IWF, as is Vice-President Cheney's wife Lynne, who has been a prominent leader in the organization since its origins. The favored position of the IWF is indicated by the fact that it was chosen in 2004 to receive part of a $10 million grant from the Bush State Department to develop programs 'to train Iraqi women in the skills and practices of democratic public life' (US Department of State 2004), an effort in which no other women's organization participated.

The Heritage Foundation

This right-wing think-tank was established in 1973 by beer magnate Joseph Coors, with ultraconservative Paul Weyrich as its first president. Major funding came from the Sarah Scaife Foundation and various corporate sponsors. The Heritage describes its mission as the development and promotion of 'conservative public policies based on the principles of free enterprise, limited government, individual freedom, traditional American values, and a strong national defense' (Heritage Foundation 2005). The largest conservative policy institute in Washington, the Heritage Foundation develops and distributes policy papers to the media, members of Congress, government leaders, and major donors. According to People for the American Way, the Heritage Foundation 'takes credit for much of President Bush's policy,' claiming it comes 'straight out of the Heritage play book' (PFAW 2005b).

Among the policies especially relevant to women promoted by the Heritage Foundation are support for 'faith-based' initiatives, opposition to abortion, 'marriage promotion,' privatization of social services, and opposition to affirmative action. Among former employees of the Heritage Foundation appointed by Bush are Secretary of Labor Elaine Chao, Director of Personnel Management Kay Coles James, and Assistant Secretary of Labor Mark Wilson (PFAW 2005b).

The Federalist Society

This association was organized in 1982 by a group of conservative law students who objected to what they considered the absence of conservative/libertarian perspectives in legal policy and education (its full name is the Federalist Society for Law and Public Policy Studies). Its membership includes some 25,000 lawyers, judges, and other legal professionals, plus law students and faculty in a nationwide network of chapters. The Federalist Society comprises libertarians and conservatives who hope to transform the American legal system through legislation, judicial appointments, and elections. The society develops conservative positions and promotes them through its network of lawyers, politicians, judges, and commentators (Federalist Society 2005).

The Federalist Society website claims that US law schools and the legal profession are now dominated by a liberal-orthodoxy, which the organization hopes to counter through its activities. In line with its values, the Society has received large financial support from such far-right sources as the John M. Olin and Charles Koch Foundations and arch-conservative Richard Mellon Scaife. Over the past two decades, the Federalist Society has become highly influential within

Republican administrations, helping to develop legal strategies for reversing previous court rulings in areas such as states' rights, civil rights, reproductive rights, corporate regulation, and religion–state separation (Fletcher 2005).

George W. Bush has named many members of the Federalist Society to offices within his administration, both executive and judicial. Among these are some of the administration's most conservative appointments, including John Ashcroft, first-term Attorney General; Spencer Abram, Secretary of Energy (first term); Gale Norton, Secretary of the Interior; and Ted Olson, Solicitor General. Other well-known members of the society are Senator Orrin Hatch (R–Utah); Supreme Court Justice Antonin Scalia; failed Supreme Court nominee Judge Robert Bork; Charles Murray (author of books claiming racial difference in intelligence as the cause of income and educational inequalities); Don Hodel, former Christian Coalition president; Judge William Pryor, controversial Bush appointee to an Appeals Court; and Kenneth Starr, Independent Counsel whose work led to the impeachment of Bill Clinton (PFAW 2005a).

Other conservative organizations with important influence in the Bush administration include:

- The *American Enterprise Institute*, a neoconservative think-tank from which Bush named over a dozen appointees to senior positions. One of the most influential conservative policy institutions, the AEI boasts such fellows (or former fellows) as Lynne Cheney, Dinesh D'Souza, Charles Murray, Newt Gingrich, and antifeminist author Christina Hoff Sommers.
- The *Family Research Council*, a right-wing Christian lobbying organization created by James Dobson of the related organization *Focus on the Family*. The FRC and its parent organization are increasingly influential in national politics, especially in the Bush years. Both groups oppose abortion, some methods of contraception, and gay rights; promote school prayer, vouchers to allow tax monies to pay for religious education, and so-called 'traditional values' in family matters and gender relations.

- *Center for Equal Opportunity* is a think-tank devoted to 'color-blind' equal opportunity. This organization opposes affirmative action, multicultural education, bilingual education, and 'racial preferences' as remedies for past discrimination. Bush's administrative 'diversity' is accomplished by drawing on this and similar organizations. Under CEO Linda Chavez, the Center has worked to oppose the kinds of diversity-related admissions policies the Supreme Court recently deemed acceptable at the University of Michigan.
- *Project 21*, an initiative of The National Center for Public Policy Research, sees itself as an alternative to 'the nation's civil rights establishment' for conservative pro-business African Americans (National Leadership Network of Black Conservatives 2005). The organization generally supports the conservative Republican agenda, including opposition to affirmative action, race-based policies, and mainstream black civil rights groups' perspectives. The group's website and that of the National Center for Public Policy Research are very critical of the Congressional Black Caucus.

If there is a theme running through this list of organizations, it is their consistent opposition to the ideals of the Great Society and the various progressive movements of the 1960s and 1970s. Their research and publications provide the ideological underpinnings for Bush administration policy, and their membership constitutes a ready source of personnel to fill the administrative structure.

CRONYISM AND POLITICAL PAYBACK IN BUSH APPOINTMENTS

Although many Bush appointments come from conservative organizations, a fair number have no relevant experience or demonstrated interest in the issues addressed by the position to which they are named. In a number of notorious cases, the appointee seems to be nominated to the position as a matter of political patronage, a reward for contributions to the political campaigns of George Bush. The most famous of these 'crony' appointments was that of Michael Brown as head of FEMA, the Federal Emergency Management Agency. This appointment received little attention until Brown's apparent incompetence and unconcern were revealed during the Katrina disaster in August–September 2005. Details of this disaster and Brown's role in it are discussed further in Chapter 11, but the fact is that Brown was just one of many such appointments to important policy positions of individuals who had few qualifications other than party and/or Bush loyalty. In many cases, this has led to 'a major exodus of experienced career officials,' who are unwilling to work under unqualified leaders who refuse to enforce the mission of their agencies (Krugman 2005f).

BUSH'S 'DIVERSITY' STRATEGY

Bush's high-ranking appointments have been noted for their diversity in terms of gender and racial/ethnic backgrounds. His Cabinet, judicial nominations, and other senior officials include a number of highly visible African Americans, Hispanics, and Asian Americans, many of whom are women. If one looks at the women and minorities that Bush appoints, however, one finds that they are hardly representative of most members of those groups. This is especially true of his African-American appointees, who are selected from the tiny percentage of black Americans who are politically conservative, even on issues directly related to racial discrimination.

Bush's appointment of minority individuals and women is part of a strategy that Republicans developed at least as far back as the George H.W. Bush presidency, when the elder Bush nominated Clarence Thomas as Supreme Court Justice. George W. Bush often brings several 'diversity' nominees up for Senate confirmation at once, on the theory that Democratic senators will be unlikely to oppose all of them for fear of being labelled racist or sexist. In fact, it is Bush who uses race and sex in order to push through some of the most far-right nominations possible. Among the most conservative and corporation-friendly members of his Cabinet have been Ann Veneman, Secretary of Agriculture, and Gale Norton, Secretary of the Interior. Yet these nominations received much less opposition in their Senate confirmation hearings than John Ashcroft. The Republican strategy of promoting conservatism by finding members of minority racial and ethnic groups and/or women to fill positions has been quite successful. This plan also provides cover for Bush for his harmful policies for women and minorities, since he can point to the diversity of his Cabinet as 'proof' of his lack of racial or gender bias. Overall, if one looks at the political views of these Bush appointees, it is clear how radically different they are from the majority of US citizens, regardless of race or gender.

A ROGUE'S GALLERY OF BUSH APPOINTEES

In this section I describe some of the most controversial of Bush's appointees to positions with influence over policymaking or implementation on women's or gender-related concerns. Many of these names are not widely known, but their attitudes and backgrounds are disturbing to supporters of women's equality. These appointees have important power to influence the direction of the country – through interpretation of laws, developing regulations, and establishing priorities – in ways that threaten women's progress. Bush may speak publicly in positive ways about his support for women, but it is in the agencies and departments and committees where many policy decisions are made, often in ways that contradict the public face of the administration.

Karl Rove

Bush's senior White House political advisor. Bush's character can be seen by the company he keeps, and Karl Rove, one of his closest, long-term advisers, does not reflect well on him. A recent article (*Boston Globe* 2005) describes Rove as a 'master of dirty tricks, divisiveness, innuendo, manipulation, character assassination, and roiling partisanship,' over his thirty-five-year career as a Republican activist. Rove has been responsible for a consistent pattern of character attacks and personal slurs against candidates who dared to run against his clients. Often these attacks appeal to the worst motives of voters, exploiting homophobic, sexist, or racist attitudes. Here are some examples of dirty tricks that seem to bear Rove's fingerprints:

- When George W. Bush was running against Ann Richards for the Texas governorship in 1994 there were rumors circulating that some of Governor Richards's appointees were lesbians, and other suggestions that the governor herself was gay. Bush himself made vague suggestions that supported the rumours.

- In the Republican primary of 2000, John McCain was running well until the South Carolina primary. In the run-up to that vote, rumours were circulated that John McCain was gay, that he had a black child, that he had a Vietnamese child, and that he had received special treatment as a prisoner of war in Vietnam.

- In the 2004 general election there were libelous attacks against decorated veteran John Kerry by the so-called Swift Boat Veterans.

According to the authors of *Bush's Brain* (Moore and Slater 2004), Rove's dirty political strategies have been consistently vindictive throughout his career. 'Rove didn't just want to win; he wanted the opponents destroyed,' they wrote (quoted in *Boston Globe* 2005).

More recently Karl Rove has been connected to the Valerie Plame CIA-leak story. Special prosecutor Patrick Fitzgerald was given the assignment of looking for the person(s) who illegally revealed Plame's identity as an undercover CIA operative. It became clear that the motive for revealing her identity was to retaliate against her husband, Joseph Wilson, who had publicly questioned some of the Bush rationale for the 2003 invasion of Iraq. Rove, though not immediately indicted, was still under investigation at this writing, and the entire affair fits his traditional modus operandi.

According to John DiIulio, the University of Pennsylvania professor who first ran Bush's 'Faith-Based Initiative' office, almost everything the White House did under Bush was done for political not policy reasons. The political team (especially Rove and Karen Hughes, along with Vice-President Cheney) was involved in practically every decision that was made. Rove was especially keen on maintaining the support of the Christian right, a political aim that was responsible for many of the most troublesome policies for women. Ron Susskind describes DiIulio's frustration in *The Price of Loyalty*:

> After eight months in the White House, DiIulio felt his initiative had been revised from Bush's campaign rhetoric about 'compassionate conservatism' – a way to support those in need – into a political and financial prop for those evangelicals who were in 'the base'. (Susskind 2004: 170)

Almost a year after leaving the White House, DiIulio told a few close White House friends,

> There is no precedent in any modern White House for what is going on in this one: a complete lack of policy apparatus. What you've got is everything – and I mean everything – being run by the political arm. (Susskind 2004: 170)

Karl Rove was at the center of this politicization of the presidency.

John Ashcroft

One of the most controversial appointments of the Bush presidency, Ashcroft served as Attorney General for the first term. *New York Times* columnist Anthony Lewis called him an 'unfit' nominee on the extreme right of American politics. 'As a member of the Senate Judiciary Committee he worked to block the confirmation process, without a hearing, of any judicial nominee he suspected of the faintest of liberal taint,' wrote Lewis, even trying to 'outlaw abortions for victims of rape or incest' (Lewis 2000). Ashcroft had a reputation for religious fundamentalism and a taint of race-baiting from his political campaigns and previous positions as state legislator, governor, and senator from Missouri. When he was governor, he had vetoed a maternity leave law and funding for domestic violence programs, and he strongly opposed the Equal Rights Amendment (Cooper 2001).

During his Senate years Ashcroft most notoriously opposed the Clinton judicial nomination of Judge Ronnie White to a federal appeals court. White, a moderate African-American justice of the Missouri Supreme Court, had upheld the imposition of the death penalty about as often as most other judges on that court. But, in a fiery speech on the Senate floor, Ashcroft denounced White as 'pro-criminal' on the basis of one particular opinion he wrote in which he objected to the death penalty in the case under review (Tiefer 2004: 38). Ashcroft privately persuaded his colleagues to oppose this moderate judge, leading to the defeat of the nomination on a strictly party-line vote. According to Charles Tiefer, after the White nomination was defeated a number of Ashcroft's colleagues realized that he had 'deceived them about the part that race played in the matter,' leaving them feeling betrayed (Tiefer 2004: 38–9). Perhaps in part due to that event, but also because of his far-right ideology, Ashcroft lost his Senate re-election bid in 2000 to Mel Carnahan, the Democratic candidate who had died in a plane crash a month before the election. Because of the voters' rejection and Ashcroft's reputation, his nomination to head the Justice Department, with its responsibility for enforcing civil rights, affirmative action, and similar laws, was the most contentious of all those requiring Senate approval. Nevertheless, Ashcroft was confirmed as Bush's first-term Attorney General by a narrow vote.[2]

Liberal fears and conservative hopes were realized with Ashcroft's leadership of the Justice Department, as he carried out many of Bush's most conservative policies, deflecting criticism from Bush himself, who could then remain above the fray. Through his own appointments and initiatives, Ashcroft moved the nation seriously to the right, especially in the areas of women's reproductive rights and general civil liberties. His use of the Patriot Act to invade the privacy and assault constitutional rights of those he suspected of wrongdoing was widely reported and criticized, but there was little his outranked Democratic opponents could do. At least one of his most outrageous suggestions was halted by public outcry: in the post-9/11 atmosphere, in a move that seemed more like the Stalinist Soviet Union than the 'Land of the Free,' Ashcroft proposed that every citizen should spy on other citizens – family, co-workers, neighbors, plumbers, and so on – under 'Operation TIPS,' which encouraged citizens to report suspicious activities to the government (Conason 2004: 106).

In terms of issues specifically affecting women, Ashcroft's opposition to abortion and related reproductive rights was the most significant. In spite of his pledge during his confirmation hearings that he would not ask the Supreme Court to overturn *Roe* v. *Wade*, he mounted a multiple-front attack on aspects of the law that could undermine the basis for Roe. Among his actions while in office was to subpoena women's medical records from health clinics and hospitals that had performed late-term abortions, stating his suspicions that these were not really medically necessary. Ashcroft's true aim in this invasive ploy was probably just intimidation, and federal judges quickly stepped in and prevented the order from being carried out. However, this action shows the extent to which Ashcroft would go to overrule women's privacy and health in order to restrain a medical procedure of which he disapproved, one that was incidentally completely legal. Instead of prosecuting serious domestic threats to abortion providers, Ashcroft went after women seeking medical treatment. It was also Ashcroft who introduced the questionable concept of 'fetal pain' into official discussions, suggesting that women seeking abortion be warned about the pain the procedure would cause the fetus and that they be offered anesthesia for the fetus during the procedure.

A supporter of 'states rights' only when it served his interests, Ashcroft brought suit against the State of Oregon on the basis of the Federal Controlled Substances Law, trying to overturn its assisted suicide law. This law had been twice supported by a majority of Oregon voters. The law allows terminally ill patients at the end of their lives to request (and receive) medication that ends their lives in a dignified and painless way, providing hope for those who have horrible illnesses that result in unbearable pain, suffering, and loss of functioning (Lane 2005). The law was ultimately upheld by the courts.

Perhaps symbolically, the action that best describes the puritanical Ashcroft was his order to put up curtains around a bare-breasted Spirit of Justice statue in the Great Hall of the Justice Department in Washington. The drapes were installed in 2000 at a cost of $8,000 for the purpose of allowing the Attorney General to speak in the Great Hall without having to fear the intrusion of a bare breast lurking behind him in a photograph or television news clip. The 12½-foot statue had been installed in the building in the 1930s, but Ashcroft was the first Attorney General to require the statue to be draped at all times (*USA Today* 2005).

In other actions, Ashcroft was able to bring in many far-right individuals to the Justice Department, resulting in many problematic decisions and policies emanating from that agency. His appointments included a number of radical anti-abortion, homophobic, authoritarian, and antifeminist conservatives. A strong supporter of fundamentalist Christian attempts to break down the wall between church and state, Ashcroft personally led prayer meetings at the beginning of each day in his office.

Always a lightning rod for criticism, Ashcroft was never part of Bush's inner circle but had been appointed in the first place to please the religious-right section of the base (Conason 2004: 98–9). He was one of the few Bush Cabinet members from the first term who left at the beginning of the second, replaced by Bush's long-time friend and advisor Alberto Gonzalez.

Claude Allen

The first-term Deputy Secretary of Health and Human Services, Allen was appointed Chief Domestic Policy Advisor to the president in January 2005, serving until his sudden resignation in early 2006. An African American, Claude Allen is a strong religious-right Republican, having once served as press secretary to the ultraconservative former Senator Jesse Helms (R–NC). Allen is an advocate of 'abstinence only' sex education, even opposing safe-sex education to combat AIDS. In an interview on Amy Goodman's *Democracy Now!*, the political journalist Doug Ireland described Allen's problematic positions:

> Claude Allen has been [one of] the AIDS community's ... number one enemies for some years, because he is an opponent of condom use. He is a proponent for years of the theory that condoms do not work to prevent AIDS. And he has worked very hard to replace science-based sex education with the failed policy of abstinence-only sex education as the only way to prevent AIDS. (*Democracy Now* 2005a)

In addition to his abstinence-only, anti-condom stance, Allen is staunchly opposed to abortion in all, or almost all, cases. In his position as Commissioner of Health and Human Services in Virginia, he opposed health coverage for abortions for underage victims of incest, rape, and other forms of abuse. When the state legislature passed the law anyway, Allen was deliberately slow to enroll eligible girls in the program (*Democracy Now* 2005a). Allen helped to draft Virginia's parental notification law and supported a 24-hour waiting period for women seeking abortions. He also supported requiring that medically misleading information be given to women seeking abortions prior to the waiting period (Feminist Majority Foundation 2003a). The Feminist Majority Foundation reports that

> during Helms' 1984 re-election campaign, … Allen accused
> Helms' opponent James Hunt, who was serving at the time as the
> Governor of North Carolina, of having ties to 'radical feminists'
> and 'queers' as well as socialists and labor unions. Incredibly, Allen
> later explained that his reference to 'queers' had not been about
> gay people but about Hunt's 'odd' campaign staff. (SIECUS 2005a)

As Deputy Secretary of HHS, Allen supported various anti-abortion and abstinence initiatives, including helping to extend insurance coverage to fetuses under the Children's Health Insurance Program (without coverage for pregnant women) (SIECUS 2005a). President Bush approved of Allen's views so much that he twice nominated him to the US Court of Appeals, Fourth Circuit, but the confirmation was blocked both times by Senate Democrats. The raising of Allen to the highest domestic policy advisory position signalled Bush's far-right ambitions for his second term. A few weeks after he resigned his position, Allen was arrested in Maryland for felony theft (Londoño and Fletcher 2006).

Scott J. Bloch

Special Counsel, US Office of Special Counsel. Brought into the Bush Justice Department by John Ashcroft, Bloch first served as Associate Director and then Deputy Director and Counsel to the Task Force for Faith-based and Community Initiatives (US Office of Special Counsel 2005). In late December 2003 he was unanimously confirmed to the position of Special Counsel in the OSC, an office that is charged with protecting federal employees from job discrimination, retaliation for whistle-blowing, partisan evaluation, and other unfair practices. Bloch seems uniquely inappropriate to carry out these important missions and has created controversy for his strong anti-gay agenda. During his relatively short tenure, Bloch has taken a number of actions that threaten, rather than protect, federal workers' right to work in a discrimination-free environment (Berkowitz 2004).

A graduate of the University of Kansas law school, Bloch had little knowledge of the job when he was nominated, by his own admission.

Soon after taking over the position he created a controversy in the agency by announcing plans to review the 1978 law that prevents the firing of an employee for non-job-related causes. His apparent purpose: to be able to fire gay or lesbian employees. The *Federal Times* reported that federal employees would no longer be protected 'if they are fired or demoted simply for being gay' if Bloch had his way, reversing a policy in effect since the Reagan era (Berkowitz 2004). Bloch also ordered the removal from complaint forms and the agency's website all references to sexual orientation as a basis of claims of discrimination, harassment, or retaliation (Berkowitz 2004). Employees of his office in early March 2004, only three months after he took office, filed a complaint against Bloch accusing him of instituting 'illegal gag orders, cronyism, discrimination, and retaliation,' the very actions the office is supposed to oppose (Seper 2004).

When members of Congress heard about Bloch's actions, they demanded that President Bush intervene and fire Bloch. But Tony Perkins, president of the Family Research Council, defended Bloch's homophobic actions as 'pro-family' and consistent with his right to interpret the law. The White House did intervene to the extent that Bloch was ordered to sign a statement reaffirming commitment to the traditional understanding of the 1978 law – that is, that gay and lesbian workers would be protected from discrimination or firing on the basis of their sexual orientation (Berkowitz 2004).

A few months later, in October 2004, a group of Democratic Congressional Representatives sent a letter to President Bush complaining that Bloch still had not restored the language he had removed from the OSC website and training materials citing sexual orientation as a protected category in federal employment (at this writing in late 2005 he still had not done so). Furthermore, when the Social Security Administration began renegotiating its contract with the American Federation of Government Employees in May, the SSA followed Bloch's lead and proposed removing protection of employees from sexual orientation-based discrimination from its contract as well. Because of widespread protests (and the ongoing political campaign), Bush ordered a change and the proposal was withdrawn, at least temporarily (Berkowitz 2004).

Bloch, a conservative Catholic and social conservative, has a history of opposing feminism, multiculturalism, and gay rights, going back to his college days in Kansas. Although Bush has often sought to portray himself as neutral on issues of sexual orientation, his appointment of people such as Bloch to an office overseeing employment discrimination and whistle-blowing can be seen as trying to have it both ways. Indeed, Bush had courted and received support in his first presidential campaign from prominent conservative gay-advocacy groups, including the Log Cabin Republicans and Republican Unity Coalition. He also appointed a few openly gay men to White House staff positions, committees, and executive offices. These groups came to view Bush with suspicion after he took a sharp right turn to please his 'Christian' conservative base with his 'marriage promotion' that explicitly leaves out gay and lesbian couples; sex education that ignores homosexuality; support for faith-based organizations that discriminate against non-heterosexuals; and appointment of individuals such as Bloch. Scott Bloch is only one of the more visible anti-gay appointees in Bush's administration – still there after all the controversy (Berkowitz 2004).

Anita K. Blair

Deputy Assistant Secretary of the Navy, Blair was named in 2003 to direct the Pentagon's investigation of sexual assaults and harassment of women at the Air Force Academy. Blair was one of the founders of the Independent Women's Forum and an opponent of co-ed training of women in the military. She had opposed the admission of women to Virginia Military Institute in 1997, causing a number of critics to question whether she was the right person to lead the inquiry into a similar institution. Sociologist Mady Segal, who had served with Blair on a Congressional Commission looking into the 1997 Aberdeen Proving Ground rape scandal, opposed Blair's appointment to head the Air Force Academy inquiry, saying 'Anita Blair is clearly identified with a position, and the position is that she is opposed to women in the military' (Soraghan 2003). Blair's nomination created so much opposition that she was replaced by Tilly Fowler, who had also worked on the Aberdeen investigation

that had found evidence of frequent sexual discrimination and harassment (Weller 2003). It was Secretary of Defense Donald Rumsfeld
who initially appointed Blair and who replaced her, showing that
sometimes public criticism can have an effect.

Gerald A. Reynolds

Named in March 2002 to be Assistant Secretary of Education for the
Office of Civil Rights (serving by recess appointment). In December
2004 Bush appointed Reynolds chair of the US Commission on Civil
Rights (US Commission on Civil Rights 2005). Reynolds has never
been a civil rights activist and has a long record of vehemently opposing affirmative action and other civil rights safeguards he is charged
with protecting. He has served as president of the conservative Center
for New Black Leadership and as a board member of Project 21.
Reynolds's nomination to the Office of Civil Rights in Education
was opposed by the traditional civil rights groups, including the
NAACP, and by women's groups, because he would be responsible
for the enforcement of Title IX, the primary gender-equity law for
federally funded educational institutions (Fears 2005; Weiburg 2001).
According to Jocelyn Samuels of the National Women's Law Center,
Reynolds was 'committed to undoing Title IX athletic policies in very
serious ways' (Stearns 2004). He views discrimination as primarily a
thing of the past, arguing that education is the answer to African-
American disadvantage (Fears 2005). According to Fears, Bush has
transformed the traditionally independent and liberal Civil Rights
Commission into a 'bastion of conservatives' by his appointment of
Reynolds and others, thus undermining its traditional role as the
'conscience of the government' on issues of discrimination.

Nancy Mitchell Pfotenhauer and Margot Hill

Named in 2002 to the National Advisory Committee on Violence
Against Women, Pfotenhauer is president and Hill is a board member
of the Independent Women's Forum, which is on record as opposing
the Violence Against Women Act, the very Act the Committee was
established to help implement. Both women have testified against
the law. In the 1990s, Pfotenhauer was an officer of Citizens for a
Sound Economy, a group that helped to defeat the Clinton health

reform proposal. She now heads the organization under its new name, Americans for Prosperity Foundation; the APF opposes most government social programs and business regulations (Women's eNews 2002; Americans for Prosperity Foundation 2003). In congressional testimony, Pfotenhauer had claimed that the Violence Against Women Act would 'do nothing to protect women from crime,' but would 'perpetuate false information, waste money and urge vulnerable women to mistrust all men' (Sourcewatch 2005).

BUSH'S AMBIVALENCE ON GAY APPOINTEES

Not all of the Bush's appointments have been as thoroughly conservative as some of those described above. In fact, Bush received a lot of criticism from his Christian right supporters when early in his first term he appointed an openly gay man, Scott Evertz, to head the White House Office of National AIDS Policy as the nation's 'AIDS czar.' Evertz, who had formerly served as president of the Wisconsin Log Cabin Republicans, was the first ever openly gay appointee in a Republican White House. His appointment dismayed many Bush supporters on the religious right, some of whom even accused him of bringing a 'gay agenda' into the White House. James Dobson of Focus on the Family was strongly critical of the appointment, given his belief that AIDS is primarily caused by 'rampant homosexual behavior' (Groening and Brown 2001). Probably due to Evertz's influence, Bush named several gay men to the Advisory Council on HIV/AIDS. These men were mostly conservative on women's issues – Evertz himself is anti-abortion, having been a fundraising executive for the Wisconsin Right to Life organization.

The White House's internal conflict over gay rights issues has led to inconsistent policies and actions, revealing some of the clashes between the socially moderate economic conservatives and religious right supporters. The confusion over the Office of National AIDS Policy is revealing. At various points there were rumors (even an announcement by Andrew Card) that the office would be closed, but it remained open in spite of some opposition (Noah 2001; Chibbaro 2003, 2004). In July 2002, Scott Evertz was replaced by Dr Joseph O'Neill, another openly gay man, but one who was expected to be less supportive of the use of condoms and needle exchange programs than his predecessor. While the appointment of a second gay man in the White House pleased the Log Cabin Republicans, it disturbed religious conservatives, especially since Evertz was kept on as a senior advisor on global AIDS issues in the Department of Health and Human Services (Cassels 2002). A year later, Bush again made a change in the White House position, transferring O'Neill out to be deputy coordinator of the Global AIDS Office in the State Department. Several months later, during which the White House position remained vacant, Bush named Carol Thompson to succeed O'Neill, ending speculation that he might shut down the office or leave the post vacant until after the election (Chibbaro 2003, 2004). The long delay led some members of the president's Advisory Council on HIV/AIDS to express concern that leaving the position vacant signalled a decline in the president's commitment to domestic AIDS issues. At the same time, the expected appointment of Christopher Bates to the White House position failed to materialize, causing further speculation that Bush was now reluctant to appoint a third gay AIDS czar, especially in an election year (Chibbaro 2004). The frequent turnover in this position, intermittent speculation about its demise, and White House silence on its existence indicate conflicts within the administration over how to handle issues relating to homosexuality.

Other controversial appointments will be discussed with relevant topics in later chapters, but the brief list in this chapter provides an insight into some of Bush's major criteria when it comes to appointments: ideological conservatism, approval by the religious right, and thus willingness to restrict rights, minimize problems, and oppose aggressive remedies for discrimination or disadvantage, backed up by the conservative organizations from which they are drawn.

4

MANAGING INFORMATION: ERASURES, MANIPULATION, DISTORTION

The Bush administration expends a great deal of energy attempting to hone its public image and promote its policies though information management, in some cases hiding behind a veil of secrecy, in others using distortion, 'junk' science, and misrepresentation to sell its programs to the public. This administration has been called the most secretive in American history, conducting business behind closed doors, closing access to papers and documents, and holding fewer press conferences than any recent president (Carter 2004; Dean 2005). Instead of providing information, Bush and his appointees prefer to 'manage' information for political purposes. When Dick Cheney held secret talks with energy company representatives to develop the administration's corporation-friendly energy policy, it was well publicized. In spite of lawsuits and many requests for information about who participated in those talks, the administration never released the information.

Another very common Bush practice is to announce publicly a popular, moderate position while taking action to undermine the very position he publicly supports. Sheldon Rampton and John Stauber write: 'Imagery substitutes so thoroughly for substance that the Bush administration's photo opportunities have often directly contradicted his actual policies' (2004: 152–3). These authors describe how in March of 2001 Bush visited the Egleston Children's Hospital in Atlanta Georgia, telling them how he planned to submit a budget to the Congress, one priority of which would be 'making sure the health care systems are funded.' Yet Bush's first budget actually proposed cutting funds to children's hospitals, including the one where he made these comments.

The same authors provide several similar examples of Bush's habit of supporting programs publicly while undercutting them by his actions. In 2002, he visited a housing project supported by a HOPE VI grant from the US Department of Housing and Urban Development. Bush was photographed standing alongside a number of satisfied residents who had received assistance from the program, which helps pay for housing construction and rehabilitation in distressed areas. In his remarks, Bush praised the project and the value of home ownership in American society; but in his 2004 budget proposal, he completely eliminated funding for HOPE VI (Rampton and Stauber 2004: 153–4).

In yet another example, Bush received much attention for promising help to police, rescue workers, and firefighters after the 9/11 events. Yet he later actually opposed funding to assist communities to hire more firefighters, in spite of the fact that fire departments across the country were understaffed. The wide gap between Bush's photo-op promises and the actual help he offered led the International Association of Fire Fighters to vote unanimously to boycott Bush's 2002 tribute to the firefighters who died in the September 11 attacks (Rampton and Stauber 2004: 153).

In still other ways, and more than is usual for American presidential administrations, the Bush team has misrepresented facts, removed useful information from government websites, and provided misleading information as if it were true and even scientifically supported, all for political purposes. Under the guidance of Karl Rove, this administration has been very successful at presenting itself in favorable images while acting in ways contrary to the public interest. No wonder there have been so many recent books about presidential dishonesty and secrecy, including John Dean's *Worse than Watergate* (2004), Al Franken's *Lies and the Lying Liars Who Tell Them* (2003), David Corn's *The Lies of George W. Bush* (2004), and

Eric Alterman's *When Presidents Lie* (2004). This Bush White House appears to do just about everything it does for political advantage, not for the good of the country or the world – and certainly not for women, children, workers, or minorities. In the remainder of this chapter I look at ways in which this distortion of information has affected women.

REDUCING PUBLIC ACCESS TO RELIABLE INFORMATION

When people need information today, their first impulse is often to look to the Internet, rather than (as in the past) to go to the library. The Internet has become the major source for all sorts of information, greatly expanding public access to all manner of data. Since websites are not monitored or rated for accuracy, most Internet users know to look at the credentials of the website under review before believing everything found on it. One source that in the past has generally been believed to have great reliability was the United States government, especially for information about health care, safety, labor and population statistics, and a variety of types of information available. Under the Bush administration, this sense of trust in government information has been betrayed, as changes have been made to government websites that actually reduce the amount of helpful information available; in other cases, the 'information' provided has been unreliable or misleading. The changes instituted by Bush appointees to websites useful to women often have had the effect of minimizing their 'problems' and presenting overly optimistic accounts of where women are today, sometimes deleting more realistic data that could support efforts to improve things. In the following pages I give several examples of how information about or relevant to women has been suppressed or distorted under this administration.

Removing information from the Women's Bureau website

In mid-April 2004, the National Council for Research on Women (NCRW) issued a fascinating report, *Missing: Information about Women's Lives* (NCRW 2004a). The document describes the removal by Bush appointees in the Women's Bureau of the Department of Labor of important information that had been available previously. The report lists twenty-five documents that had been removed from the Women's Bureau website. These included: *Don't Work in the Dark: Know Your Rights*, *Handbook on Women Workers*; and fact sheets on *Domestic Violence: A Workplace Issue*, *Earning Differences between Women and Men*, *Women Who Maintain Families*, *Black Women in the Labor Force*, *Working Women Count*, *Equal Pay: A Thirty-five Year Perspective*, and *Women's Earnings as a Percent of Men's 1979–1997* (NCRW 2004a: 14).

These missing reports and fact sheets (along with many others) are no longer available through the Women's Bureau; nor are most being updated. Gone also is any information at all about sexual harassment in the workplace, how one might deal with it, and how to protect oneself from harassers. In place of the removed documents are a few left over and some new ones, mostly with flashy and upbeat titles such as: *Hot Jobs for the 21st Century*, *Women Business Owners*, and *Women in High Tech Jobs*. I used to access the Women's Bureau website myself as a quick data source for comparing earnings of women and men by education and by specific occupation, important evidence on continuing wage differentials. These useful tables are no longer available at the website.

In the past, the Women's Bureau was a nonpartisan unit concerned with doing research and providing information of assistance to women workers, advocates, scholars, and others with an interest in understanding women's issues and promoting equality. Under Bush and Secretary of Labor Elaine Chao, the mission has become a less engaged and informative one. The NCRW report quotes the former mission statement (as of 1999) as including 'the responsibility to *advocate* and *inform* women directly and the public as well, of women's *rights* and employment issues. … To ensure that the *voices of working women are heard*, and their *priorities represented* in the public policy of the Women's Bureau' (emphasis added). The former activities of the Women's Bureau included alerting women about their workplace rights, proposing 'policies and legislation to benefit working women,' and performing and disseminating research on issues of women and work. By stark contrast, the Bush-revised mission is more employer- and business-oriented.[1] A recent (2005) revision of the mission statement contains no language about women's rights, the need to include their voices or serve as an advocate. The new mission is more narrow: 'to promote the well being of wage-earning women, improve their working conditions, increase their *efficiency*, and advance their opportunities for profitable employment.'

Women's Bureau programs now focus more on providing resources to women employers and business owners, rather than on the needs of women wage earners and their rights. The current Women's Bureau names its major initiative 'Strengthening the Family,' placing women's economic activity within the frame of their family roles. Under that rubric, there are four initiatives with subheadings 'Better Jobs,' 'Better Earnings,' 'Better Living,' and 'Value-Added Partnerships.' Under 'Better Jobs' are listed just three current projects supported by the Bureau, one an Internet-based project to 'increase awareness of the benefits of a career in nursing;' a second on entrepreneurship for women with disabilities; and another to help military spouses to access training and job opportunities. Under 'Better Earnings,' an online course on money management for young women is listed, along with related conferences. Under 'Better Living,' the Bush administration's 'Flex-options' program is described, a program that seems to be designed with employers in mind, not workers.[2]

The 'Value-Added Partnerships' section gives an email newslist that announces programs of the Bureau and describes a series of 'leadership forums' whereby women 'leaders' participated in conferences to discuss the Bureau's 'demonstration projects.' In keeping with the pro-business (and conservative religious) agenda, the participants listed in these forums did not include representatives of women's labor organizations, but instead consisted of representatives of 'faith-based organizations, chambers of commerce, employers, local industry and state and local governments,' and the events often had corporate sponsorship. Thus, the business-oriented, conservative philosophy of Bush and Chao has seemingly completely taken over the office that was designed to assist women workers to know their rights and improve working conditions and opportunities.

Removing guidelines about sexual harassment in schools

In January 2001, just before the Clinton administration left office, a *Revised Sexual Harassment Guidance* was issued by the Office of Civil

Rights (OCR) of the Department of Education, intended to replace a similar 1997 document. The revision was developed 'in light of subsequent Supreme Court cases' about schools' responsibility for preventing and stopping harassment (US Department of Education 2001). Under the new Bush administration, OCR 'archived' this revised *Guidance* with no notice or explanation, leaving the 1997 version in place, thus obscuring from public view the implications of more stringent recent Supreme Court rulings (NWLC 2004b: 17–18).

Removing documents of the US Commission on Civil Rights

The US Commission on Civil Rights lists a number of 'Documents removed from the US Commission on Civil Rights website,' including some that are highly critical of the Bush administration for its lack of commitment to civil rights, including women's rights.[3] The documents were removed by the reconstituted committee with a new Republican chair, based on what the Commission's website calls a 'new policy on the public release and posting of documents.' Among the removed documents were several draft reports 'that failed to receive a majority of Commissioners' votes' (Hibbitts 2005). A week after one scathing report was submitted, the chairperson of the Commission, Mary Frances Berry, was forced to resign and the report was never published (Jackson 2005). The documents removed include briefings on Civil Rights issues facing Muslims and Arab Americans after 9/11; a summary of voting rights problems in Florida; and other reports on racial and gender discrimination in the United States.

Misinforming the press (and the public) about the global gag rule

On Bush's first day in office, he reinstated the 'global gag rule,' thus preventing foreign recipients of US family-planning aid from even discussing abortion as a medical option, lobbying or advocating for legal reforms, or promoting greater public awareness of abortion options. This ruling, as discussed in Chapter 6, has resulted in reduced family-planning services, higher unwanted pregnancy rates, and higher maternal and abortion-related mortality in many poor countries. However, in order to sell the controversial policy to the press, the White House 'employed a careful misinformation strategy,' according to Jennifer Pozner of the media watchdog organization FAIR (Fairness and Accuracy in Reporting) (Pozner 2001). Bush justified his action in a memo to the US Agency for International Development by asserting: 'It is my conviction that taxpayer funds should not be used to pay for abortions or advocate or actively promote abortion.' Press Secretary Ari Fleisher promoted this rationale as well, and it was this reasoning that was carried forth by the media to explain the policy (Pozner 2001).

The rationale was misleading, however, since it had already been illegal (since 1973) to use US taxpayer funds to finance foreign abortion services or promotion. What the gag rule did was to withhold monies for other family planning services from organizations that wished to use *other* funds (their own, or donations from other countries) to pay for abortions, to advocate for liberalization of abortion law, or even to discuss the possibility of abortion as a solution for pregnant women in the midst of life crises. Thus US funds that might have supported family planning education, provision of contraception, well-baby care, and anti-AIDS programs were unavailable to any organization that had anything to do with even discussing abortion as an option with patients or referring them elsewhere for the procedure. As Pozner points out, most initial press reports failed to correct Bush's error, or, if they did, they placed it in inconspicuous places in their reports, with the result that the public was mostly misled as to the real impact of the gag rule.

Removing emergency contraception from rape victim treatment guidelines

In January 2005, the Justice Department released a new national set of guidelines to be issued to law enforcement agencies and health workers for the immediate treatment of rape victims. These guidelines will likely be used by medical personnel across the nation to guide their procedures in dealing with survivors of rape. Most advocates say that health workers should advise rape victims of the possibility of pregnancy and inform them of the availability of emergency contraception, offering it to them if they want it. The initial drafts of the new federal guidelines included these actions in the protocol. However, in the process of review within the Bush Justice Department, this key provision was removed, leaving no mention of emergency contraception in the final protocol. In its place is a vague suggestion that providers should discuss 'reproductive health options' with the victim. The decision to remove the explicit directives about emergency contraception was widely condemned (Lewis 2005; ACLU 2005).

This issue is not merely academic or technical. In a National Public Radio *Morning Edition* program aired on 14 February 2005, a rape victim told how she was devastated when, six weeks following her rape, the same doctor who examined her following the trauma told her she was pregnant. He had failed to inform her on the first visit that emergency contraception was available. Had she known, she would have taken it and avoided the double trauma of discovering the pregnancy and obtaining an abortion (Lewis 2005). Apparently this scenario is not all that rare – reinforcing the need to include emergency contraception instructions explicitly in the protocol.

Even though the US Centers for Disease Control (CDC) recommends giving emergency contraception to rape victims, and the American Medical Association recommends informing and giving victims the option of choosing it, the Bush Justice Department chose to go along with the minority of radical anti-abortion supporters who claim that emergency contraception is really a very early abortion, contradicting the overwhelming medical consensus. Given the fact that the majority of Americans support the use of emergency contraception (and even abortion) in the case of rape, the omission again shows the Bush team to be clearly out of the mainstream and hazardous to women's health needs (Lewis 2005).

Removing information on sex education and condom use

Under Bush administration directives, the CDC dropped a project called 'Programs that Work' that aimed to identify and share information about sex education programs that were successful at reducing early sexual activity and teen pregnancy. The five programs that met the criteria of success in 2002 all used 'comprehensive sex education,' teaching methods of contraception and protection while encouraging abstinence for teenagers, not 'abstinence-only' approaches.[4] According to an anonymous source within the CDC interviewed by authors of a March 2004 Union of Concerned Scientists report, the agency was forced to discontinue the project 'at the behest of higher-ups in the Bush administration' and to remove all information about the programs from its website (UCS 2004a: 12).

The same website in 2000 had a fact sheet on the proper use of condoms, their effectiveness in preventing sexually transmitted diseases, and comparisons of different types of condoms, with links to the 'programs that work' information described in the previous paragraph. In December 2002, the condom information was revised, removing the guides to correct use and emphasizing instead the failure rates of condom use and promoting the effectiveness of abstinence (NCRW 2004a: 8–9). Thus the ideological emphasis on abstinence, to the exclusion of information on contraception or prophylactics, is not only affecting the sex education of adolescents, but has reduced information about successful sex education programs that could be useful to scholars, educators, citizens, and public health workers.

Attempting to close down the Government Printing Office

Author Joe Conason reports that the Bush White House at one point sought to shut down the Government Printing Office, the main agency that has provided information from the executive and legislative branches of government 'since the earliest days of the Republic.' Justified as a cost-cutting measure, in effect such a measure would shut down one more source of information needed by the public in exercising their democratic responsibilities of keeping a watchful eye on the government's activities (Conason 2004: 105).

Discontinuing data collection on women's employment

In the fall of 2004, the US Bureau of Labor Statistics (BLS) announced its intention to discontinue data collection by gender in their *Current Employment Statistics* (CES) survey. This survey is a nationwide monthly survey of payroll records for workers covering over 300,000 businesses, providing important information on women's employment by industry. The data allow analysts to track where women and men are gaining or losing jobs in response to various economic conditions. The stated reasons for the action, according to the BLS, were that it imposed too heavy a burden on the reporting businesses, that the data were 'little used,' and that the *Current Population Reports* would provide similar information.

The Institute for Women's Policy Research (IWPR) in Washington DC, a think-tank on women's economic issues, registered strong objection, pointing to the uniqueness of the CES data, which are 'extremely useful for research on women's employment.' The Institute also stated that since the proposed revisions involved expanding data collection on other items, it seemed unreasonable not to include data on gender also.

> As we all know, women and men generally work in very different places in the labor market; occupational segregation by sex is a persistent feature of U.S. employment. Job losses and job gains over the course of a recession and recovery vary tremendously by industry, leading to unpredictable differences between women's and men's experiences over the business cycle and in response to structural change. Without accurate, timely data, we may develop misleading pictures of employment changes for both men and women and institute ineffective policy solutions. (IWPR 2004)

The IWPR objection also noted that the *Current Population Reports* do not provide the same information, since they are collected from households, not business establishments. 'Without information on [gender from the CES data], important questions regarding women's employment and job loss across the business cycle will be impossible to answer,' they asserted (IWPR 2004). In spite of calls to continue the collection of the CES gender data, the BLS in August 2005 discontinued the series. In a *Boston Globe* article critical of the action, Derrick Jackson wrote:

> The ending of the data collection comes from a Bush administration that has repeatedly deleted the hard truths from official documents – from global warming to racial discrimination at the Justice Department to disparities in healthcare.... I think that in the political arena generally, there's an unwillingness to consider women's issues in employment as being important and different from men. We don't have a lot of willingness among political leaders to address the barriers women face. (Jackson 2005)

Jackson quotes research director Vicky Lovell of the IWPR as saying:

This is the kind of data that can tell you whether women or men are being walled off from certain industries or walled into certain industries. There is still so much difference between the types of work of men and women and still so many barriers to horizontal mobility between industries. (Jackson 2005).

Apparently these are questions the Bush administration does not want analysts to be able to answer.

POLITICAL MANIPULATION OF SCIENTIFIC RESEARCH AND INFORMATION

One of the key principles of science is that empirical results and observations must be accurately and completely reported without political manipulation. Of course, politics and values have an impact on the type of research one does, but most scientists make every effort to be fair and objective and will not, for example, suppress some results in order to promote a preferred outcome. The entire basis of scientific knowledge comes into question when it becomes politicized (as it was in the former Soviet Union, for example), and progress in medicine, technology, and so on, is impeded. That is why the Bush administration's policies with respect to scientific review and information distribution on issues related to women's health and sexuality are so disturbing.

The Union of Concerned Scientists released two reports in 2004 protesting the misuse, manipulation, distortion, and suppression of scientific research for political aims by the Bush administration (UCS 2004a, 2004b). Likewise, the Association of Reproductive Health Professionals lists a number of 'examples of political interference with science' on its webpage (ARHP 2005a). I present some examples of the manipulation of scientific results concerning sexual health, pregnancy prevention, and similar topics for conservative political purposes in the following sections.

Posting junk science on National Cancer Institute website

When the Bush administration took over in 2001, the National Cancer Institute's (NCI) website displayed a *Fact Sheet* that clearly discredited the claim by anti-abortion activists that abortion may increase the risk of breast cancer. The NCI fact sheet drew on the results of a large and definitive study published in the *New England Journal of Medicine* that had refuted the purported abortion–cancer link (NCRW 2004a: 8). Nevertheless, without any scientific justification, NIH officials in 2002 changed the online material so as to imply the strong possibility of a link between abortion and breast cancer, even though staff members of the CDC pointed out that researchers had long dismissed this claim. In a highly critical editorial, the *New York Times* (2003a) called the revised item 'an egregious distortion of the evidence.' After widespread public protest the web information was corrected to state firmly that hypothesized links between breast cancer and abortion find no support in careful medical research. In reporting this incident, the Union of Concerned Scientists concludes that 'it is troubling that public pressure was necessary to halt this promotion of scientifically inaccurate information to the public' (UCS 2004a; Malek 2003).

'Editing' scientific reports for political purposes

In some cases scientific reports have been 'edited' by Bush administration officials to make them more consistent with Bush political goals or to present a more favorable picture than the research supports. A report on socio-economic health disparities requested by Congress was released by the Health and Human Services Department (HHS) in December 2003. The original draft documented 'pervasive' racial disparities in the US health-care system. However, the final report had been redacted at the request of HHS officials so as to present a much rosier picture of the US health-care system than the data justified and to downplay racial and other inequalities in access and quality of care. The introductions to the two versions are revealing. The original draft version began:

> Inequalities in health care that affect some racial, ethnic, socio-economic, and geographical subpopulations in the United States ultimately affect every American. From a societal perspective, we aspire to equality of opportunities for all our citizens. Persistent disparities in health care are inconsistent with our American values. (Jackson 2004)

The edited version began with a much cheerier picture:

> The overall health of Americans has improved dramatically over the last century. Just in the last decade, the United States has seen significant reductions in infant mortality, record-high rates of childhood vaccinations, declines in substance abuse, lower death rates from coronary disease, and promising new treatments for cancer. (Jackson 2004)

The entire report was changed to downplay racial disparities and even to suggest that some 'priority populations' (i.e. Asian Americans) do better than the general population in some aspects of health care. In addition, many other negative facts were deleted:

> Eliminated from the final report was any reference to health care disparities being costly to taxpayers. Eliminated was 'The personal cost of disparities can lead to significant morbidity, disability, and lost productivity.' Eliminated were examples that patients of color were more likely than white patients to be diagnosed with late-stage breast and colorectal cancers; that people of color and people of low income are more likely to die from AIDS, and Latinos are less likely to receive the best care for myocardial infarction. (Jackson 2004)

Once the politicized editing was discovered and made public, Tommy Thompson (then secretary of HHS) was asked by the House Ways and Means Committee to explain the revision, and he had to admit that it was a 'mistake.' Because of the controversy, he agreed to release the original report. However, the fact that the politicized editing had been done in the first place is more evidence of the Bush tendency to place politics before science when reporting information to the public.

A similar incident occurred in 2003 when an EPA report drastically reduced and watered down references to climate change (Revkin and Seelye 2003). The report had been ordered by then-EPA administrator Christine Todd Whitman to provide a complete review of environmental problems for policy assessment. Once the draft reached the White House, requests for changes in the document were made, over the objections of EPA analysts. The requested changes eliminated references to many studies that identified smokestack and auto emissions as partially responsible for climate changes that might threaten health and ecosystems. Entire discussions of climate change were either deleted or changed to imply that scientific data on the issues were still inadequate for making policy decisions. The changes were controversial among some scientists in EPA and were strongly criticized by some nongovernmental environmentalists. Jeremy Symonds of the National Wildlife Federation accused the White House political staff of 'forcing agency officials to endorse junk science.... This is like the White House directing the secretary of labor to alter unemployment data to paint a rosy economic picture' (Revkin and Seelye 2003).

Statistician demoted for refusing to massage report

A *New York Times* article reported in August 2005 that Lawrence A. Greenfeld, head of a small Justice Department office that conducts statistical studies of law-enforcement issues, was ordered to delete references to racial disparities in police traffic stops from a news release he had prepared to announce the results of study (Eggen 2005a). The survey report, based on interviews with 80,000 people, was eventually issued without publicity. The study found that 'minority drivers were three times as likely to have their vehicles searched during traffic stops as white drivers.' After Greenfeld protested the requested deletions, he was reportedly asked to resign. By invoking personnel rules, he was able to remain employed until he was eligible for pension benefits. Although the Justice Department denied any wrongdoing, representative John Conyers requested an investigation of the incident by the General Accounting Office (Eggen 2005a).

In another case, Interior Secretary Gale Norton used data from an oil company instead of more negative findings from the Fish and Wildlife Service on the effects on caribou of drilling in the Arctic National Wildlife Refuge, in order to support the administration's quest to drill in the Arctic refuge (Piven 2004: 58). These examples make one wonder what can be trusted coming from Bush administration official sources. Women's lives are seriously affected by health and environmental issues, and distortions such as these simply prevent the development of policies that would seriously and adequately deal with the problems they present. We all need to know about instances of racial profiling or other discrimination.

The habit of Bush and his appointees of subordinating scientific integrity to short-term political goals has important implications for women and their advocates, since many of the issues about which women care need careful scientific assessment in order to develop sound policy.

Misrepresenting stem cell line availability

In a televised address to the nation on 9 August 2001, President Bush announced his limitations on federal funding for new stem-cell research, claiming that there were more than 60 genetically diverse stem cell lines already in existence that would be sufficient for research that might lead to new therapies and cures for a number of diseases. White House officials later raised the estimate to 'as many as' 78 cell lines that might be available. These claims were never accurate and were vastly exaggerated.

> Shortly after the president's announcement, stem-cell researchers immediately expressed skepticism about the number and quality of available cell lines. This skepticism, while disregarded by the Administration, has proven to be justified. Some of the institutions that had stem cell lines did not have the resources to ship them safely to other labs; others have not developed the lines to the stage necessary for research. Still other lines may have genetic problems. (Waxman and Slaughter 2005a)

In February 2004, the head of stem-cell research at the National Institutes for Health wrote that *at best* there were only 23 cell lines that might be available at some point for medical research under the Bush limitations. That assessment was never released to the public by the administration, which may be just as well, given the fact that the previous April the *New York Times* had reported that there were not 60 lines but only 11 (Reported in Tiefer 2004: 45).

Stem-cell research is considered very promising and important for many of the diseases that disproportionately affect women, such as diabetes and Alzheimer's. In addition, since women are the primary caregivers in most families, their lives are especially impacted when their husbands, brothers, sons, or other family members develop chronic diseases. Bush's refusal to allow embryonic stem-cell research is widely viewed as just one more gift to his ultra-right religious conservative base, since protecting embryos is one aspect of their war against abortion, without regard for the larger health needs of the public. The embryos saved by not being used for research are mostly destroyed. If Bush were truly concerned about the welfare of embryos, he would also oppose the fertility procedures that create them, but he has been silent about *in vitro* fertilization and similar pro-fertility measures.

Politicizing advice to the World Health Organization

In yet another example of the politicization of science, the Department of Health and Human Services has announced that it will henceforth control who may serve as scientific advisors from the US to the World Health Organization. Previously, the WHO invited scientific advisory experts directly, but now the organization must submit its requests to the Office of Global Health in HHS, whose staff will then decide which advisor to appoint. The new policy is presented by HHS as improving accountability, but the written directive to HHS employees notes that in their advisory capacity they act as 'representatives' of the US government, who must therefore 'advocate government policies' (*Lancet* 2004: 114). Similarly, in 2002 the Department of Agriculture announced new rules for the release of scientific information from its Agriculture Research Service. Scientists working for the agency were told they would need prior approval before they could release information having to do with so-called 'sensitive issues' (Carter 2004: 98).

Thus, the subordination of scientific knowledge and expertise to political goals is expanding in this administration, in spite of strong criticism from many quarters. The impact of this attitude can be seen in the attempts by US representatives to question and block global initiatives to reduce global warming, to improve women's status, to promote women's health, and a myriad other worthy goals. In the long run these actions hurt women by promoting as fact incomplete or erroneous information and limiting access to needed resources; but they also undermine the very credibility of government agencies as sources of information while demoralizing serious government scientists.

Stacking scientific panels to get the 'right' recommendations

One of the ways the Bush administration has attempted to control scientific recommendations for its policies has been to replace members of scientific review committees who disagreed with its policies, adding new members who were more politically acceptable. This practice has been widely criticized by members of the scientific community, since decisions should be made on the basis of data and not ideology. In a later chapter I describe this type of action with respect to women's access to certain reproductive drugs, but here I present three examples affecting other issues important to women.

Dismissing members of the President's Council on Bioethics

In February 2004, two distinguished members of the President's Council on Bioethics were dismissed from membership, for the stated reason that the White House wanted individuals with 'different expertise and experience.' Both members who were removed were highly qualified, but they had disagreed with the president's policy limiting research on embryonic stem cells. One of the two was cell biologist Dr Elizabeth Blackburn, who was removed soon after she objected to problems in the Council's report assessing the current state of stem-cell research. Dr Blackburn suggested that the report was misleading in its overly positive presentation of the promise of *adult* stem cells as a substitute for embryonic stem cells. Following her prompt dismissal from the Council, Dr Blackburn wrote: 'The public is done a disservice when science is presented incompetently; myths are then perpetuated' (Waxman and Slaughter 2005a).

Bush's refusal to fund stem-cell research except on very limited 'lines' has been strongly criticized by the medical research community in the United States. A scientific consensus has emerged that supports the need for research on additional stem-cell lines not approved by the president. Writing in the *New England Journal of Medicine*, Dr George Daley pointed to 128 new cell lines that are ineligible for federal funding, resulting in many opportunities lost for working toward potential cures. According to Dr Elizabeth Nable of NIH, the Bush policy has cost the agency its previous leadership in the field, and as a consequence has led many of the best scientists to leave the agency (Waxman and Slaughter 2005a).

Again, as already noted, stem-cell research is important to women not only in its promise for finding cures and treatments for women's diseases, but also because women are the primary caregivers for those who are ill. Moreover, changing the membership on scientific committees in order to promote a particular political agenda threatens the integrity of science, constrains medical discovery, and violates scientific ethics as well.

NIOSH grant-review panel appointees are screened for political views

In November 2002, officials of the National Institute for Occupational Safety and Health had proposed three new members for a panel that evaluates research grant applications in the area of occupational safety. Previously, under Democratic and Republican administrations, the panel members had been selected on the basis of scientific expertise. However, the proposed members in this case were rejected by the Office of the Secretary of Health and Human Services, Tommy Thompson, without explanation. According to a *Wall Street Journal* editorial, at least two of the proposed members were experts in ergonomics who had supported an ergonomics standard that Bush had rejected in 2001. As discussed further in Chapter 9, the ergonomics standards overturned by Bush were especially important to women workers, who sustain many injuries as a result of repetitive-motion work at keyboards, sewing machines, and factory assembly work. Further evidence of the political motivation behind the rejection of proposed members came in a report that the candidates had been asked for their views on ergonomics and other policy issues, as well as how they had voted in the U.S. presidential election of 2000 (Begley 2002). This type of questioning was strongly criticized by scientists and other observers. In this case the administration seemed to be attempting to ensure that the panel's recommendations on ergonomics injuries and remedies fit their already-determined policies.

According to the Union of Concerned Scientists,

> highly qualified scientists have been dropped from advisory committees dealing with childhood lead poisoning, environmental and reproductive health, and drug abuse, while individuals associated with or working for industries subject to regulation have been appointed to these bodies.

Across a wide range of agencies, the Bush administration 'has undermined the quality and independence of the scientific advisory system and the morale of the government's outstanding scientific personnel (UCS 2004c).

Stacking the President's Advisory Council on HIV/AIDS

The President's Advisory Council on HIV/AIDS, known as PACHA, was established in 1995 by the Clinton administration to advise the president on policies, programs, and research on HIV/AIDS. The committee of thirty-five members was intended to bring together medical and scientific expertise to provide advice, information, and recommendations to promote effective prevention and treatment programs. As with other scientific panels, Bush has appointed members who satisfy his political criteria rather than the scientific criteria intended for committee members. Although not all of the Bush appointments would fit that description, some definitely appear to have been appointed primarily for their support for the president's abstinence-based approach to HIV. Among the most controversial are the following three nominees.

- *Joe McIlhaney*, appointed to the Council in 2002, is the founder and head of the Austin, Texas, Medical Institute for Sexual Health, a nonprofit organization that sponsors seminars and produces educational materials endorsing sexual abstinence. McIlhaney opposes the use of condoms or comprehensive safe-sex education in fighting HIV/AIDS, accepting only 'abstinence until marriage, faithfulness in marriage' approaches. According to one report, McIlhaney and the Institute promote marriage as 'the best public health strategy' for fighting premarital pregnancy and sexually transmitted diseases. Dr Scott Spear, who once served with McIlhaney on a committee to develop a curriculum for sex education in the Austin schools, commented, 'I found him very difficult to work with ... his argument was that because condoms were not 100 percent effective, we shouldn't talk about them. But in terms of prevention, there's nothing we do that is 100 per cent effective.' Although McIlhaney has authored a number of books, he does not publish in standard peer-reviewed medical journals. Spear questioned McIlhaney's scientific background and experience, averring that the appointment was made to please 'a group of religious extremists who helped put Bush in office' (Apple 2002).

- *Jerry Thacker*, nominated in early 2003 to serve on the Advisory Council, had no scientific expertise, instead having a background in religious activism and marketing. Thacker teaches 'gay reparative therapy' and argues that homosexuality is a 'deathstyle' and a sin from which 'Christ can rescue' the sinner. He has referred to AIDS as a 'gay plague' (*San Francisco Chronicle* 2003). According to a *San Francisco Chronicle* report, Thacker's appointment 'stunned' many AIDS researchers and activists, who noted that Thacker had argued that religious faith could cure homosexuals, that condoms do not stop the spread of HIV, and that people choose to be gay. 'When you appoint someone with this social view, it is dangerous,' said James Weiss, deputy director of health for AIDS programs with the San Francisco Health Department. 'This individual is an extremist ideologue who persecutes and demeans an entire class of people impacted by this disease,' said David Smith, spokesman for the Human Rights Campaign. 'That type of person has no business advising the president of the United States on how the government should address the epidemic' (*San Francisco Chronicle* 2003). This nomination was so outrageous and raised enough outcry that Bush quickly withdrew it before Thacker was ever seated as a Council member.

- *Freda McKissic Bush*, another nominee to PACHA, was a board member of Joe McIlhany's Medical Institute. Dr Bush shares McIlhaney's pro-abstinence, anti-condom approach to AIDS and STDs. She belongs to a medical group in Jackson, Mississippi, whose mission statement begins with an acknowledgement of the 'Lordship of Jesus Christ' in their professional as well as personal lives. Dr Bush speaks frequently on sex education and sexually transmitted diseases, encouraging 'a lifestyle of abstinence until marriage and fidelity within marriage' (Medical Institute 2005). According to her biography on the Medical Institute website, Bush has also been the medical director of the Center for Pregnancy Choices–Metro, Jackson, and co-president of the Mississippi Family Council, both Anti-abortion 'pro-life' organizations. Like many conservative 'crisis pregnancy centers,' the Center for Pregnancy Choices in Jackson today includes a great deal of misinformation about abortion on its website. For example, visitors to the website who explore the link 'considering abortion' are warned not to have an abortion before eight weeks because of the danger of perforation or incomplete removal, which can lead to infection, infertility, toxic poisoning, and even death. The website claims that 10 per cent of women undergoing elective abortion will suffer 'immediate complications, of which 2 per cent are considered life-threatening.' Another claim is that patients who undergo abortion have a 50 per cent higher chance of breast cancer, and that 50 per cent of abortion patients have emotional and psychological disturbances lasting for months or years. Finally, the website implies that most people who provide abortions are unethically doing so for financial gain (Center for Pregnancy Choices 2005). All of these claims are unsupported by standard scientific and medical research. Dr Bush's association with these types of organization has raised questions about the appropriateness of her appointment to PACHA.

These nominations illustrate the Bush administration's preference for making appointments on the basis of ideology rather than solid public health science where conservative policy issues are at stake.

REACTION OF THE SCIENTIFIC COMMUNITY

The serious nature of the distortions and misuses of science by this administration is indicated by the strong reaction of many working scientists. In February 2004 over sixty leading scientists, including Nobel laureates, former federal agency directors, leading academics, and medical experts, signed a statement condemning the Bush administration's unprecedented disregard for science. They claim that

> when scientific knowledge has been found to be in conflict with
> its political goals, the administration has often manipulated
> the process through which science enters into its decisions ...

by placing people who are professionally unqualified or who have clear conflicts of interest in official posts and on scientific advisory committees; by disbanding existing advisory committees; by censoring and suppressing reports by the government's own scientists; and by simply not seeking independent scientific advice. (UCS 2004b)

The open letter goes on to assert that the administration has at times misrepresented scientific knowledge and misled the public in order to gain support for its policies. While other administrations have occasionally acted similarly, the UCS scientists claim that the level and breadth of scientific manipulation and distortion of the current Bush administration is unprecedented. By March 2005, over 6000 scientists had signed the document (UCS 2004c).

THE DANGERS OF POLITICIZING INFORMATION

The level of disinformation and manipulation of science perpetrated by this administration in the interest of its narrow political goals is unprecedented in American history. Since the ability to move forward depends on a correct assessment of our current situation and its problems, this interference with scientific reports and public information is injurious to those who seek to promote change. By stacking scientific committees to achieve the desired results, the integrity of the entire advisory system is brought into question. The production of bogus scientific results and the biased reviews of scientific knowledge on such issues as the health effects of abortion, the best way to prevent HIV/AIDS, the proper use of condoms, and the availability of scientific resources provide cover for policies that are not based on accurate information. They also misinform the public in ways that can be harmful, even though they serve the purpose of maintaining the support of social conservatives or anti-regulation business interests. In the long run, however, the politicization of science is a dangerous trend that will lead to a weakening of the respect that American scientists have held for generations.

REPRODUCTIVE RIGHTS, SEXUALITY, AND ABSTINENCE: LIMITING WOMEN'S FREEDOMS

THE BIRTH CONTROL REVOLUTION

The ability to control pregnancy with contraception has been one of the most liberating elements of change in women's lives in the past half-century. Even through the 1950s, contraceptive methods were difficult to obtain and lacked effectiveness, with the result that many women faced more pregnancies, births, and childrearing than they wanted. However, with the introduction of oral contraception in 1960, women's lives rapidly changed. The pill led to many changes in women's roles in society. Reliable fertility control allowed women to move into the job market and higher education without fear of disruption by unplanned pregnancies. With the pill, women's sexuality also began to change, and the so-called 'sexual revolution' gained momentum. Women who chose to do so could express themselves sexually without fear of pregnancy, which meant they could begin to pay more attention to their own sexual needs. Women were able, for the first time, to live their lives without taking into consideration the random threat of disruption by pregnancy and childbirth. Throughout the 1960s and 1970s, birth rates declined rapidly.

Studies carried out in the 1960s showed that low-income women were twice as likely as others to have unwanted children, due partly to lack of access to family planning services and resources. Over time a growing consensus developed that family planning should be made available through federally funded programs to help women control their childbearing, thereby encouraging economic development, poverty alleviation, self-support, and better health for women and their families. In 1965, federal funds for family planning were authorized through the Johnson War on Poverty, and later state welfare agencies were required to provide family planning services to women receiving assistance. In 1970 Title V of the Public Health Service Act was signed by President Nixon, initiating a comprehensive federal program devoted to providing family planning services nationwide (Alan Guttmacher Institute 1997).

Birth control was still not perfect, however, and as women gained independence and confidence in their expanding roles they began to push for relaxation of laws they now perceived as restrictive – including laws that severely restricted abortion at any stage of pregnancy. By the early 1970s, the women's movement was in full bloom, and with it growing public pressure to legalize abortion. In 1973, the Supreme Court handed down the important *Roe v. Wade* decision denying states the ability to prohibit abortion in the first three months of pregnancy, and allowing restrictions only to protect the woman's health in the second trimester. Thus contraception allowed women more control over their lives, and abortion provided a back-up for those whose circumstances would not reasonably allow them to have a child when contraception failed. Death and morbidity rates from illegal abortion declined dramatically after these events.

SEX EDUCATION WARS

Some women did not immediately benefit from the greater access to birth control – especially teenage girls, whose rates of sexual activity increased without a concomitant rise in the use of reliable contraception. Throughout the 1970s, 1980s, and 1990s, US teenagers had higher rates of pregnancy and unprotected sex than their counterparts in Europe. The HIV/AIDS epidemic and the increase in sexually transmitted diseases (STDs) also raised the alarm among the population, who came to realize that more needed to be done to educate teenagers and to help prevent early pregnancies and/or STDs. Although sex education was always somewhat controversial in the US, by the late 1980s most states had programs of sex education that discouraged early sexual activity but at the same time provided students with a range of information about sexuality, reproductive health, pregnancy, abortion, and contraception (Levine 2004).

Conservatives often opposed these courses in the public schools, and over time they had some success in persuading school boards to eliminate or limit them, arguing that the comprehensive sex education courses actually encouraged teens to engage in sexual intercourse by showing them how to do so safely.[1] This backlash was led mainly by Christian conservatives, who often misunderstand or misrepresent comprehensive sex education, arguing that it does not encourage abstinence and that it teaches what they consider 'immoral' behavior as normal. In the latter category would be information about homosexuality, abortion, premarital sex, and the use of contraception. While most comprehensive sex education programs do encourage abstinence and provide ways to deal with pressures to engage prematurely in sexual behavior, they make an effort to present sexuality as a positive aspect of human relationships if handled well and provide information about pregnancy and STD prevention (Levine 2004).

'Abstinence-only until marriage' programs have been funded by the federal government for two decades, in spite of the dearth of evidence of their effectiveness in preventing early sexual activity, pregnancy, or STDs. Federal funding of such programs increased dramatically after 1996, when Title V of the Social Security Act was established as part of the welfare reform with little publicity or debate. Under this law, states can receive grants from the federal government for developing and teaching abstinence-only programs (SIECUS 2004). The federal definition of 'abstinence education' includes strict guidelines that must be followed in order for states to be eligible to receive funds. These include a specification that 'a mutually faithful monogamous relationship in the context of marriage is the expected standard of all human sexual behavior,' thus immediately marginalizing such common behaviours as adult cohabitation, single adult sexuality, or same-sex relationships. The 'standard' assumes that all persons will marry unless they plan to remain celibate, and that they will not engage in sexual intercourse or other sexual behavior until they are married. Given that the average age at marriage for men in the US is now 27, and for women 25, this seems quite unrealistic and far removed from actual behavior. Nevertheless, these curricula ensure that young people in such classes will not receive solid information about contraception, 'safe sex' practices, and the establishment of healthy sexual relationships. Indeed, the guidelines require that students be taught that all sexual activity 'outside the context of marriage is likely to have harmful psychological and physical effects' (SIECUS 2004; see also Levine 2004).

Originally these programs were an experiment funded through the Department of Health and Human Services (HHS), authorized for five years; but, instead of being phased out in 2000, they have been expanded under the current administration. Now, in addition to state grants from HHS for abstinence-only education, programs are being funded by a number of other federal sources, including funds allocated for the prevention of HIV/AIDS (SEICUS 2004).

Research shows that comprehensive sex education is successful in encouraging teenagers to use contraception if they engage in intercourse, thus reducing the number of unwanted early pregnancies and sexually transmitted diseases. Other research shows that while abstinence-only education may delay the onset of sexual activity by a few months, it also reduces the probability that young couples will use condoms, since they have been told in their classes that such methods are unreliable (Levine 2004: 451). Thus, by promoting abstinence, omitting critical information about sexual health, and discounting the value of condoms, these programs may actually be leading to a greater incidence of sexually transmitted disease and more early pregnancies.

Under President Bush, comprehensive sex education programs have received decreasing support, while funding and priority have increased for 'abstinence-only' approaches. In abstinence-only courses, discussion of the use of condoms or contraceptives to prevent pregnancy or sexually transmitted diseases is not allowed, and abstinence is presented as the only appropriate sexual behavior prior to marriage. The problems with these courses are serious, even where they are well designed, since they offer little help to those who will be initiating sexual relationships, as the majority do now in the high-school years. However, problems with the most popular Bush-funded programs go even further, as they have been found to contain misinformation and false and harmful stereotypes of women and men. They also usually present a very negative view of premarital sexuality as dangerous, a claim that is bound to discredit them in the eyes of most teenagers. In addition, the programs are now often designed and run by federally funded conservative religious organizations, under Bush's 'faith-based initiatives,' and their ultimate religious purposes are not always hidden.

In a recent review of six popular curricula based on abstinence-only (*Choosing the Best PATH, Choosing the Best LIFE, I'm in Charge of the FACTS, FACTS and Reasons, Sex Respect*, and *A.C. Green's Game Plan*), SIECUS noted that the curricula all 'are based on religious beliefs, rely on fear and shame, omit important information, include inaccurate information, and present stereotypes and biases as facts' (SIECUS 1996–2005)[2] The abstinence-based curricula portray premarital sexual behavior as 'universally dangerous' and omit discussions of safer sexual practices, since their answer is that the person must 'just say no.' Moreover, there is little federal oversight of these programs, even when they are federally funded.

In December 2004, California Representative Henry A. Waxman (D) issued a report of an investigation of the content of several federally funded abstinence-only education programs (Waxman 2004). The chapter headings of the report illustrate the study's findings:

- Eleven of Thirteen Abstinence-Only Curricula Contain Errors and Distortions
- Abstinence-Only Curricula Contain False and Misleading Information about the Effectiveness of Contraceptives
- Abstinence-Only Curricula Contain False and Misleading Information about the Risks of Abortion
- Abstinence-Only Curricula Blur Religion and Science
- Abstinence-Only Curricula Treat Stereotypes about Girls and Boys as Scientific Fact

- Abstinence-Only Curricula Contain False and Misleading Information about the Risks of Sexual Activity
- Abstinence-Only Curricula Contain Scientific Errors

The report points out that a number of the organizations receiving funds under the one main federal abstinence-education program are openly opposed to abortion. These organizations include a number of 'crisis pregnancy centers,' anti-abortion agencies that have been repeatedly criticized for distorting information about the risks of abortion. According to the Waxman report, several of the curricula used by these and other taxpayer-funded programs provide clients with misleading information about the physical and psychological effects of legal abortions either by exaggerating their dangers or by using out-of-date statistics about complication rates. For example, one curriculum states that sterility results in up to 10 per cent of women who undergo abortion; in fact, contemporary obstetrics textbooks say that fertility is not affected by elective abortion. In other distortions, the curriculum claims that abortion increases the risk of premature birth, ectopic pregnancies, mental retardation in children born subsequent to abortion, and serious mental health problems to the woman, contrary to current medical research.

The curricula examined in the Waxman study were found to promote stereotypes about sex differences in roles, abilities, and psychological traits. Among the stereotypes uncovered in the study (found in the curricula being funded by the US government) are the notion that 'girls care less about achievement and their futures than do boys' (Waxman 2004: 16). Another example was the following quotation from one of the curricula being used:

> Just as a woman needs to feel a man's devotion to her, a man has a primary need to feel a woman's admiration. To admire a man is to regard him with wonder, delight, and approval. A man feels admired when his unique characteristics and talents happily amaze her. (Waxman 2004: 16)

The same curriculum lists 'financial support' as one of the five major needs of women, but not men, whereas 'domestic support' is one of the five major needs of men, but not women (Waxman 2004: 17).

Other curricula describe girls as 'helpless or dependent on men,' using stories and teacher directives that sound as if they might have come from the Victorian age. For example,

> One book in the 'Choosing the Best' series presents a story about a knight who saves a princess from a dragon. The next time the dragon arrives, the princess advises the knight to kill the dragon with a noose, and the following time with poison, both of which work but leave the knight feeling 'ashamed.' The knight eventually decides to marry a village maiden, but did so 'only after making sure she knew nothing about nooses or poisons.' The curriculum concludes: Moral of the Story: Occasional suggestions and assistance may be alright [*sic*], but too much of it will lessen a man's confidence or even turn him away from his princess. (Waxman 2004: 17–18)

Such sexist stereotyping by materials funded by the United States government, which has laws supporting equal rights and opportunities, seems incredible; but under the Bush administration these types of messages are being promoted to children across the country with tax dollars. The Waxman report concludes:

> Under the Bush administration, federal support for abstinence-only education has risen dramatically. This report finds that over two-thirds of abstinence-only education programs funded by the largest federal abstinence initiative are using curricula with multiple scientific and medical inaccuracies. These curricula contain misinformation about condoms, abortion, and basic scientific facts. They also blur religion and science and present gender stereotypes as fact. (Waxman 2004: 22)

Again, independent scientific research questions the value of abstinence-only programs, supporting the superiority of traditional programs that teach about contraception and protection from STDs and pregnancy, while still encouraging abstinence (Levine 2004). Nevertheless, the Bush administration has increased funding for abstinence-only programs every year, ignoring scientific data on the subject.

There is little doubt that the motivation behind Bush's insistence on abstinence-only has less to do with a desire to protect young people from the consequences of unprotected sex and more to do with a punitive and negative attitude toward non-marital sexuality.

Whether this is a cynical pandering to his religious right supporters or a true belief in such values is an open question. Whatever
its origin, its effects are to put more young women at risk and to
reinforce negative attitudes about their sexuality.

In a related matter, the measures of success of sex education
programs were revised by Bush appointees so as to mask the failure
of the administration's 'abstinence-only' programs (NCRW 2004a:
8–9). In previous administrations, government guidelines required
assessments of sex education programs by following up the female
participants and measuring their sexual activities and/or pregnancies
and birth rates, with comparisons to averages for their social groups.
Under the new Bush guidelines, programs are deemed successful if
participants have a high rate of attendance and if they respond in
the approved way to questionnaires at the end of the course (NCRW
2004a: 8–9). Thus, the standard of evaluation has been lowered,
making true assessments impossible, while providing political cover
for the administration's ineffective programs.

MISINFORMATION AND INEFFECTIVE ADVICE FOR PARENTS

Bush has carried his abstinence message, along with its associated misinformation, further in an outreach effort to parents. In
March 2005, the Department of Health and Human Services (HHS)
launched a website for parents of teenagers (www.4parents.gov) with
the stated aim of helping them discuss 'healthy choices, sex and
relationships' with their teenaged children. The website presents
sex before marriage as dangerous and always unacceptable, while
providing little support for parents who wish to communicate with
their children effectively about responsible sexuality.

The 4parents website was almost immediately called into question
by traditional sexuality educators and public health experts for its
'fear-based, biased, and inaccurate information' (SIECUS 2005b).
According to SIECUS, for example, the 4parents site 'does not
address the needs of many youth, including sexually active youth,
youth who have been or are being sexually abused, and lesbian, gay,
bisexual, transgender, and questioning (LGBTQ) youth.' SIECUS
calls on the government to suspend the website, set up a group of

experts in public health, sexuality, and communication to review its presentation, and revise it to be more inclusive, less fear- and shame-based, and more respectful of diversity.

Representative Henry Waxman of California had several experts in sexuality-related issues review the website and has posted their reviews on a House website.[3] The review from Professor John Santelli, head of Columbia University's Department of Population and Family Health, is illustrative of the critiques of 4parents.gov: 'My overall impression is that, while the website has some correct facts about sexually transmitted infection (STI) risk, its primary message – that sex outside of marriage is extremely dangerous and the only solution is to abstain – is unrealistic and unlikely to work' (Santelli 2005). Professor Santelli goes on to explain that the information in the website is incomplete and misleading, lacking any discussion of contraception to prevent pregnancy, for example. The abstinence-until-marriage message is so overwhelming that it 'virtually abandons' parents whose children are sexually active, providing them with no advice on how to reduce risks of pregnancy or STIs. Santelli criticizes the website's message for its lack of awareness of research on communication between parents and teens on sexual issues, as well as its disregard of the scientific research on the effectiveness of condoms and contraception. He gives several examples of important results of research that are left out of the discussion on the 4parents website and criticizes the sources and accuracy of the information presented. Waxman's posting includes his own letter to Secretary Michael Leavitt and the responses of four experts (including Santelli), all of which note inaccuracies, incompleteness, and likely ineffectiveness in the 4parents presentation.

THE PARTIAL-BIRTH ABORTION BAN

On 5 November 2003, President Bush signed new legislation that would limit women's access to safe abortion while instituting criminal penalties against physicians who perform them. The so-called 'partial-birth' abortion ban is based on political misrepresentation of medical procedures, its backers implying that it would only apply to certain rare, late-term abortions that use a procedure known as 'intact dilation and extraction.' Many legal and medical experts disagree, noting that its vague wording places in jeopardy many of the safest abortion procedures commonly used today, even at relatively early stages of pregnancy. More importantly, and contrary to many recent court rulings, the law contains no provision to allow such procedures in order to protect the health of the pregnant woman. In a symbolically revealing photograph, President Bush was shown signing the bill surrounded by a smiling, self-congratulatory group of nine apparently all-white, all-male (mostly aging) congressional supporters of the bill. Immediately after he signed the bill into law, three lawsuits were filed challenging its constitutionality, and all three were successful. Federal District Judges in New York, California, and Nebraska all agreed that the law was unconstitutional because it contained no exemption for the health of the woman (IWHC 2005e).

In late September 2005, US Solicitor General Paul Clement filed an appeal before the US Supreme Court asking that it reinstate the ban. Even though Nebraska's similar state law had been overturned by a 5:4 Supreme Court ruling, Bush was apparently hoping that by the time the current case was decided the balance of the court would have changed to uphold the ban. In submitting the appeal, Clement argued that the Court should ignore the medical evidence that showed that the ban would prevent doctors from being able to protect women's health in some cases. Instead, said Clement, the Court should defer to the wishes of Congress (James 2005). At this writing, the case is pending, but it should be decided by the summer of 2006, now by a Roberts-led court that includes conservative justice Samuel Alito, who replaced the moderate Sandra Day O'Connor.

REDEFINING THE STATUS OF THE FETUS, AT THE EXPENSE OF WOMEN

The Bush administration and its appointed representatives have made some headway in redefining the fetus, even the fertilized egg, as a person with legal rights, in a strategy moving toward outlawing abortion. In October 2002, embryos were given a new status in the revised Charter of the HHS Secretary's Advisory Committee on Human Research Protections. The purpose of this committee is to oversee research, to protect human subjects from unethical or unsafe research practices. The previous Clinton-appointed committee was disbanded and a new, smaller committee was formed and given a new charter. The new charter states that the group is to review research on human subjects, 'with particular emphasis on ... pregnant women, embryos, and fetuses,' thus defining even early embryos in experiments as 'human subjects' (Weiss 2002).

In a related move, following the passage of the partial birth abortion ban, Attorney General John Ashcroft assigned responsibility for its enforcement to the civil rights division of the Justice Department, thus framing the law in terms of the 'civil rights' of the fetus. Since the same office is charged with protecting women's health clinics from harassment or violence, such a redefinition establishes a conflict of interest for civil rights enforcers – whether to protect women from harassment or their fetuses from 'murder' by abortion. The delegation of enforcement to the civil rights office provoked strong objections, especially from proponents of traditional civil rights issues. Democratic members of the House Judiciary Committee sent a letter of protest to Ashcroft calling the move 'Orwellian,' since the law itself had been found by the courts to violate women's civil rights (Egelko 2003). The implications of such a Justice Department ruling are disturbing for supporters of women's rights to control their bodies.

In a similar vein, Bush supported the passage in 2004 of the 'Unborn Victims of Violence Act,' another new law that defines the rights of the fetus separately from those of the pregnant woman (*Guardian* 2004; PPFA 2004a: 25–7). The law was presented as a protection for women ('not about abortion') but alternate bills that would have simply added to the normal assault penalty if a woman is pregnant and/or for harming her pregnancy or fetus were defeated. Thus, an assault on a woman that causes a miscarriage could potentially result in a murder charge as well as an assault charge. More significantly, it seems reasonable to assume that, once this precedent is established, medical procedures that harm the fetus could likewise be considered illegal.

In still another move to enhance the legal standing of the fetus, the Children's Health Insurance Program (CHIP) guidelines were extended to provide health coverage to fetuses of pregnant women (now covered from conception to age 19), but not to pregnant women (*Guardian* 2004). Bush's prohibition on embryonic stem-cell research, similarly, is based on the ultimate notion that a human embryo deserves the protections granted to a 'person' under the law. Overall, then, on several fronts, moves have been made to elevate the status of the embryo or fetus to that of a person with separate rights and protections, actions that are aimed ultimately at outlawing abortion.

REDUCING ACCESS TO CONTRACEPTION FOR EVERYONE

In 2005, a 'federal refusal clause' became law as an amendment to a major appropriations bill, without debate and without a vote in the Senate. The bill was presented in terms of 'nondiscrimination' against health-care providers who oppose abortion, including physicians, hospitals, health insurance plans, or 'any other kind of health-care facility, organization, or plan' (NWLC 2005b).

Under law existing before this bill, it was already the case that no hospital could be compelled to perform abortions, except in medical emergencies. And most states had individual refusal laws, so that anti-abortion physicians had the right to refuse these procedures. What the new law does is to further encourage health-care entities to impose abortion prohibitions on physicians who work for them in hospitals or clinics. Clients of health insurance companies or HMOs that receive federal monies for Medicaid might also be affected. According to the National Women's Law Center, the impact of the law is unclear, but the intent was that it be applied very broadly, such that it might have the following consequences:

- Health-care corporations could issue gag rules so that physicians working for them would be prohibited even from making referrals for abortion, or even providing any information on abortion as an option. This sort of 'gag rule' has been issued in the past for clinics receiving federal funds, but this new law could expand the reach of such rules.

- The rule could also stop states from funding abortions for low-income women through Medicaid, for abortions not covered by the 'Hyde Amendment'. That amendment prohibits the use of federal funds to pay for abortions except in cases of rape, incest, or to save the life of the woman. Thus, states' own rules, paid for by their own funds, might be overridden by federal rules.
- The ruling might reduce states' ability to protect women's access to reproductive services, where the state has laws prohibiting community-based hospitals from refusing to provide these services. The penalty for noncompliance as specified in the new law is not only the loss of family-planning funding, but of *all* federal funding for health, education, and labor. Thus the federal government could force states to shut down most abortion-related health services. (NWLC 2005b)

DOES BUSH OPPOSE CONTRACEPTION? TROUBLING QUESTIONS

As we saw in Chapter 2, early in his first term Bush proposed dropping a requirement that all health insurance programs offered to federal employees provide coverage for contraception. According to the *Washington Post*, 'the move sends a message of support to social conservative groups that do not believe the federal government should be in the business of making contraceptives available at all' (Nakashima 2001). This action was condemned by many women's advocates as discriminatory, since it affected only women and was contrary to the president's stated desire to reduce abortions and unwanted pregnancies. Bonnie Erbe, writing for Scripps Howard, expressed puzzlement at the president's action.

> It is news to a lot of people that Bush is symbolically opposed to the use of contraception, or would single out its coverage in this way.... It also seems bizarre to single out one category of drugs, used almost entirely by women, for exclusion from a federal program. It would not seem so bizarre if, for example, the president's budget disqualified coverage for prescription forms of birth control and for Viagra, a drug that treats erectile dysfunction. Then the administration would at least be consistent in its distaste for coverage of any drugs having to do with sex. But Viagra was apparently not targeted. (Erbe 2001)

Erbe notes that the Alan Guttmacher Institute estimates that without the requirement, only about a third of the policies held by federal workers would cover oral contraception, even though 97 per cent of the policies cover prescription drugs in general. In the end, the contraception exclusion was removed from the budget that was passed by the Congress. But this early Bush action raised troubling questions in the minds of many as to the president's concern for women's lives and health.

Further questions were raised the following July, when the state of New York requested permission to expand contraceptive coverage for Medicaid recipients in the state by raising the income limits for eligibility. Medicaid recipients have long been eligible for contraceptive coverage, but only if their incomes are less than 185 per cent of the poverty line. New York wanted to expand eligibility to those under 200 per cent of poverty level, making contraceptive coverage available to thousands more women. The poverty level at the time for adults was $8,590 per year. In July 2001 the Bush administration denied New York's request (McCaffrey 2001).

After four years of his administration's support for abstinence and lack of support for family planning, the question of Bush's attitude toward contraception came up in a press conference. On 26 May 2005, White House Press Secretary Scott McClellan was asked publicly if Bush supports contraception. Ominously, McClellan refused to answer, instead going round and round in an attempt to deflect the question. The questioner in this case was Les Kinsolving:

Q   There are news reports this morning that parents and children who were guests of the president, when they visited Congress, wore stickers with the wording, 'I was an embryo.' And my question is, since all of us were once embryos, and all of us were once part sperm and egg, is the president also opposed to contraception, which stops this union and kills both sperm and egg?

Mr McClellan   I think the president has made his views known on these issues, and his views known –

Q   You know, but what I asked, is he opposed – he's not opposed to contraception, is he?

Mr McClellan   Well, and you've made your views known, as well. The President –

> *Q*   No, no, but is he opposed to contraception, Scott? Could you just tell us yes or no?
>
> *Mr McClellan*   Les, I think that this question is –
>
> *Q*   Well, is he? Does he oppose contraception?
>
> *Mr McClellan*   Les, I think the president's views are very clear when it comes to building a culture of life –
>
> *Q*   If they were clear, I wouldn't have asked.
>
> *Mr McClellan*   – and if you want to ask those questions, that's fine. I'm just not going to dignify them with a response. (White House 2005a)

McClellan's refusal to affirm that the president supports contraception, and his allusion to the 'culture of life,' raised red flags among many observers. 'Culture of life' is a code word for Bush's extreme anti-abortion stance, which for many of his base supporters includes opposition to most methods of birth control – that is, those other than abstinence during high-fertility periods or 'rhythm.' In an attempt to clarify the issue, nineteen members of Congress wrote to Bush asking for a clear answer to the question of his support for contraception. The question came up again during a press briefing in June 2005, as Kinsolving pressed the issue:

> [*Kinsolving*]   Nineteen members of Congress from seven states have written a letter to the president saying that they are still waiting for an answer to a May 26th question: Is the president opposed to contraception. And my question is, could they now have an answer to my question? Or do you regard them, too, as not to be dignified with a response?
>
> *Mr McClellan*   No, I think we've talked about these issues before and these issues when it comes to the federal government and programs aimed at promoting abstinence and how those ought to be funded on at least equal footing with other programs, so I think we've addressed the president's views in that context. (White House 2005b)

Representative Carolyn Maloney of New York has posted on her website the texts of the two Congressional representatives' letters to Bush asking for a clear response to Kinsolving's question. (A second letter was sent after the June refusal to respond.) She comments:

It is absurd that the president's spokesperson is unable to answer this simple question.... He can't even give a straight answer. The continued failure of the White House to answer this question is evidence of the mounting attack on access to birth control. (Maloney 2005)

Her posting goes on to say

The White House's silence on birth control comes at a time when women's access to birth control is threatened. Individual pharmacists across the country have recently refused to fill prescriptions for birth control because of personal objections, the House of Representatives has voted to strike any mention of contraception from legislation on family planning, and the president has nominated a man with no clear record on women's rights to replace the first woman to serve on the Supreme Court. (Maloney 2005)

As of late 2005, Bush had not answered this question.

ABORTIONS RISE UNDER BUSH

A study by a professor at Fuller Theological Seminary, a relatively conservative California evangelical institution, showed that the Bush anti-abortion policies and rhetoric have failed to reduce abortions in the United States. Contrary to widespread assumptions, abortion rates rose during the Bush presidency, in large part due to his economic policies (*Sojourners* 2004). Professor Glen Stassen reported that 'under President Bush, the decade-long trend of declining abortion rates appears to have reversed.' Abortion rates had declined by 17 per cent in the 1990s to a 24-year low by 2000, but they had risen after Bush took office. Stassen estimates that there were 52,000 more abortions in 2002 than would have been expected had the pre-2000 conditions continued. The study found that economic hardship was a major cause of abortion. Two-thirds of women choosing abortion give as a reason the inability to afford a child, and half say they do not have a reliable partner or co-breadwinner. In addition, women of childbearing age are disproportionately among those who lost health insurance coverage since 2000.

In response to the Stassen findings, Jim Wallis, editor of *Sojourners* magazine, a progressive evangelical publication that generally opposes abortion but strongly criticizes Bush's policies, stated:

We have seen once again in this campaign the issue of abortion used as a partisan wedge rather than having a serious discussion on how to act to reduce the number of abortions.... [I]f we're to be truly pro-life, we must focus on real people and the conditions that lead women to seek abortions.... Jobs, health care, and a living income must be part of a pro-life agenda. (*Sojourners* 2004)

IDEOLOGICAL APPOINTMENTS TO
REPRODUCTIVE POLICY POSITIONS

Bush's anti-reproductive rights agenda can be seen in the appointments he has made to offices involved in health-related policy. Since it is often lower-ranked officials who actually carry out policies, much of their activity remains relatively invisible to the public. Once John Ashcroft was confirmed as Attorney General and Tommy Thompson as Secretary of HHS, for example, it was they who made many controversial appointments of officials in their departments. Both Ashcroft and Thompson were strongly anti-abortion and antifeminist, and their appointments and actions reflect those values – this in spite of Bush's claim that abortion attitude would not be a litmus test for appointments (Wokusch 2004).

The case of Claude Allen of Virginia can be used as an illustration of the pattern. Allen was appointed as Bush's first Deputy Secretary of Health and Human Services; he was twice unsuccessfully nominated to the Fourth Circuit Court, in 2003 and 2004; and in early 2005 he was named Bush's Domestic Policy Advisor, a position he held until his sudden resignation in February 2006. An extreme conservative, Allen opposes legal abortion, birth control for unmarried persons, and comprehensive sex education. He has opposed safe-sex education to combat HIV/AIDS and health coverage for abortions for underage victims of incest and rape survivors; and during his time at HHS he helped to develop an extension of children's health insurance to fetuses (see the more detailed discussion in Chapter 3). While many have believed that Bush was making such extremist appointments to consolidate his conservative religious base, the fact that in his second term he appointed such people to more central positions indicates that he himself wants to promote these views and enact them into policy and law. Whether he has acted for strongly held beliefs or merely for cynical political purposes, the end result has been a growing threat to women's health and freedom.

The FDA and reproductive health drugs

The FDA Reproductive Health Drugs Advisory Committee reviews drugs related to reproduction, primarily contraceptives, for safety and effectiveness before allowing them to be prescribed or sold over the counter. By law, recommendations by this committee about new drugs must be made solely on scientific grounds, not political leanings. This committee has incurred controversy during the Bush years for its refusal to approve emergency contraception for over-the-counter sales. To accomplish this, Bush had named a few ultraconservative members to the committee who were reliably opposed to expansion of women's reproductive options. Even though Bush's ideological appointees do not make up the majority of the committee, their presence and votes provide some cover for the administration's negative decisions about reproductive health drugs.

The two most controversial appointees were Drs Joseph Stanford and David Hager. Stanford, a conservative Mormon, is a Utah physician who believes the only acceptable form of contraception is 'natural family planning,' or the 'rhythm method.' In his view other forms of birth control are incompatible with the 'Christian values' of the sanctity of life and marriage (ARHP 2005b; Feminist Majority Foundation 2002). He has published an article arguing that birth control pills should be considered abortifacients and should be restricted on that basis (FDA Advisory Committee 2005). In his role on the committee, Stanford is supposed to review objectively the safety of drugs that he disapproves of on 'moral' grounds.

David W. Hager is a physician who joined the committee in 2002, first nominated as chair but finally seated as a regular member because of widespread opposition. Hager is a fundamentalist member of the conservative Christian Medical Association, who had written several books before his nomination, including one on women's health in which he argued that Bible reading and prayer might be effective treatments for some of women's common health problems (IWHC 2005a). Hager had served on the Physicians Resource Council for Focus on the Family and prior to his nomination had actively petitioned the FDA to reverse its approval of RU-486, the 'abortion drug.' It is widely reported that he refuses to prescribe contraceptives to unmarried women. Hager himself has been accused by his former wife of sexual and marital abuse (McGarvey 2005).

David Hager's role in the FDA's rejection of proposals to make emergency contraception available to women as an over-the-counter drug provides revealing insight into the Bush strategy for pushing back women's progress in the realm of reproductive health and choice. Dr Hager was appointed to the FDA Advisory Committee in 2002 and reappointed for a one-year extension when his term ran out in late 2004, both times over strong protests from women's health advocates (PPFA 2004b).

Although Hager had promised to be objective in carrying out his duties and not to allow his personal beliefs to influence his decisions, in December 2003 he was one of four members of the advisory panel (of twenty-seven) to vote against allowing emergency contraception (known as Plan B) to be sold over the counter. This drug has proved highly effective in preventing pregnancy if taken within seventy-two hours (preferably within twenty-four hours) of unprotected intercourse, but its effectiveness declines rapidly after that. The need to obtain the drug quickly was one of the primary reasons supporting over-the-counter access. The other twenty-three advisors were strongly supportive of the proposal, citing its demonstrated safety and potential benefits to women (McGarvey 2005).

Hager's stated reasoning for his opposition suggests that his vote was not based on the safety of the drug, but instead on his punitive attitude toward women's sexuality. According to *US Newswire* (2004), Hager explained his opposition as follows: 'What we heard today [in the discussion of the need for the availability of Plan B over the counter] was frequently about individuals who did not want to take responsibility for their actions and wanted a medication to relieve those consequences.' Hager represents the concerns of the religious conservatives who argue that emergency contraception is in fact an 'abortifacient,' a claim rejected by the great majority of medical experts as inconsistent with standard definitions of pregnancy. In a highly unusual step, the FDA followed the decision of the committee's minority instead of its clear majority, announcing its intention in May 2004 to delay its decision for 'further study.' In January 2005, the FDA once again announced a delay in the decision to approve Plan B for over-the-counter availability, promising a decision by the following September (McGarvey 2005).

In May 2005, the *Washington Post* reported that Dr Hager had sent a separate memo (outside of the advisory committee channels) to the FDA commissioner urging rejection of the emergency contraception application after the supportive panel vote in early 2004. The article suggested that this memo might have swayed the decision of the FDA commissioner (*Washington Post* 2005a; see also McGarvey 2005). In fact, someone in a higher position may have requested that Hager send this memo, to be able to use it as justification for a negative decision – a move that, if true, would have been at variance with regulations and standard procedures for drug approval. Evidence for this was reinforced by a sermon that Hager gave at Asbury College in the fall of 2004, in which he claimed that he 'was asked to write a minority opinion that was sent to the commissioner of the FDA' (McGarvey 2005). When journalist Ayelish McGarvey of *The Nation* asked other panel members if they knew anything about this minority report, none of them did, and McGarvey was unable to learn who had asked Hager to write the dissenting report. Whatever the case may be, Hager's presence on the committee appears to have had undue influence on the decision to delay the approval of emergency contraception for over-the-counter sales.

After having made several promises that a decision would definitely be made by September 2005, in late August the FDA again postponed approval of nonprescription sales of emergency contraception, restating concerns about its safety, especially for teenagers who might obtain the drug illegally. Again the decision was announced with the excuse that still more time was needed for study and public comment (*Washington Post* 2005b). The administration's actions were praised by social conservatives, but the continued delay in accepting this important drug for wide distribution was decried by scientists, health providers, and women's advocates. The decision, in addition to the omission of emergency contraception from medical guidelines for the victims of rape (see Chapter 4), shows the administration's extreme disdain for women's right to make their own decisions about pregnancy when conservative political support is at stake.

Negative fallout: criticisms and resignations

The latest postponement prompted widespread criticism and disapproval. A report released by Representatives Henry Waxman and Louise Slaughter calls the FDA's rationale for its decision misleading. It disputes Commissioner Crawford's claim that 'the agency is unable at this time to reach a decision on the approvability of the application because of ... unresolvable regulatory and policy issues that relate to the application we were asked to evaluate.' In fact, Plan-B producer Barr Labs had designed their revised application precisely according to guidelines given by the FDA itself in its July 2004 letter to the company explaining its earlier rejection (Waxman and Slaughter 2005b).

On 31 August 2005, Dr Susan Wood resigned from her position as FDA Assistant Commissioner for Women's Health, stating her strong dissatisfaction with the FDA's action. Dr Wood criticized the administration's political interference in the decision that she believed should have been based solely on science. In her letter of resignation Wood stated: 'I can no longer serve as staff when scientific and clinical evidence, fully evaluated and recommended for approval by the professional staff here, has been overruled' (*New York Times* 2005c).

The *New England Journal of Medicine* likewise condemned the action in an editorial, stating that 'recent actions of the FDA leadership have made a mockery of the process of evaluating scientific evidence, disillusioned many of the participating scientists both inside and outside the agency, squandered the public trust, and tarnished the agency's image.'

In October 2005, Dr Frank Davidoff, an eminent scientific consultant to FDA, resigned in protest. In his resignation letter, Davidoff wrote: 'I can no longer associate myself with an organization that is capable of making such an important decision so flagrantly on the basis of political influence, rather than the scientific and clinical evidence' (Waxman and Slaughter 2005b). Davidoff stated that he believed Plan B met all the criteria for approval of an over-the-counter drug, based on the large amount of evidence that was presented to the committee (CNN.com 2005b).

In October 2005, a report by the nonpartisan Government Accounting Office (GAO) was released, investigating the FDA's actions in failing to support Plan B for over-the-counter access. The report concluded that the decision-making process had been 'very unusual,' involving extraordinary involvement from top agency officials and unnecessary delays in resolution (Kaufman 2005). The most troubling finding was that high-level officials had reportedly made the decision to reject the application even before it was submitted. In an editorial in response to the GAO report, the *New York Times* wrote:

> It seems pretty clear that those running the agency were looking desperately for a reason – any reason – to prevent easy access to a contraceptive that is a red flag to the administration's conservative base. In doing so, they tarnished the reputation of an agency whose decisions are supposed to be based on science. (*New York Times* 2005g)

The August 2005 decision to postpone approval of the proposal again was announced by Lester Crawford, the acting Commissioner of the FDA at the time; Crawford himself resigned soon after this decision was announced.

BUSH BRAVELY PROTECTS MARRIAGE

On 25 February 2004, Bush announced his support for a constitutional amendment restricting marriage to a contract between a man and a woman. 'The union of a man and a woman is the most enduring human institution, honored and encouraged in all cultures and every religious faith,' Bush proclaimed (CNN.com 2004). 'Marriage cannot be severed from its cultural, religious, and natural roots without weakening its good influence on society,' he continued. This came up because the Massachusetts Supreme Court had decided recently that same-sex couples could not constitutionally be denied the right to marry in the state, and the San Francisco mayor had also decided to offer marriage licenses to same-sex couples. Conservative homophobes were alarmed, and Bush–Rove saw an opportunity to rev up support for the coming election.

Bush was responding to pressure from the religious right to outlaw same-sex marriage, an arrangement that had been gaining support among the public. The usual conservative statements about the historical, religious, and cross-cultural universality of marriage as a 'natural' institution between one man and one woman was, of course, false. Bush and his team simply do not know (or want to admit) the facts, but neither do their supporters, so the claims make for good politics even if they are not true. The issue has been extremely useful for Republicans in motivating their conservative religious base to vote.

The truth is, of course, that human 'marriage' comes in many forms and has not usually been beneficial for women, as it is not always beneficial today. The most common preferred form of marriage historically, in fact, has been polygyny, in which one man is allowed to have more than one wife (but not the other way around). It is true that in most of these cases marriage was between members of two sexes, but even same-sex marriage is not unknown in the diversity of family forms seen historically and cross-culturally (Coontz 2005).

For Bush and conservative Republicans, of course, facts are not important when discussing marriage and sexuality or other issues important to the Christian right. Their use of such emotional issues as gay marriage and abortion to motivate support from religious conservatives is a purely political ploy, but one that has proved very successful in winning elections. Unfortunately, this overheated rhetoric also encourages discrimination and harassment against gays, their supporters, and women's health clinics. The real motivation of these political tactics is to use these hot-button issues to win elections so as to be able to implement the economically retrograde policies that favor big business and affluent Americans – tax cuts, deregulation, and defunding of social welfare programs. As Thomas Frank wrote in his insightful *What's the Matter With Kansas?*,

> The leaders of the backlash may talk Christ, but they walk corporate. Values may 'matter most' to voters, but they always take a backseat to the needs of money once the elections are won. ... Abortion is never halted. ... The trick never ages; the illusion never wears off. *Vote* to stop abortion; *receive* a rollback in

capital gains taxes. *Vote* to make our country strong again; *receive* deindustrialization. (Frank 2004: 6–7)

Unfortunately, as the need to motivate voters becomes more important in a closely divided country, some groups and constituencies may be sacrificed in order to maintain the support of the religious right for the Republican cause. The groups most threatened include supporters of abortion, gay rights, and reproductive health resources. At the very least, the increasingly hostile anti-feminist rhetoric over these issues presents a real problem for women in their struggle to overcome the many barriers to full equality that still exist.

6

RESTRICTING REPRODUCTIVE RIGHTS AROUND THE GLOBE: THREATENING WOMEN'S LIVES TO PLEASE THE RIGHT

These acts are a testament to the Bush administration's war against women and his overall contempt for their fundamental civil and human rights.

> Dr Steven Sinding, Director General,
> International Planned Parenthood Federation

Most Americans would be shocked at the lengths American representatives are going to in their international war against women's right to control their bodies.

> *New York Times*, 19 January 2005

In presidential campaigns and publicity, Bush and his supporters have often included support for international women's rights as an integral part of their message. Laura Bush is frequently brought out to speak on this issue, as when she declared that the Afghanistan war was successful in freeing women. Indeed, when one searches the White House website for 'women,' various actions of the First Lady pop up, as if these issues are not appropriate matters for the president himself to worry about. Here, as with other issues, the Bush rhetoric is not matched by his actions – in fact the opposite is often the case.

The rhetoric *is* very positive, revealing White House recognition that Americans *want* their government to promote women's rights in the global arena. In a campaign speech in 2004, Bush, flanked by Laura and high-ranking administration women, boasted of his record in 'advancing human rights for women' in Afghanistan and Iraq, according to a *Boston Globe* story.

> 'Just think about it,' Bush said at the White House in a speech marking the close of International Women's Week. 'More than 50 million men, women, and children have been liberated from two of the most brutal tyrannies on earth – 50 million people are free. And for 25 million women and girls, liberation has a special significance. Some of these girls are attending school for the first time. Some of the women are preparing to vote in free elections for the very first time.' (Washington 2004)

The *Globe* story went on to suggest that Bush's remarks were meant to counter increasing criticism of the Iraq war and to shore up support among women.

Similarly, the US Department of State has a website under the Office of International Women's Issues (OIWI) that presents the official positive story of the administration's attitude toward women around the world:

> The United States is deeply committed to addressing issues that are important to American women and women throughout the world. Promoting women's political and economic participation in their countries is an important element of US foreign policy. (US Department of State 2006)

The Undersecretary of State for Global Affairs, Paula J. Dobriansky, was quoted on the 2003 version of the OIWI website as follows:

> Ensuring women's rights benefits individuals and their families, strengthens democracy, bolsters prosperity, enhances human rights and advances religious tolerance. It is at the core of building a civil, law-abiding society, which is an indispensable prerequisite for true democracy. The advancement of issues of concern to women has been a long-standing American goal. This administration has intensified that pursuit. (US Department of State 2003)[1]

Thus, the public face of the administration promotes a very positive image of its concern for women around the world. Dobriansky's statement even makes the astonishing claim that the Bush administration has 'intensified' the pursuit of advancing issues of concern to women. Unfortunately, as with Bush's domestic policies on women, the reality is not always matched by the rhetoric, especially in the critical area of reproductive rights.

REPRODUCTIVE RIGHTS AS HUMAN RIGHTS

Reproductive rights are among the most important human rights for women, important in maintaining their own health and having implications for economic development and well-being in general. These rights involve the right to both (1) reproductive health care – access to safe and effective health services such as prenatal care and postnatal care, cervical smears to detect cancer, contraceptive education and provision, and other gynecological services; and (2) reproductive self-determination – the right of each individual to make decisions, free of coercion, about when and how many children to have. The Beijing Platform for Action, developed at the worldwide conference on women's rights in 1995, declared reproductive and sexual rights to be every woman's human right:

> The human rights of women include their right to have control over and decide freely and responsibly on matters related to their sexuality, including sexual and reproductive health, free of coercion, discrimination, and violence. (Burke and Shields 2005: 247)

Providing accurate and easily accessible information and services for family planning is a key to reproductive health, which in turn can reduce maternal deaths by an estimated 25–30 per cent by reducing unwanted pregnancies. According to the editors of the scientific journal *Contraception*,

> The inability to meet these needs is one reason that maternal mortality has remained high in much of the developing world. Each year, up to 200,000 maternal deaths result from lack of contraceptive services and 68,000 from complications of unsafe abortion. Failure to guarantee the right to family planning results in deprivation of the basic right to survival. (Burke and Shields 2005: 248)

The editors go on to point out that family planning is critical in poor countries in ways other than mere survival, leading to higher standards of living and health for everyone. When women are able to limit and plan their pregnancies and births, they are able to provide more resources for each child in terms of health care and education. Lower population growth also means better opportunities for employment and economic growth for the country, as poverty and hunger are reduced. Child mortality is also substantially reduced by allowing greater spacing between births, permitting parents to devote more attention, protection, and nutrition to each child (Burke and Shields 2005: 247). Finally, family planning is basic to a woman's individual quality of life, opening up options to develop her own talents and abilities in pursuit of goals other than motherhood.

Since the 1960s, the United States had been considered a world leader in the provision of family planning education and funding throughout the world. Unfortunately, with the election of George W. Bush, US policies have radically changed, at a very high cost to the world's women. In the very first days of his administration, Bush signaled a retreat from support for international women's reproductive and sexual rights. His policies are calculated to please his social-conservative supporters by promoting a restrictive anti-abortion and anti-sexuality program abroad, while not upsetting his more moderate domestic supporters, many of whom pay little attention to this area of foreign policy and its effects. The media have not treated US international family planning policy as a high-profile issue, leaving most US citizens unaware of these actions, even though the effects of Bush policies have been far-reaching and devastating to women in poor countries.

REINSTATING THE GLOBAL GAG RULE

On 22 January 2001, his first business day in office, Bush reinstated the 'global gag rule' first formulated by President Reagan in 1994, maintained by George H.W. Bush, and overturned by President Clinton in 1993. This rule, also called the Mexico City policy,[2] prohibits foreign agencies receiving US family planning funds through the US Agency for International Development (USAID) from performing abortions and requires that they provide no information or counseling to clients about abortion, including information about the dangers of illegal or self-induced abortion, how one might obtain a safe abortion, or when abortion might be medically necessary to protect the health of the woman. Agency personnel also are not allowed to refer patients for abortions or to advocate for abortion law relaxation. The agencies cannot do these things even using non-US funds if they are to receive US assistance. The only exceptions are very narrow: providers are only allowed to tell a woman 'passively' where she can obtain a legal, safe abortion, if the woman first clearly states that she has already made the decision to have an abortion and the counselor believes it is ethically necessary to respond with the information. The 'provision of abortion services in cases of rape, incest, or threat to the pregnant woman's life' (but not her health) is also permitted (Center for Reproductive Rights 2003). However, many agencies are so intimidated by the possible loss of funds that they refuse to say anything about abortion in any case.

These agencies have been forbidden to use US funds to pay for abortions (even where legal and necessary) since 1973,[3] but the gag rule forbids the agencies to use their own funds for the procedure or even to discuss the issue with patients. Organizations that refuse to go along with the guidelines lose more than monetary support: they also lose important technical assistance and US-donated contraceptives, including condoms, vital resources for the women of the recipient countries. According to the International Women's Health Coalition (IWHC), a New York-based organization that supports women's health services internationally, 'This policy stifles free speech and prevents medical professionals from offering the full range of legal, medically acceptable options to women. It is contrary to US law and would be held unconstitutional if imposed on US-based organizations' (IWHC 2005a). The global gag rule endangers women's lives by restricting access to family planning, forcing the closure of clinics and the cut-back of services due to lack of funds, and consequently increasing the number of illegal abortions and maternal deaths (Population Action International 2005).

In spite of widespread harsh criticism of the policy, in August 2003 Bush actually extended the gag rule to foreign organizations that receive funds from the US Department of State, including vulnerable groups such as immigrant and refugee women displaced by war and civil violence (IWHC 2005a). The Congress has attempted unsuccessfully to overturn this rule.

The consequences of the global gag rule have been enormous. Developing countries must rely on funding from wealthier countries to provide family planning services and the infrastructure to supply such services to all parts of their countries. The ideologically based restrictions imposed by the Bush administration have had highly adverse consequences in many countries, damaging the health and lives of millions of women. The policy sets in motion a vicious cycle: where contraception is restricted, unplanned and unwanted pregnancies occur; this often leads to unsafe abortion, since funded agencies are not allowed to provide, refer, or advise about safe abortions. As a result, higher maternal health impairment and mortality follow: some 78,000 women die each year worldwide from complications of unsafe abortion (Center for Reproductive Rights 2003; Grundy 2003). The very policy intended on the face of it to lower abortion rates has the consequence of increasing them while assuring that they are unsafe. The cruel irony is that abortion now is safer than childbirth under appropriate conditions. But when safe abortion is not available, either due to illegality or lack of access due to inadequate funding or political opposition, desperate women resort to unsafe means.

African impacts

Across the African continent, women have limited access to contraception, prenatal care, and good medical care due to the prevalence of poverty and lack of public health infrastructure. Abortion is illegal in every country except South Africa, which as a result has one of the continent's lowest maternal death rates (230 deaths per 100,000 live births, as compared to the African average of 830) (du Venage 2003). In the past, the United States has been a major benefactor of African nations in its family planning funding through USAID. The global gag rule has led to a major cutback in funding for these programs and in the services provided to poor African women.

Ethiopia

The very poor country of Ethiopia in northwestern Africa has been especially hard-hit by the Bush policies. Its infant mortality rate is 113 deaths per 1,000 live births in the first year of life, a high figure (by comparison, the infant mortality rate in the UK is 5 per 1,000, and in the US 7) (Global Virtual University 2005). In Ethiopia, where abortion is legal only in cases of 'danger to the health of the mother,' unsafe abortion is the leading cause of maternal mortality, accounting for more than half of maternal deaths (du Venage 2003; Loder 2003). Because of the global gag rule, many local organizations decided to decline US funds in order to continue providing a full range of reproductive health options; as a result, their ability to provide contraceptive services has been reduced. Those organizations that agreed to follow the Bush rule, on the other hand, are unable to provide any assistance or advice with respect to unsafe and illegal abortion, leaving women who wish to terminate pregnancies without a safety net (Burke and Shields 2005: 248).

According to a December 2003 *San Francisco Chronicle* report, giving birth in Ethiopia is already a high-risk matter due to poor health care, high poverty rates, and inadequate nutrition. As a result of health risks and the need to preserve scarce resources for the children they already have, many women without access to contraception terminate their pregnancies as a method of birth control. Because of this situation, family planning experts argue that responsible health care needs to include safe-abortion counseling, even where abortion is not provided by the agency doing the counseling. An official of the Ethiopian National Family Guidance organization reported that 'Hospitals tell us they still see many deaths from illegal abortions.... If we are going to keep women healthy and alive, we have to provide abortion-related advice' (du Venage 2003).

The London-based Marie Stopes international family planning agency working in Ethiopia lost its US-based funding because it refused to stop providing abortion counseling for women as part of their health-care program. Similarly, the Ethiopian Family Guidance Association lost almost $4 million in US funds in 2002, 60 per cent of its annual budget, because it engaged in lobbying the government to legalize abortion in order to make it safe (Loder

2003). The agency soon lost its supply of contraceptives from their USAID-related supply source, which in turn led to more women using unsafe abortion to terminate unwanted pregnancies that could have been prevented with the contraceptives (du Venage 2003).

The drying up of US funding almost forced the complete closure of several clinics until the US-based David and Lucile Packard Foundation stepped in to make up the loss. The clinics are especially important to young women under 18, who make up 45 per cent of women seeking abortions. These young girls, if unable to obtain abortions, frequently drop out of school, are rejected by their families, and may end up in prostitution, where they would be in danger of contracting HIV/AIDS (du Venage 2003).

Zambia

The Planned Parenthood Association of Zambia (PPAZ), one of the best-known providers of reproductive health services for the women of Zambia, was the only major family planning organization in the country to refuse to go along with the global gag rule restrictions. As a result of the restrictions, PPAZ lost 24 per cent of its main grant from its parent organization, International Planned Parenthood Federation (which also refused to accept the Bush-mandated restrictions), and additional USAID funding for its Zambia Integrated Health Program. The latter project provided integrated health services in family planning, HIV, and malaria prevention to many clients. It was terminated in 2004, resulting in service disruption and the loss of 26 of 68 staff members. The agency has been forced to scale back its services and the number of communities it serves, especially in rural areas that still have severe needs. Once a vibrant agency that most Zambians used for reproductive health care and AIDS prevention, PPAZ has now been forced to end its programs providing health information and contraceptive supplies, exacerbating the supply shortage in rural areas (Population Action International 2006).

Yet the needs of Zambia for strong and effective reproductive health care and education are great: about 17 per cent of Zambians aged 15–49 were living with HIV/AIDS in 2004, including many women. It is well known that HIV-prevention programs are not effective without family planning education and resources, but increasingly these services in Zambia are separated, with family planning funding declining while HIV/AIDS funds grow. A recent report on the impact of the global gag rule in Zambia concludes, 'Family planning providers ... are in despair, given that HIV prevention cannot be tackled effectively unless broader sexual and reproductive health issues are addressed' (Population Action International 2006).

Asian Impact: Nepal

The South Asian country of Nepal has had the fourth highest maternal mortality ratio in the world, with 830 deaths from pregnancy-related complications per 100,000 live births in 1995, more recently down to 539 (Global Virtual University 2005; Feminist Majority Foundation 2003a). The UN estimates that about half of these deaths are due to unsafe abortion. The infant mortality rate in Nepal, a poor country, is 64 deaths per 1,000 live births in the first year of life.

In September 2002, the Nepalese king signed a new law permitting abortion on broad grounds (Center for Reproductive Rights 2003). Unfortunately, due in part to the Bush policies, safe abortions remain inaccessible to many poor, mostly rural, women, as agencies that provide or refer for this service risk losing their US funding (Feminist Majority Foundation 2003a).

Before the reform, Nepal had one of the most restrictive and punitive abortion laws in the world. A number of women are still in prison for having obtained abortions before the procedure became legal. In one famous case, a 13-year-old girl who had been impregnated as a result of rape by a relative had been taken by another relative for an abortion. Another family member turned her in for having had the abortion. Found guilty, she was sentenced to twenty years in prison. The Family Planning Association of Nepal advocated for her release and that of other women prisoners. These actions disqualify the agency for US assistance under the global gag rule (Population Connection 2003).

Latin American impact: Colombia

In the South American country of Colombia, abortion is illegal in all circumstances, with no exception even for saving the life of the woman, rape, or incest. According to the law, a woman who has an abortion can be sentenced to three years in prison, along with her abortion provider (WHRNet 2005). Because of the law, women are forced to risk their lives and health when they obtain illegal, unsafe abortions, making abortion the third most common cause of maternal mortality in the country.

Attorney Monica Roa is campaigning to change this extreme law by filing a lawsuit challenging its constitutionality. Her suit argues that 'the criminalization of abortion, when the woman's life or health is in danger, the pregnancy is the result of rape, and/or the fetus has impairments incompatible with life outside the womb' violates a number of women's basic rights as guaranteed in the Constitution (WHRNet 2005). Roa's campaign to reform Colombian abortion laws has the widespread support of much of the population, but it has met with vociferous opposition from powerful leaders of the Catholic Church in the country. Ms Roa also reports that the Bush gag rule has undermined her efforts:

> It's been crucial. I have had lots of people saying they support what I am doing but they cannot say so publicly. People cannot speak about it. They lose their funding from USaid that goes to other projects in Colombia. (Buncombe 2005b)

The Colombian Social Welfare Ministry reports that some 300,000 illegal abortions take place in the country annually; hence the ban does not eliminate abortions but makes them dangerous. They have to be done in secret, and women with complications are reluctant to seek help. In spite of the high maternal death rate from abortions, Catholic opposition has been 'loud, vociferous, and threatening,' even comparing abortion to death-squad massacres and murder. Family planning groups and leaders used to be at the forefront of efforts to change the highly restrictive abortion law, but now they remain silent in order to maintain their USAID funding (Buncombe 2005b). This in turn has a negative impact on efforts to change the law, even in the most extreme circumstances stipulated in Monica Roa's petition. In Colombia it is clear that Bush's global gag rule interferes with the democratic process by suppressing discussion and efforts to reform these oppressive laws that harm women's lives and health.

Access denied

A large multi-country research report sponsored by a coalition of international women's health care groups was released in 2003, documenting the harmful effects of the Bush gag rule. One of the sponsoring organizations was Ipas, an international organization whose mission is to stop preventable deaths and disabilities due to unsafe abortion. The study, called *Access Denied*, looks at the consequences of the Bush policy in four countries, Ethiopia, Kenya, Romania, and Zambia (Ipas 2003).

The report summarizes some of the worst effects of the global gag rule's limitations on access to vital health services and family planning resources. The study (Ipas 2003) found that the policy hurts women by:

- Forcing established family planning organizations and clinics to close. The study found that five clinics in Kenya that provided family planning as well as pre- and postnatal care for mothers and well baby care for their infants have been closed due to loss of income from the US gag rule policy.
- Cutting off supplies of contraceptives to organizations that don't follow the restrictions. In Ethiopia, where maternal death and rates are extremely high and women desperately seek contraception, one rural clinic that had provided 70 per cent of its clients with Depo-Provera has run out of its stock after having been cut off by USAID.
- Preventing health-care workers from informing women who have abortions about to how to prevent more pregnancies, and from providing them with the means to do so, thus failing to intervene at this important point to prevent further abortions. The study found that in Romania, where abortion is common and where unsafe abortions account for many maternal deaths and injuries, the gag rule has limited the ability of providers to engage in post-abortion family planning counseling.

Barbara Crane, Ipas executive vice-president, said of the policy,

> By denying access to a full range of reproductive health services – including safe abortion in circumstances where it is legal – the

policy only leads to more unwanted pregnancies, more unsafe abortions, and tragically, preventable deaths and injuries to the world's most vulnerable women and girls. ... And by prohibiting doctors and others working in local U.S.-funded NGOs from speaking out to their own policy makers, the Global Gag rule stands in the way of efforts to end this carnage. (Ipas 2003)

Ipas has worked throughout the developing world to provide medical equipment and training to prevent the injuries and deaths associated with unsafe abortion, a cause of death for some 70,000 women each year. A US-based group, Ipas has refused to accept the global gag rule, and thus has lost its government funding (Ipas 2003).

At least one major Kenyan women's health organization was forced to close clinics that also provided prenatal care and children's immunizations because it declined to go along with the US requirements for aid (Burke and Shields 2005: 248). Thus the consequences of restricting family planning support, abortion counseling, and similar services, are far-reaching in ways not well understood by politicians in Washington. These examples are simply indicative of the thousands of stories of the impact of the Bush restrictions imposed on women's health-care organizations around the world. Presented as a means to lower the incidence of abortion, the policy in fact everywhere creates an increase in unsafe abortion and maternal health risks, while reducing family planning services that could prevent unwanted pregnancies and the very need for abortion in the first place. Given the vast array of criticisms of the policy, the Bush administration is well aware of these problems, but they remain unmoved by the suffering of women when right-wing religious votes are at stake.

FIGHTING AIDS WITH ABSTINENCE

The spread of HIV/AIDS has been dramatically slowed in many parts of the world through the use of safe-sex practices, especially the consistent use of condoms. Family planning clinics developed the expertise to education people about safer sex, help people understand how to avoid high-risk behaviors, and screen for and treat sexually transmitted infections. Educating people about safer sex and condom use was the primary means for fighting HIV/AIDS by the US government before the Bush administration came to power, with its persistent attention to the desires of its fundamentalist religious conservative base.

In his 2003 State of the Union address, Bush promised to devote $15 billion to the eradication of AIDS around the globe, somewhat to the surprise and appreciation of many of his critics. However, soon it became apparent that the funds granted by the Global AIDS Act of 2003 came with strings attached to please the Christian right. Incredibly, instead of condoms, Bush officials promoted 'abstinence until marriage' and fidelity within monogamous marriage as the primary solution to the HIV pandemic. This approach had never worked in the United States, but it was even more inappropriate and ineffectual in many other countries with completely different cultural beliefs and social arrangements. Yet the fact that the United States has great sums of desperately needed money to provide to those who accede to its demands has led to the weakening of efforts in many countries to fight HIV/AIDS.

As if that were not enough, Bush proposed in 2003 to use his celebrated AIDS-funds program to extend the global gag rule further to health clinics receiving AIDS funds (Stevens 2003; PPFA 2003b). This proposal generated strong criticism and led the administration to withdraw the plan. However, the administration substituted restrictions that were called 'draconian' by one writer:

> Last month, amid a blaze of publicity, the American president appeared to make a magnanimous gesture when he announced that $15bn of US Aids funding would not be subject to the [Global Gag] rule. However, critics have accused him of actually using the new cash to impose draconian new restrictions on American funding. The gag rule has never applied to Aids funding, but now groups that provide Aids prevention as well as abortion services must keep their abortion and family planning operations separate. (Grundy 2003)

The new rule would force clinics that provided both abortion and AIDS-related services to spend unnecessary and scarce monies to separate completely their operations – providing separate buildings, even separate bookkeeping – in order to receive the US funds. The ruling was expected to force many agencies to choose between family planning and AIDS programs, the former likely to lose out. Health workers, human rights activists, women's advocates, and others urged the administration to abandon this plan, which is designed for domestic political purposes instead of adhering to established medical and scientific health care. An emergency summit meeting of hundreds of African health officials expressed outrage at the 'arrogance' and lack of understanding of the problem by the American government (Grundy 2003).

To make matters even worse, Bush inserted his 'faith-based' bias into the anti-AIDS program, making clear his preference for religious groups as providers of these social services. Women's advocates were afraid that 'missionaries might soon partly replace experienced medical technicians who are demanding that African women and girls be afforded clean and safe clinics and hospitals where abortions can be carried out' (Grundy 2003). There were questions also about whether evangelical Christian groups that opposed homosexuality, premarital sex, contraception, and abortion could provide the kind of care really needed to manage and prevent AIDS while maintaining adequate health care for women.

Falling backwards in Uganda

A United Nations envoy, Steven Lewis, charged recently that US pressure had caused the government of Uganda to change its approach to HIV/AIDS by 'demeaning' the usefulness of condoms while preaching abstinence (BBC News 2005b). The country had already been facing a shortage of condoms, but since 2004 the utilization of condoms had decreased significantly, according to Lewis, while the supply had dwindled and the price tripled (BBC News 2005b). Similar criticisms were voiced by Human Rights Watch (2005c), a US-based organization. Until 2003, Uganda had been widely praised for its strong program promoting a three-pronged approach to HIV/AIDS involving (1) encouraging delayed sexual initiation; (2) encouraging monogamy among sexually active couples; and (3) promoting the correct and consistent use of condoms. This program was highly successful in lowering Uganda's HIV/AIDS infection rate from 15 to 6 per cent between 1992 and 2002. But

Human Rights Watch presents evidence that since 2003, under the influence of the Bush administration's policies, Uganda's government has begun emphasizing abstinence and minimizing condom use. In a letter addressed to Uganda's Minister of Health and signed by 54 Ugandans and endorsed by 58 organizations or individuals outside of Uganda, the government's move toward abstinence-based programs is denounced:

> Since 2003, we have watched as the Ugandan government downplays its own proven track record in an obvious attempt to please international donors such as the United States. We have watched as our own leaders rewrite history and misleadingly attribute reduced HIV prevalence to adoption of sexual abstinence. We have watched as the U.S. government pours millions of dollars into HIV-prevention programs that provide misleading information about the effectiveness of condoms and that fail to equip people – particularly women – with the essential skills needed to negotiate safer sex. We have seen billboards throughout the city of Kampala, sponsored by the U.S. Agency for International Development (USAID), the Office of the First Lady of Uganda and the Global Fund to Fight AIDS, Tuberculosis and Malaria, that exaggerate the failure rate of condoms and present 'abstinence-until-marriage' as a complete HIV-prevention strategy, despite the fact that a large share of women are getting infected *within marriage*. We have seen Ugandan organizations stop supplying condoms either to gain or to avoid losing U.S. funding. (Human Rights Watch 2005c)

As a result of the anti-condom campaign, there are now widespread condom shortages in Uganda, its public has lost confidence in the effectiveness of condoms against HIV, condom prices have greatly increased, and usage is down. Tragically, rates of infection have begun to rise again.

INHIBITING SUCCESSFUL SEX-WORKER ANTI-AIDS PROGRAMS

Another aspect of the Bush AIDS policy has been the requirement that groups receiving US funds pledge their opposition to prostitution and refuse to support it in any way. This policy has been in effect since 2003 for foreign agencies receiving US funds, but in 2005 the Bush administration extended it to American organizations as well (*New York Times* 2005b). While this policy may sound reasonable at first glance, in many countries prostitution is culturally acceptable, and many women are forced by circumstances into the profession. Sex work is the primary source of new HIV infection, and as such it is important to provide education and services to prostitutes. Some of the most successful anti-AIDS programs work in a nonjudgmental way with prostitutes to provide them education about safe-sex practices, medical examinations and care, condoms, and other support so as to help protect them and their clients from infection or its spread. Many of these programs are undermined by the US policy, which has been criticized as uninformed, judgmental, and disastrous in its impact.

The government of Brazil refused a $40 million grant from the US because of its opposition to this requirement, which it said would require it to give up some of its most successful programs. The Bush policy suggests that 'anything that makes life more tolerable for prostitutes encourages prostitution.' But the *New York Times* editors pointed out that the Bush plan would disallow funding programs that organize sex workers 'to stand up to abusive clients' or help them with resources needed to be able to visit clinics for health checks (*New York Times* 2005b). In Brazil, officials opposed the rule because 'it would hamper the treatment of infected sex workers and their clients' (BBC News 2005a). The extension of the rule to US-based organizations was questioned also on constitutional free-speech grounds by the *Times* editorial, and suspicions were raised about the administration's underlying motives for this ruling:

> The new anti-prostitution requirement may have a hidden purpose: to take away the right of American groups working on family planning overseas to counsel abortions. On his first day in office, President Bush signed a reinstatement of [the global gag rule]. The abortion gag rule has never applied to American groups, for the same First Amendment reasons that the prostitution pledge did not. But the decision to strip Americans of their First Amendment right to speak as they please on prostitution opens the way to an attempt to keep them silent on abortion, too. (*New York Times* 2005b)

The aggressive stance of the Bush administration and its allies against programs that work with prostitutes was highlighted in another *New York Times* opinion piece published in late August 2005. Helene Cooper (2005) describes a number of successful programs aimed at teaching women who work in brothels in Central America about the dangers of HIV and AIDS and how to protect themselves and others. In one program funded by Population Services International, the teachers were former prostitutes themselves, enhancing the credibility of the program with the target group. Lessons took place in local bars and included a simple game-like presentation for the mostly illiterate prostitutes. The game maintained the interest of the women and at the same time provided the frame for teaching them how to protect themselves from HIV.

Unfortunately, Senator Tom Coburn, extreme-right Republican from Oklahoma, heard about the program and wrote to President Bush to demand a stop to US funding of what he called 'prostitute parties' held in bars and brothels. Coburn is a strong supporter of abstinence as the primary solution to AIDS. Soon after his letter was mailed, the nonprofit funding agency Population Services International received word that its USAID funding would not be continued (Cooper 2005).

In May 2005, Human Rights Watch and more than two hundred leading human rights experts and organizations sent a letter to President Bush opposing the anti-prostitution provisions of his AIDS funding requirement, especially its extension to US-based organizations. 'None of these organizations promotes prostitution,' said Jodi Jacobson, executive director of the Center of Health Equity. 'Instead, they use advocacy and other strategies to address violence against sex workers, reduce their social isolation, and increase their access to health services' (Human Rights watch 2005a). The requirement also makes it difficult to assist the people who are at most risk of HIV/AIDS. Assistant Professor Alice Miller of Columbia University pointed out other flaws in the policy:

> Evidence from India, Thailand, and Cambodia shows that these restrictions have already undermined promising interventions.... In Cambodia, for example, NGOs discontinued plans to provide English-language classes – which could provide a path out of sex work – for fear that they would be seen as 'promoting prostitution.' (Human Rights Watch 2005a)

Overall, then, Bush's anti-prostitution policy prevents the kind of intervention that could protect sex workers and their clients and that could assist them out of prostitution in the end. As with other policies, the stated intent of the Bush regulations is undermined by the details of their implementation.

WITHDRAWING FUNDING FROM THE UNFPA

The United Nations Population Fund (UNFPA) aims to promote the well-being of 'every woman, man, and child' on earth in terms of health and equal opportunity. Supporting population policies, broadly conceived, UNFPA is strongly supportive of women's rights, aiming to 'reduce poverty and to ensure that every pregnancy is wanted, every birth is safe, every young person is free of HIV/AIDS, and every girl and woman is treated with dignity and respect.[24] The agency helps governments to formulate policies in the areas of reproductive health, gender equality in education, improved maternal health, and HIV/AIDS prevention, as well as providing funding for these and other development efforts. The agency spent some $220 million in developing countries in 2004, the largest share going to reproductive health programs – UNFPA supports locally administered family planning programs in over 130 countries. The United States in the past had supported the agency, which has been called 'a leading voice for human rights' (EngenderHealth 2005).

Since fiscal year 2001, President Bush has held back funds appropriated annually by Congress for the UNFPA, citing unfounded allegations that the organization supports coercive abortion policies in China. These charges have been investigated and refuted by a number of groups, including the US State Department, but Bush and his conservative supporters continue to make the unsubstantiated claims. The latest action (September 2005) was widely denounced by population groups, especially as it came in the same week that Bush appeared before the UN General Assembly pledging his support for the Millennium Development Goals, which include support for women's health care and poverty reduction. A letter to the US State Department signed by the directors of twenty-one population, environmental, and religious groups protested the action, stating,

> A U.S. decision to restore funding to UNFPA would have been
> a swift and concrete indication to the rest of the world that the
> reality of U.S. policy now matches U.S. rhetoric. Instead, just one
> day after President Bush's speech to the U.N. General Assembly,
> your office once again has chosen politics over saving the lives
> of women living in the most vulnerable circumstances who are in
> need of life-saving reproductive health care. (Lobe 2005a)

The Bush rationale for withholding the funds is 'simply incorrect,'
according to the director of UNFPA, who pointed out that the agency
works hard to end coercion by promoting voluntary family planning.
In order to protest China's past coercive policies, Congress had required UNFPA to make sure than none of the US contribution went
to China, a policy accepted by presidents Reagan and George H.W.
Bush but still unacceptable to George W. Bush. In fact, not a single
dollar of the US contribution would have gone to China because of
this stipulation, but this fact has been conveniently overlooked by the
current president, in a move obviously meant to please his Christian
right supporters. According to the letter from the groups previously
cited, none of the money, 'had it materialized, would have gone to
China, or to promote or perform abortions anywhere in the world.'

> Rather it would have helped provide critical services to women in
> 139 countries in sub-Saharan Africa, Asia, the Middle East, and
> Latin America. The U.S. hands-off policy has had no impact on
> China's behavior, but it has caused measureless suffering world-
> wide. (Lobe 2005a)

Given the long list of Bush's restrictive reproductive-health actions
and the implausible stated excuses for defunding UNFPA, it is highly
doubtful that Bush has any real concern about China's policies;
instead, that concern provides a weak excuse for his callous refusal to
fund UNFPA's programs in support of gender equality and women's
reproductive rights. Moreover, the UNFPA asserts that its work in
China has led to greater reproductive choice and freedom in that
country. The United States is the only UN member-country ever to
have denied the UNFPA funding for other than budgetary reasons
(EngenderHealth 2005). Since 2001, the total amount appropriated by
Congress for this purpose but withheld by the Bush administration
has been $136 million.

EngenderHealth executive vice-president Maurice Middleburg expressed the disappointment and frustration of the organization (echoed by many others):

> We are dismayed at the Bush administration's decision to deny funding that could prevent as many as 2 million unwanted pregnancies and 4,700 maternal deaths in developing countries.... It is disturbing that the Administration could take this step just one day after President Bush's proclaimed commitment to promoting women's equity and universal reproductive health care at the United Nations World Summit. (EngenderHealth 2005)

The UNFPA estimates that Bush's refusal to fund its programs has resulted in 2 million unwanted pregnancies, leading to 800,000 abortions, 4,700 maternal deaths, and 77,000 deaths of children before they reach the age of 5 (Feldt 2003).

OPPOSING THE WORLD HEALTH ORGANIZATION

In yet another attack on women's health, the Bush State Department in 2002 froze some $3 million intended for the World Health Organization (WHO), in response to conservative complaints that the organization supports a Geneva-based research project on human reproduction studying mifepristone or RU-486, the 'abortion pill.' Three years later the US tried to block the World Health Organization from endorsing abortion pills by adding them to its list of 'essential medicines' that all doctors should have. The list is used by governments in an advisory capacity in developing health resources for their countries. The WHO estimates that the pills could save the lives of up to 68,000 women who die each year from unsafe abortion practices, since their risk of negative side effects is much lower than the risks of surgical abortion in most developing countries (Boseley 2005).

In March 2005, when a committee of experts met to consider updates to the list, they approved the two drugs (mifepristone and misoprostol) to be used in combination for early-pregnancy termination, 'where permitted by national law and where culturally acceptable' (Ipas 2005). The US Department of Health and Human Services lobbied the WHO to block the approval of the pills over the unanimous advice of the committee. The committee had supported the pills because it believed their use would greatly reduce the deaths and damage caused by unsafe abortion in poor countries, where the risk of dying from abortion is a hundred times as great as in many developed nations. The abortion pills have been licensed and used successfully in both the UK since 1991 and in the US since 2000 (Boseley 2005). Although the pressure from the US delayed the approval of the drugs for the list of essential medicines, news of US interference led to strong expressions of support for their inclusion by members of the worldwide medical, public health, academic, and development community. The British medical journal *The Lancet*, in an editorial published in May 2005, likewise expressed strong support for the committee's recommendations. The World Health Organization approved the inclusion of the abortion pills in June 2005 (Ipas 2005).

CONCLUSION: UNDERMINING WOMEN'S REPRODUCTIVE FREEDOM IS A BUSH PRIORITY

The actions described in this and the previous chapter reveal the deep disregard Bush and his associates have for women's health and independence. His claims of 'pro-life' concern fall flat when placed in the context of the millions of lives of women lost, harmed, or limited by their lack of freedom to control their own bodies, to say nothing of the lives lost unnecessarily in the Bush-initiated military actions in Iraq. The attacks on women's health and reproductive rights seem to be among Bush's major priorities, generally hidden from view but relentless and consistent in their aims. Even the highly respected mainstream newspaper the *New York Times* supports this view. In an editorial published on 17 January 2003 the *Times* denounced the 'lengthening string of anti-choice executive orders, regulations, legal briefs, legislative maneuvers and key appointments emanating from [Bush's] administration.' The editors go on to assert that the long list of actions 'suggests that undermining the reproductive freedom essential to women's health, privacy and equality is a major preoccupation of his administration – second only, perhaps, to the war on terrorism' (*New York Times* 2003b).

BUSH VERSUS THE WOMEN OF THE WORLD:
ARE WOMEN'S RIGHTS HUMAN RIGHTS?

Bush's anti-woman approach has not been confined to issues relating to abortion or reproductive rights. Even while publicly promoting 'respect for women' and women's rights as justifications for his military ventures in Afghanistan and Iraq, his administration has attempted to thwart women's progress in the international arena as well. For years, scholars and development specialists have pointed to the importance of women's education, security, and economic resources and opportunities as a necessary condition for true economic development of a country. The UN Millennium Development Goals recognized this as a critical goal for the twenty-first century, and US government agencies such as the US Agency for International Development (USAID) have recognized the importance of 'women in development' issues in the past. But under the Bush administration there have been various troubling signs of insensitivity to women's needs, ignoring women's rights, and even opposition to inexpensive and simple measures that might help women. The result is that women have suffered and their attempts to redress grievances have been rebuffed.

An incident that symbolizes the lowered priority the Bush administration gives to international women's issues occurred in September 2005, when Secretary of State Condoleezza Rice missed an important opportunity to show her solidarity with women in other nations by turning down an invitation to meet with other female foreign ministers gathered at the UN General Assembly. Feminist-leaning women who have made it to powerful positions often create networks among their ranks to discuss issues of particular relevance to women and create a sense of solidarity. Rice has never been a strong advocate of women's rights, preferring the male-dominated world of diplomacy and military policy. Madeleine K. Albright, Secretary of State under President Clinton, had initiated the tradition of the women's dinner while serving as ambassador to the United Nations, and she continued the practice after becoming Secretary of State. Swedish Foreign Minister Laila Freivalds, who attended the 2005 dinner, commented that the relatively low number of female counterparts (nineteen in all) makes it even more important for them to get together. Secretary Rice, one of only two female foreign ministers who failed to attend, cited a 'busy schedule' as the reason for skipping the event. This was simply one small decision, but it seems to indicate the low priority given to women's issues and a lack of desire to make common cause with Rice's female counterparts to promote better conditions for women around the globe and in government positions (*Washington Post* 2005c). Unfortunately, a failure to act vigorously in support of women's human rights, and indeed setting up barriers to progress in this area, have been hallmarks of the Bush foreign policy.

OPPOSING COMFORT WOMEN'S SUIT AGAINST JAPAN

One of the earliest opportunities for Bush to show his support for women's global human rights occurred early in his first term, but his administration instead stood against the claims of women seeking redress for grievances. In September 2000, fifteen former 'comfort women' from Korea, China, and other countries filed a class action lawsuit in a US federal court, charging the government of Japan with violations of international law in its treatment of the women during World War II. This lawsuit was one of a series of actions by representatives of some 200,000 women who were kidnapped and forced against their will to serve as sexual slaves for the Japanese military during the war. The conditions under which the women were held were horrendous; they were subjected to torture, incarceration, and repeated rape by Japanese soldiers, sometimes up to thirty times a day. As could be expected, many of the survivors were left physically and psychologically damaged for life. The Japanese government denied for many years that it had engaged in such practices, but finally admitted to them in 1995 in the face of overwhelming evidence, but it has yet to issue a formal apology or provide compensation (Miller 2001a).

In response to the women's lawsuit, the Japanese government filed a motion to dismiss it on the basis that the US court did not have jurisdiction to interfere with Japan's 'sovereignty' and that post-war treaties had resolved all the issues. In a completely unnecessary move, the US State Department in April 2001 entered the case by filing a 'Statement of Interest' in support of the Japanese government position, and against the women. The US claimed to have 'deep sympathy' for the women but said it was bound by international law to join the case on the side of Japan. This was not a settled question, and of course the same administration later had no problem with acting outside of international law in the invasion of Iraq and other matters. Attorney Michael D. Hausfeld challenged the US position, calling it 'one of the most outrageous actions I've ever seen the United States take on issues involving fundamental human rights' (Miller 2001b).

A district court ruled in October 2001 that the US courts had no jurisdiction in the matter, since issues related to the war were settled in treaties. An appeals court upheld this decision. However, the US Supreme Court overturned the decision and ordered the appeals court to reconsider the case. In June 2005, the appeals court rejected the damages lawsuit for a second time, again citing lack of jurisdiction (*Sydney Morning Herald* 2005). The Alien Tort Claims Act, under which the lawsuit was brought, allows citizens of other countries the right to sue other foreign citizens in US courts for abuses of international law.

The women achieved a symbolic victory in December 2001, when a Women's International War Crimes Tribunal in The Hague upheld all but one charge, including rape, torture, and slavery. Organized by Asian human rights and women's organizations, the tribunal held hearings before highly respected jurists, following strict international norms. Among their recommendations was that an advisory judgment be sought from the International Court of Justice in The Hague. Although the judgment was not binding, it provided a hearing and a sense of moral justice for the victims of these war crimes (Rodgers 2001). The US government, on the other hand, refused to stand aside to allow the case to go forward, but actively entered on the opposing side instead.

REFUSING ASYLUM TO DOMESTIC VIOLENCE VICTIMS

In another famous case, Bush's Attorney General John Ashcroft intervened in the case of a woman seeking asylum in the United States based on gender-related violence in her home country of Guatemala. As Amnesty International describes the case, the facts are 'undisputed.' After suffering for ten years extreme abuse at the hands of her husband in Guatemala, and after receiving no help from legal authorities in that country, Rodi Alvarado fled to the United States in 1995. She petitioned for asylum, claiming that her husband's abuse and the government's failure to protect her constituted persecution on the basis of her gender. A US immigration judge agreed and granted Alvarado asylum in the United States in 1996. Officials within the US Immigration and Naturalization Services appealed the decision, however, and the Bureau of Immigration Appeals reversed it. In 1999, President Clinton's Attorney General Janet Reno vacated that decision and set in motion new regulations that would allow asylum on the basis of gender-related persecution. Reno directed the Bureau of Immigration Appeals to reconsider the case after the new regulations were finalized, and it was expected that Alvarado's case would be decided in her favor. Unfortunately, the new regulations were not finalized before the Bush administration took over and the effort was again delayed (Amnesty International 2005a).

In March of 2003, Attorney General John Ashcroft took over the case and announced that he would make the decision whether to grant Rodi Alvarado asylum. Ashcroft's action alarmed many women's advocates, who were concerned that he would use the case to broadly limit the ability of women to seek asylum on grounds of gender-based persecution. These types of cases involve fleeing from government-condoned domestic violence, honor killings, sex trafficking, and other abuses. Because of the widespread support Alvarado received from a very broad coalition of supporters, including members of Congress, religious groups, human rights organizations, and women's groups, Ashcroft did not decide against the petition but instead delayed it, leaving Alvarado's fate in limbo. In February 2004, the Department of Homeland Security filed a brief in support of Alvarado. Nevertheless, Ashcroft failed to act until 21 January 2005, just before he left office, when he sent the case back to the Board of Immigration Appeals with no decision. Although he failed to rule in her favor, many of Alvarado's supporters were relieved that he had not ruled negatively (Human Rights First 2005).

Rodi Alvarado has been in limbo for a decade, waiting for a decision about her status, during which time she has been unable to see her children or to petition that they be allowed to join her. The Bush administration appears to be opposed to establishing women's right to request asylum on grounds of gender-based persecution, preferring instead to leave things undefined. Perhaps with Bush's approval, legislation was introduced in Congress in early 2005 that would limit such rights. Amnesty International states that the US failure to recognize gender-based violence as a legitimate basis for asylum has serious implications. If Alvarado's petition were denied, she would be deported to Guatemala, where she would face serious abuse and possibly death at the hands of her husband. Such a decision would also set an unfortunate precedent by disallowing severe gender-related human rights violations as grounds for asylum. In addition, it would place the United States in conflict with recent UN guidelines on gender persecution and out of step with countries such as Canada, Australia, New Zealand, and the United Kingdom, all of which recognize government-tolerated gender-based persecution as a general ground for asylum claims (Amnesty International 2005).

As of late 2005, the Alvarado case was still undecided. Thus, for five years the Bush administration has delayed justice for this woman and has stood in the way of justice for thousands more who might seek asylum in the future. A decision in Alvarado's favor could have been made very easily, and the regulations proposed by Janet Reno could have been finalized as well. But, as we have seen, women's rights and women's needs do not occupy a high priority with this administration.

RETREAT FROM INTERNATIONAL
WOMEN'S RIGHTS GOALS AND TREATIES

In the year 2000, over 150 heads of state came together at a UN World Summit to develop goals for the new millennium. Out of the summit came the UN Millennium Development Declaration, by which the participants declared their commitment to work with the United Nations organization and its Charter as 'indispensable foundations of a more peaceful, prosperous and just world.' The leaders also adopted a number of Millennium Development Goals (MDGs) that establish targets for the reduction of poverty, increasing educational achievement, and improving health among the world's nations. The eight general goals include such aims as eradicating extreme poverty and hunger, achieving universal primary education (especially important for girls), reducing child mortality, and ensuring environmental sustainability. In addition, some of the goals are aimed specifically at improving the status of women in poor countries. These include promoting gender equality and empowering women, improving maternal health, and combating HIV/AIDS, malaria, and other diseases (DFID 2005).

The goals included specific targets that were to be met by signatories at various points, targets that would encourage specific actions on the part of governments and that included measurable indicators to assess progress. For example, the 'gender equality and women's empowerment' goal treated these as basic human rights, rights that are crucial for sustainable economic and social development. These rights included ensuring women's equal rights to property, inheritance, equal wages, job opportunities, and health care. Another goal was to increase women's representation in national governing bodies. Overall, the targets and goals were very laudable, and even though many countries lagged in progress toward the goals by the first checkpoint of 2005, some 190 countries had signed on to the goals, showing at least a nodding commitment to women's equal rights (DFID 2005).

In September 2005, 120 heads of state and other world leaders came together in New York for a World Summit to assess progress toward the goals and to renew commitments and make plans for moving further toward the required outcomes. In preparation for the meeting an 'Outcomes' document had been drafted, outlining targets and goals to be reached by the year 2015. This would have been a reaffirmation of the basic commitment to global development as outlined in the Millennium Development Goals. Since the document had been circulated to the member countries and had been under negotiation for six months, it was anticipated that it would be quickly affirmed and the summit could be spent discussing progress and needs for the future (Stapp 2005).

A mere two weeks before the meeting, John Bolton, Bush's controversial new recess-appointed ambassador to the UN, outraged many of the member states by submitting a list of 750 amendments to the UN draft of the Outcomes document, potentially blocking many of the aims of the summit (Stapp 2005). According to Yifat Susskind, Bolton's revisions would 'block potential progress on issues that are critical to everyone in the world, including development, nuclear disarmament, and global warming' (Susskind 2005a). Susskind goes on to point out that Bolton attempted to delete *all mention* of the Millennium Development Goals, even though assessing progress toward those goals had been the purpose of the meeting!

> To most of the world, Bolton's obstructionism looks more like bullying than negotiating. It's a tactic that we've seen before from the Bush administration: barge in at the final hour of negotiations, demand drastic changes, and then gradually relent, but only to the point that you were willing to accept all along. (Susskind 2005a)

Scholarly research, development workers, and various international agencies for the past three decades have demonstrated that protecting women's human rights and promoting their well-being is an important key to the economic uplift of an entire society. Even though the MDGs do not mention human rights or sexual and reproductive rights (due to previous compromises with US negotiators and fundamentalist governments), they represent an important step toward economic, educational, and health-care progress for poor countries, with women's issues fully recognized as a priority. But the United States under Bush seems reluctant to support even these basic rights in an international forum.

The Gender Monitoring Group of the World Summit, composed of three major women's nongovernmental organizations, accused Bolton of attempting to undermine the Outcomes document and weaken progress toward economic development and women's rights. According to their press release,

> What's at stake for women are all the promises of equality, empowerment and women's human rights contained in CEDAW (the 'Women's rights' treaty), the Beijing Platform for Action, Cairo Programme of Action and other government agreements of the 1990s. Women are concerned that their voices will not be fully heard and their perspectives will not be fully incorporated into the proposals that come out of the World Summit. (Gender Monitoring Group of the World Summit 2005)

On 14 September 2005, George W. Bush spoke to the summit, failing to acknowledge the widespread international outrage over Bolton's attempts to derail its goals. In his speech Bush proclaimed 'We are committed to the Millennium Development Goals,' even though Ambassador Bolton had tried to delete every mention of them from the Outcomes statement. Bush called on the world leaders to 'to implement the Monterrey consensus,' which includes a commitment by wealthy countries to spend 0.7 per cent of their national income on foreign development assistance. In fact, the US spends less than 0.2 per cent of its income on development and has fought against this requirement. What Bush likes about the Monterrey agreement is its insistence on neoliberal economic reforms, including austerity programs that reduce public services, trade liberalization, and openness to international corporate investment, in exchange for aid and debt forgiveness (Susskind 2005b).

In his address to the summit, Bush also brought up the goal of eradicating AIDS in Africa that had been agreed to at the G8 summit in Gleneagles, Scotland, in July 2005. He challenged every UN member to take 'concrete steps' to reach the goal. Here again,

Bush showed his hypocrisy. Some of the 'concrete steps' that he had taken were reported by Susskind (2005b):[1]

- Bush demanded that African governments spend the US funding exclusively on drugs patented by US companies, instead of generics (the patented drugs cost about $15,000 a year per patient compared to $350 a year for generics).
- Bush's ambassador refused to allow the World Summit to 'encourage pharmaceutical companies to make anti-retroviral drugs affordable and accessible in Africa.'
- Bush insists on prevention programs that promote abstinence over proven 'safer sex' approaches, put stringent restrictions on condom use, and demand that groups receiving funds formally oppose abortion and prostitution.
- Bush promised in 2003 to spend $15 billion to fight AIDS, but took most of this from existing programs, including child vaccination initiatives – a move the *New York Times* described as 'forcing the babies of Africa to pay for their parents' AIDS drugs.'

Susskind's analysis documents a number of other ways in which Bush's claims were disingenuous.

The US actions at this conference were just the latest in a series of similar efforts of Bush representatives to disrupt or oppose efforts to move forward on women's rights in the international context. The administration's position at several UN-sponsored international conferences has isolated the United States from the overwhelming majority of governments and aligns it with only a few very conservative Muslim governments and the Vatican. For example, in March 2004 the US was the only one of thirty-eight countries at the Economic Commission for Latin America and the Caribbean to oppose a declaration calling for increased reproductive health and AIDS/HIV services and better protection of reproductive rights for everyone (UN News Centre 2004).

Earlier, in December 2002, US anti-reproductive/sexual rights proposals at an International Asian/Pacific Population Conference were defeated by a vote of 32 to 1. The conference was held to assess progress toward the Program for Action goals established at the 1994 UN International Conference on Population and Development

(ICPD), held in Cairo. The Cairo conference had accomplished a breakthrough in international support for women's rights, in that it issued 'the first official expression of a new consensus that population stabilization and development strategies are inextricably linked, that women's economic and social empowerment lie at the center of both, and that women's reproductive health and rights are fundamental to their empowerment' (Cohen 2003).

At the 2002 conference, the US delegation objected to the Cairo support for 'reproductive health services,' claiming it was a code word for abortion, which it opposed. The US delegates also opposed the promotion of condoms to help prevent HIV/AIDS, attempting to substitute abstinence as a solution to both fertility and HIV problems. These attempts were overwhelmingly rejected by conference participants. The United States finally signed up to the conference agreement, but inserted a long dissenting reservation into the record, specifying its nonsupport for abortion or for family planning for adolescents. Cohen notes that 'the most stunning policy pronouncement' in the US reservations statement put the country on record 'as supporting "innocent life from conception to natural death" and ... stressing its opposition to "the use of abortifacients"' (Cohen 2003). This statement appears to call into question the administration's support for contraception itself (Cohen 2003). It is ironic that the United States, only recently viewed as a major world leader in family planning and women's development, has come to be viewed in the world community as one of the major obstacles toward further advancement of women.

Over the years of his presidency, Bush has stepped back from many UN treaties and agreements formerly supported by the United States having to do with women's rights. In another case, in October 2004, Bush formally declined to sign a declaration reaffirming US commitment to the Cairo Plan of Action, a document that had been signed by over 250 global leaders, including 85 heads of state. His stated reason was the inclusion of the phrase 'sexual rights' (Lederer 2004). This language was intended to support women's rights to freedom from violence and coercion in sexuality, but Bush officials insist on reading it as containing some unwritten support for abortion, which it consistently opposes (Cohen 2003; Lederer

2004). In general, Bush representatives usually justify their opposition to women's rights initiatives in terms of abortion issues, but in fact their negative actions have implications for a much broader range of rights.

THE BEIJING PLUS TEN CONFERENCE

In March of 2005, in another widely publicized example of this trend of interference with the global trend toward recognizing women's rights, Bush representatives held up the Beijing Plus Ten conference in New York, delaying and limiting discussion of progress on the Platform for Action and planning for the future, actions that caused almost universal outrage among other conference participants.

The Beijing Platform for Action, developed at the UN Fourth World Conference on Women, held in Beijing in 1995, called on governments to strengthen their support for women and girls by, among other things, providing universal education for girls, expanding access to reproductive health services, and ending gender-based violence and discrimination. The Beijing platform was ratified by 189 countries, including the United States. The March 2005 conference was held in New York to assess progress toward the goals and to discuss further measures that could be taken to eradicate poverty, violence, and gender-based discrimination at the ten-year anniversary of the agreement (Stevens 2005b).

The UN Commission on the Status of Women had drafted a brief document prior to the meeting reaffirming support for the Beijing declaration and for continued efforts to implement its program. It was expected that conference participants would quickly sign up to the document and then move on to substantive discussions of ways to advance women's economic equality and political participation, reduce violence against women, and work toward other gender-equity goals. But the Bush delegation held up the conference for days and created great consternation and anger when it raised objections to the brief reaffirmation statement (Lederer 2005).

The US delegates again objected to language about 'sexual rights,' which they claimed might be interpreted to imply a right to abortion. The Beijing Platform says nothing about abortion, as that language had been too controversial at the original Beijing conference to win passage. But the platform does say that women have the right to 'decide freely and responsibly on matters related to their sexuality … free of coercion, discrimination and violence.' It also asserts that where abortion is legal, it should be safe; and where it is illegal, women who obtain abortions should not be subject to criminal charges. Apparently these passages were objectionable to the Bush administration. Ellen Sauerbrey, head of the US delegation, proposed adding an amendment to the reaffirmation document stating that the platform does not create any 'new human rights,' including the right to abortion (Lederer 2005). The US representatives also demanded an amendment stating that a commitment to 'reproductive health services' does not include a right to abortion. After tremendous pressure from other member countries, the United States finally withdrew its demand for an amendment. However, the 6,000-plus delegates from over a hundred countries were almost universally outraged that the United States had diverted the conference from its important work to squabble over this very narrow and unnecessary issue. Taina Bien-Aime of the international human rights organization Equality Now said it was 'unconscionable that the United States would hijack this very important meeting' to talk about abortion, which does not even appear in the platform (Lederer 2005). A French government official worried that attempts to change a declaration that had been affirmed by 189 countries ten years ago could be seen as 'a step backward for women's rights' (Lederer 2005).

Journalist Sheryl McCarthy, writing in New York *Newsday*, commented that

> [T]his bit of grandstanding was nothing more than a sop to the administration's conservative supporters here at home. The time that could have been spent discussing how much progress these nations have made since Beijing and what obstacles stand in their way was wasted on political posturing. There was no support for the U.S. proposal, which only served to annoy the other nations before our delegation backed off and joined the consensus anyway. (McCarthy 2005)

Human rights activist Charlotte Bunch pointed out that the argument over the abortion language not only advanced a conservative religious agenda but also served as 'a stalling tactic to prevent the conference from moving forward' on other vital issues for women (Stevens 2005b).

Stevens (2005b) provides more insight into the problems surrounding this conference. Carolyn Maloney, a Democratic Congress member from New York, had asked the Bush administration if she could participate as a member of the US delegation. Maloney had co-chaired a bipartisan congressional delegation of four lawmakers to the Beijing conference, and in 2000 she had been one of the major speakers at the five-year anniversary of that conference. Maloney has spent much of her career advocating for women's rights, and she was eager to bring her experience and expertise to the Beijing Plus Ten event. Having received no reply to her initial request, Maloney sent a second request to President Bush. White House officials denied Maloney a seat in its delegation, offering her only 'observer' status without privileges to attend all sessions (Stevens 2005b). This decision to exclude Maloney is more evidence of the administration's lack of willingness to take women's interests seriously or to incorporate pro-feminist views in its discussions.

The actual selection of delegates to the conference reaffirms this suspicion. Representing the United States at this international conference on women's rights were Patricia Brister, state chair of the Republican Party of Louisiana; Susan B. Hirschmann, a Washington lobbyist and former chief of staff to the ultraconservative House Majority Leader Tom DeLay of Texas; Janet Parshall, a conservative religiously oriented radio talkshow host and author; and Ellen Sauerbrey, two-time candidate for governor of Maryland and chair of the Bush election campaign in that state in 2000, whom Bush had named for the UN Commission on the Status of Women (Stevens 2005b). With representatives like these, we cannot expect support for progress for the world's women, since none of these delegates has had any experience or awareness of the complex issues facing women in other countries. The behavior of Bush representatives at this conference and similar ones represents a major retreat from previous US leadership in the areas of family planning and women's rights over the past few decades (Goldenberg 2005).

BUSH ADMINISTRATION BACKS OUT OF SUPPORT FOR CEDAW

Soon after taking office, Secretary of State Colin Powell and President Bush recommended that the Senate ratify CEDAW, the UN Convention on the Elimination of All Forms of Discrimination against Women, an international agreement that includes a broad range of basic human rights that governments sign up to. The declaration was developed in the early 1970s and was signed by President Carter, but it had failed Senate ratification. The convention has been ratified by 180 nations (WomenWatch 2005), and pressure for US support had been growing among the public and from political leaders.

The convention is a very significant international treaty establishing women's rights as part of the UN Human Rights system, developed with the intention of improving women's status and eliminating gender discrimination internationally. CEDAW 'promotes women's equal attainment of economic, social, cultural, civil and political rights' (UNIFEM 2004: 1). The treaty defines discrimination against women comprehensively as

> any distinction, exclusion or restriction made on the basis of sex which has the effect or purpose of impairing or nullifying the recognition, enjoyment or exercise by women, irrespective of their marital status, on the basis of equality of men and women, of human rights and fundamental freedoms in the political, economic, social, cultural, civil and any other field. (UNIFEM 2004: 1)

The Convention is important because it is the first UN human rights agreement focusing specifically on women and establishing a wide range of rights for women under international law. It also provides an agenda for action for its signatories and requires frequent reports and monitoring on progress. Although some countries have made reservations to various articles, CEDAW is one of the most widely ratified conventions of the UN, leaving the United States isolated in its refusal to ratify the accord (UNIFEM 2004: 8).

Under CEDAW, discrimination is clearly defined, and governments are expected to abolish laws and customs that are discriminatory. The binding treaty commits governments to take affirmative action to ensure the equality of men and women, even to eliminate cultural and traditional stereotyping of women. The convention also commits parties to work to eliminate trafficking in women, to integrate women into all levels of the political life of the country, and to work toward equal education, employment, and legal status for women. Women are also to be guaranteed access to health care, including family planning. The treaty also covers equal rights in marriage and divorce, and in 'all matters relating to the birth, adoption, and raising of children' (UNIFEM 2004: 10–11).

Thus CEDAW is a revolutionary document that sets new international standards for the treatment of women. Unfortunately, and predictably, Bush reversed his early support for CEDAW, probably because of objections from Ashcroft and other conservatives, though against the wishes of Powell. In the summer of 2002 Bush asked the Senate to delay a vote on ratification, pending 'further study' (Kristof 2002). As of late 2005 the vote still had not taken place; nor has there been any recent mention of it by the administration (Logan 2004; WomenWatch 2005).

BUSH APPOINTEES WITH INTERNATIONAL WOMEN'S RIGHTS RESPONSIBILITIES

As with other types of appointments, the individuals Bush has nominated to develop policy and represent the United States on international women's issues have often been unqualified and unsympathetic to women's global concerns. Here I describe three of these appointments.

Ellen Sauerbrey

In October 2005, Bush nominated Ellen Sauerbrey to be Assistant Secretary of State for Population, Refugees, and Migration, a nomination strongly opposed by a coalition of women's health and rights groups, who assailed it as 'yet another in a long string of crony nominations of unqualified individuals for critical positions' (Lobe 2005b). Sauerbrey had twice run unsuccessfully for governor of Maryland in the 1990s and had served in other Bush State Department positions since 2001, recently as the US representative to the Economic and Social Council of the UN Commission on the Status of Women. Before that she served in the Maryland State Legislature and was a leader of the state's right-wing faction. In 2000, Sauerbrey had been state chair of the Bush presidential campaign. After Bush took office in 2001, he named Sauerbrey a 'public member' of the US delegation to the UN Human Rights Commission in Geneva. She told her hometown newspaper at the time that she opposed providing aid, including medicine for AIDS victims, to countries where such assistance could 'perpetuate dictators and tyrants.' As representative to the UN Women's Commission, she attracted much attention and criticism when she asserted that women 'by nature' are not risk-takers (Lobe 2005b).

Sauerbrey also vigorously supported the Bush administration's opposition to ratification of CEDAW and was widely criticized in March 2005 for her disruption of the Beijing Plus Ten conference. According to June Zeitlin of Women's Environment and Development Organization, 'This unilateralist tactic alienated many countries and totally undermined Sauerbrey's credibility as an effective leader or spokesperson for the US government' (Lobe 2005b). Not a strong proponent of women's rights, Sauerbrey had once commented, 'I always feel when I'm being introduced as a representative of the United Nations that I have to say I'm a conservative, I'm not a feminist' (Stevens 2005b).

The post for which Sauerbrey was nominated in 2005 has major responsibilities and an annual budget of over $700 million; the position usually goes to a senior professional career officer, or at least someone with major relevant experience. Women's rights groups opposing the nomination urged its withdrawal on the basis that Sauerbrey had no experience either in refugee or humanitarian crises, or in administering large programs and budgets. In addition, Sauerbrey 'has expressed ardent opposition toward efforts to strengthen multilateral cooperation at the United Nations and to U.N. treaties affecting the rights of women and girls,' according to Zeitlin (Lobe 2005b). Sauerbrey, if confirmed, would work with the US Agency for International Development to determine which countries would receive aid, and with UN and private agencies concerned with refugee-related issues.

Sauerbrey's well-documented stand against women's reproductive health protections and similar issues could seriously impact her ability to deal with women refugees and disaster victims. For example, Sauerbrey has objected to language in UN documents that would require countries to 'condemn violence against women' and that forbids countries to invoke excuses of 'custom, tradition, or religious consideration' to avoid their obligations in the UN goal to eliminate violence against women (as affirmed in the Declaration on the Elimination of Violence Against Women). According to Jodi Jacobson of the Centre for Health and Gender Equity,

> [Sauerbrey] has shown outright hostility toward women's human rights and toward reproductive health services, such as family planning and maternal and child health, a stand which is particularly problematic given that the majority both of refugees and of clients of family planning services worldwide are women, and that these programmes also are directly under the purview of PRM. (Lobe 2005b)

Sauerbrey does not consider abortion a legitimate part of reproductive health aid; nor does she believe adolescents have a right to make their own decisions about reproductive health matters. Sauerbrey is a close associate of John Bolton, Bush's controversial UN ambassador.

On 31 October 2005, the *New York Times* ran an editorial condemning the Senate for its intention to confirm Sauerbrey for the position, stating that her nomination 'conjures up memories of Michael Brown, the former head of the Federal Emergency Management Agency,' whose incompetence caused so many problems in the post-Katrina disaster. The *Times* editors write that Sauerbrey

> is currently serving as the American representative to the United Nations Commission on the Status of Women, where she has zealously pursued an anti-abortion and anti-family planning agenda. She has alienated many human rights groups, but endeared herself to the White House and her party's far-right wing.... Senate Republicans should think hard about the mismatch between Ms. Sauerbrey's credentials and the life-and-death responsibilities of this job. (*New York Times* 2005f)

The *Washington Post* and the *Baltimore Sun* published similar editorials critical of the nomination (Feminist Majority Foundation 2005c).

The Senate Foreign Relations Committee on 2 November 2005 took the unusual step of delaying a vote on Sauerbrey's nomination following the announced opposition of ten women's rights and health organizations. Senators expressing strong reservations about Sauer-brey's appropriateness were concerned about her lack of qualifications, especially since she admitted that she had no experience in dealing with refugees, a 'major responsibility' of the position (Feminist Major-ity Foundation 2005c). Bush avoided further Senate battles by giving Sauerbrey a recess appointment in January 2006 (Edsall 2006).

Louise V. Oliver

Oliver was appointed ambassador to the UN Educational, Scientific, and Cultural Organization (UNESCO) in 2003. The UN agency was established in 1945 to promote international exchange of a scientific and cultural nature, in the interest of building 'peace in the minds of men.' The UNESCO mission is to promote 'international cooperation among its [members] in the fields of education, science, culture, and communication' by promoting dialogue 'based on respect for shared values and the dignity of each civilization and culture.'

> The role is critical, particularly in the face of terrorism, which constitutes an attack against humanity. The world urgently requires global visions of sustainable development based upon observance of human rights, mutual respect and the alleviation of poverty, all of which lie at the heart of UNESCO's mission and activities. (UNESCO 2006)

Based on this broadly humanistic organizational mission, one would think that appropriate ambassadors to this agency would be chosen so as to promote an agenda of international cooperation, exchange, tolerance, and education. Traditionally the position had gone to individuals who support these goals, usually receiving strong bi-partisan support.

Louise Oliver[2] is a conservative political activist who fails to meet any of these criteria. Her last previous professional position was as president of GOPAC, the aggressive anti-government, socially conservative political action committee founded by Republican Newt Gingrich. Oliver's connection to GOPAC was not mentioned in the White House nomination announcement; instead, she was presented as 'president of Oliver Management Consultants' and as having been 'previously appointed by the president to be Commissioner of the National Council on Children.' The Congressional news journal *Roll Call* reported that it was unable to locate 'Oliver Management Consultants' on the Internet, and, further, that there was no such agency as the National Council on Children. The misleading statement in the White House announcement was apparently referring to Oliver's having been appointed to the National Commission on Children (NCPOC) by President Reagan in 1988 for a term ending in 1989. The NCOC, according to *Roll Call*, was abolished in 1993. Oliver also served for a time in Reagan's Education Department under William Bennett (Lobe 2003).

When Oliver was named for the UNESCO position, some Democrats raised strong questions as to her fitness for the post. New York Representative Carol Maloney, noting that a key part of UNESCO's mission is to promote tolerance and understanding among peoples of different cultures, suggested that Oliver's background was uniquely unsuited for the position. 'GOPAC is distinctly undiplomatic,' Maloney said, referring to its aggressive habits of attacking political opponents as 'sick' or 'traitors.' In addition, she pointed out, Oliver is listed as an emeritus director of the Independent Women's Forum, an organization on record as opposing 'multiculturalism' (Lobe 2003).

In addition to her GOPAC activity, Oliver is listed as a former employee of the Heritage Foundation, an organization that was active in the 1984 campaign that led the United States to withdraw from UNESCO, over charges by the Reagan administration that the organization was 'anti-Western' and 'anti-American' (Lobe 2003). According to Global Policy Forum's *OneWorldUS* newsletter, Bush approved returning the United States to membership of UNESCO (after a nineteen-year hiatus) at least partly in the hope that the organization could be used to promote 'pro-western values in the educational systems of Arab and Islamic countries, a priority in the ... "war on terrorism"' (Global Policy Forum 2004) – hardly in keeping with UNESCO's goals of true multiculturalism. For Bush's Western-cultural-dominance goals, however, Oliver seems the 'right' choice.

Charlotte 'Charlie' Ponticelli

Ponticelli was named Senior Coordinator, International Women's issues, Department of State on 7 April 2003. As Director of Human Rights and Women's Affairs during the Reagan and George H.W. Bush administrations, Ponticelli worked to prevent US ratification of the Convention on the Elimination of All Forms of Discrimination Against Women (CEDAW), a policy continued under George W. Bush (IWHC 2005b). In her current position, Ponticelli has become a cheerleader for Bush's policies in Afghanistan and Iraq, frequently painting a rosy picture of the impacts on women in those countries of the Bush wars of 'liberation.' She appears to have taken few initiatives to oppose global gender discrimination, instead serving primarily as a public relations agent for Bush policies. For example, in March 2004 Ponticelli called the progress of women in Afghanistan 'unstoppable' and claimed that their situation had 'categorically' improved. An article in the British publication *New Statesman* disputes this claim:

> Most Afghan women would be astonished by her description. Although girls can now go to school, few have discarded the burqa, which for the West came to symbolize Taliban repression. And in recent weeks there have been a spate of self immolations from women forced into marriage.... 'Any advances are relative advances tempered with neo-Taliban practices against women,' said Sima Wali, head of Refugee Women in Development. 'Women are still subjected to sexual violence, torture, trafficking in women, forced marriage, domestic violence – the list goes on and on.' (Lamb 2004)

The article suggests that one possible reason for Washington's 'self delusion' about the situation of women in Afghanistan is that their representatives' visits to the country are limited to a relatively small and highly protected section of the capital, Kabul. Seemingly unaware of the severity of women's problems in Afghanistan, Iraq, and in other poor nations, Ponticelli continues to praise the accomplishments for women by Bush policies.

In this chapter we have seen clear evidence of a turning away from support for women's global human rights, in the failure to support the Millennium Development Goals and CEDAW and in rejection of a number of population accords. We also saw that the administration unnecessarily supported the Japanese government against actions aimed at redressing some of the wrongs done to the so-called comfort women during World War II, and that it was unwilling to support vigorously asylum seekers persecuted on the basis of gender. In a later chapter we will look at further damage to women's human rights caused by the Bush 'war on terror,' with its secret detentions, violations of international human rights law, and the increasing militarization of culture associated with the invasions of Afghanistan and Iraq.

In spite of rhetoric to the contrary, the George W. Bush regime has actively sought to restrict women's rights and to push back on the substantial progress that the world community had made over the past two decades. It remains to be seen whether the United States will be able to reverse this trend and return to its previous support for reproductive, political, and economic rights for women. To do so will require a change of government leadership. Yet the damage already done to women around the world, and to the US's reputation internationally, may take decades to correct, if it is possible at all.

8

STACKING THE DECK AGAINST WOMEN:
BUSH AND THE COURTS

The federal judiciary is an extremely powerful branch of government, charged with determining the limits of law and federal power, based on its interpretation of the Constitution and previous legal precedent. For decades conservatives have attempted to 'take back' the courts by supporting appointees who would go along with restrictions of women's reproductive rights, minority rights and initiatives, and civil liberties involving such areas as speech, privacy, defendants' rights, and family choices. The religious right has especially hoped to fill the courts with those who would overturn *Roe* v. *Wade*, allow mandatory prayer in public schools, allow federal support for religious indoctrination in schools, and oppose affirmative action, abortion, and gay/lesbian rights. Since Bush owed his electoral victory largely to the activist religious right, he rarely acted in ways to displease them. One of the most transparent means to pay back his right-wing supporters has been through his judicial nominations, a large number of whom have been well out of the mainstream in their attitudes about civil rights, reproductive rights, and women's roles. Bush's appointments threaten to overturn many of the gains women have made since the early 1970s, especially with vacancies appearing on the Supreme Court early in his second term. Among his appointees have been some of the most extreme ideologues in the courts' history, although many of these have received relatively little mainstream press attention. The total impact of Bush's judicial appointments may be his most dangerous legacy for women's rights, one that will be felt for a generation since federal judges receive lifetime appointments.

BUSH SELECTION STRATEGIES

Although judges traditionally have been chosen to represent the general philosophy of the president who appoints them, in the past they have rarely been so ideologically defined as Bush's appointees. The unfortunate circumstance of conservative Republican control of the Senate, the huge debt owed by Bush to his ultraconservative supporters, and public distraction by fears of terrorism coincided to make possible a virtual 'revolution' in basic rights by shifting the courts sharply to the right.

Fewer women and moderates selected

Until the 1970s, the federal judiciary had been made up almost entirely of white men. President Carter broke with tradition when he appointed a number of minority and women judges – 40 women in all. Presidents Reagan and George H.W. Bush named some women to the federal bench (29 and 36, respectively), but Bill Clinton more than doubled these figures, with appointments of at least 80 women judges to district and circuit courts (Segal 2000). Of all his nominees, 30 per cent were women and 25 per cent were racial/ethnic minorities (Aron 2004). Clinton's appointments were generally moderates whose rulings were not out of line ideologically with previous judges (Segal 2000), in spite of Republican claims to the contrary. Since the average president puts in about a third of the federal judiciary in two terms, Bush's re-election was very significant in this sense. Research by political scientists has found Bush's nominees to be more conservative in their decisions than even the appointees of Nixon, Reagan, and George H.W. Bush (Feminist Majority Foundation 2004a), and only about 21 per cent of his nominees have been women and 19 per cent minorities, lower percentages than Clinton's (Aron 2004).

Elimination of American Bar Association review

George W. Bush's approach to judicial nomination has been controversial from the beginning, consistent with progressive fears expressed during the election campaigns. Early in his first term, Bush eliminated the long-standing practice of submitting potential court nominations to the American Bar Association (ABA) for preliminary screening. The ABA had been consulted by all presidents since Eisenhower began the practice in 1952, providing an independent review and vote by a fifteen-member committee on the legal qualifications of the candidate. The committee had ruled on nominees' qualifications without regard to political leanings or judicial philosophy, giving positive and negative ratings to both conservatives and liberals. In recent years, however, conservatives had criticized the ABA ratings as having a liberal bias. The ABA continues to rate nominees, but they do not receive prior notification and their views are not taken into account by the Bush nominating procedures (Tiefer 2004: 283–4).

Concealment of nominees' conservatism

In order to get his nominees confirmed, Bush has used a strategy of concealment, a tactic that was made easier by the elimination of the ABA vetting process. Charles Tiefer describes the strategy this way:

> Typically, the administration spoke with apparent frankness but in general about nominees' conservatism, while looking for ways to conceal their more specific, controversial positions, especially in opposing women's rights or civil rights. With the obscuring of many facts about nominees' records and ideologies, confirmation struggles now often shifted largely to arguments about the administration's refusal to provide specifics. (Tiefer 2004: 284)

When Democrats refused to accept a nominee for lack of documents or information, Bush and Republicans could then attack Senate Democrats as obstructionist, thus keeping from public view the real problem of the administration's refusal to admit the extreme views of its nominees.

Most nominees confirmed without controversy

While almost all of Bush's over 200 judicial nominees (in the first term alone) have been very conservative, the great majority were easily confirmed by the Senate. For example, of 52 judges nominated to federal appeals courts, the Senate failed to allow a vote on 10 who were considered so extreme and out of the mainstream that Democratic Senators went to the mat to oppose them. In an 'in your face' move of defiance in December 2004 (following the closely won election), Bush announced his intention to renominate 20 judges who had already been rejected by the Senate, either by being voted down in committee or blocked by filibuster. The most contentious nominees had very extreme records on civil rights, property rights, and women's issues, especially on abortion, contraception, sexual rights, and sex education.

In the spring of 2005, Republican Senate Majority leader Bill Frist intensified the conflict by threatening to change long-standing Senate rules, proposing to exempt judicial nominations from filibusters (the so-called 'nuclear option').[1] In an attempt at compromise, a small coalition of more conservative Democrats and 'moderate' Republicans (the 'Gang of 14') agreed to accept a small number of controversial Bush nominees in exchange for keeping the right to filibuster in 'extreme' cases. Although the press framed this decision as a reasonable compromise, in fact Democrats gained very little and Bush succeeded in placing some of his most anti-women, pro-business, anti-civil rights, and anti-environmentalist judges on the courts.

A SAMPLING OF BUSH'S COURT NOMINEES

In this section I describe some of Bush's most controversial nominations to the courts, most of whom have now taken their place in the United States judiciary.[2] The long-term impacts of these placements can hardly be overrated. From support for the right of a president to take away completely a citizen's rights to due process on the basis of 'suspicion' of terrorist activity, to opposition to the provision of contraception to unmarried women, these appointments threaten the ability of future legislators to pass laws to sustain or enhance protections for the rights of women, labor, minorities, consumers, and other vulnerable groups. It should be noted that many of the appointments are themselves members of racial minorities and/or are women. This cynical approach to nominations follows the successful strategy of George H.W. Bush in the nomination of Clarence Thomas, on the theory that liberal members of the Senate would have a harder time opposing such candidates when they could then be accused of racism or sexism for their opposition. In addition, there is the notion that a president who has won an election should be able to nominate those who represent his 'philosophy.' The success of Bush in his appointments shows that the 'advice and consent' function of the Senate in judicial nominations is in deep trouble, far too influenced by narrow and short-term political interests and not by any concern for the long-term welfare of the country.

Janice Rogers Brown

Brown was re-nominated in February 2005 to the US Circuit Court of Appeals for the District of Columbia, after having been rejected in 2003. She was described by People for the American Way as 'to the right of Thomas and Scalia,' the most inflexible and conservative members of the Supreme Court. At the time of her nomination, Brown was a member of the California Supreme Court. When nominated to the California court, she had been found 'unqualified' by the state's bar evaluation committee because of her inexperience and lack of respect for established precedent. Brown was also accused of frequently basing her judgments on political rather than legal considerations. Her many dissents while on the California court showed that she had been reluctant to find in favor of any victim of discrimination, rejected the idea of a constitutional right of privacy, opposed many civil rights protections, and did not believe in a right to birth control or abortion (Holland 2003; PFAW 2003). Brown publicly pronounced her disapproval of the Depression-era New Deal legislation (Social Security, minimum wage laws, and child-labor limitations, for example) for its 'socialistic' tendencies. In addition to all of this, she has a reputation for an acerbic personality and lack of collegiality (PFAW 2003). The *New York Times* referred to Brown as among the 'very worst' of a list of 'unworthy judicial nominees' put forward by Bush, a sentiment that was echoed by many editorial pages and women's and civil rights advocates (NWLC 2005e).

According to the National Women's Law Center, while serving on the California court Brown took positions that could undermine legal protections against sexual and racial workplace harassment.

> She would have struck down an injunction against the continued use of obscenities and ethnic slurs like 'wetback' against Latino employees, and she even raised doubts about whether women subjected to offensive verbal conduct of a sexual nature can challenge it as sexual harassment under Title VII, despite well-established, longstanding U.S. Supreme Court precedents finding that such conduct is illegal. (NWLC 2005e: 2)

In addition, Brown supported permitting employers to exempt prescription contraceptives from their prescription coverage plans, on the basis that women for whom the need for contraception was a 'critical concern' were free to look for work elsewhere. She questioned the California rule that forbade prosecutors from discriminating against black women in jury selection. In one case she tried to argue that federal and state laws against workplace discrimination did not apply to the banking industry. In many cases she had been the lone dissenter and had been accused by her colleagues of incorrect and unfair decisions. In general, Brown supports an extreme position that opposes most government protective legislation of any kind while allowing maximum freedom from regulation for businesses (NWLC 2005e: 2–4).

In summing up its opposition to Brown's nomination, a National Women's Law Center (NWLC) report claims that her views 'threaten the progress that has been made over the last 30 years' in the application of the Equal Protection Clause of the Constitution to cases of gender discrimination and in protecting women's rights to terminate pregnancy on the basis of a constitutional right to privacy. The NWLC further maintains that Brown's appeal to 'natural law' as a basis for legal decisions 'could turn the clock back to the time when the 'laws of nature and God' were explicitly used by the courts to justify sex discrimination' based on stereotyped notions of women's nature and roles (NWLC 2005e: 4). The spring 2005 deal between conservative Democrats and moderate Republicans that postponed the threat of the nuclear option led to the confirmation of Brown along with several other very controversial candidates.

Leon Holmes

Nominated by Bush and confirmed to the US District Court in Eastern Arkansas in 2004, Holmes has been a longtime opponent of women's equality and reproductive choice. At the time of his nomination, Holmes was a lawyer in private practice and an adjunct professor at the University of Arkansas School of Law. An Alliance for Justice press release after he was confirmed describes Holmes as having consistently and actively 'worked to undermine women's reproductive rights.' He had compared legal abortions to the Holocaust and had written that 'women should subordinate themselves to their husbands,' casting doubt on his ability to judge gender-based cases fairly. In addition, Holmes's public statements about gays and lesbians and religion raised 'serious concerns about his ability to remain objective in cases involving issues of sexual orientation or the separation of church and state' (Alliance for Justice 2004).

People for the American Way (PFAW) portrayed Holmes as 'far outside any mainstream understanding of constitutional values.' Holmes, PFAW continued, had been callous in his dismissal of the concerns of women desiring abortion. His statement that 'concern for rape victims is a red herring because conceptions from rape occur with approximately the same frequency as snowfall in Miami' was especially egregious, as serious estimates place the annual number of women who become pregnant by rape in the US as between 25,000 and 32,000; about half of these pregnancies are terminated by abortion (PFAW 2004).

Holmes has stated that he believes *Roe* v. *Wade* and other abortion-related decisions were incorrectly made, because they 'constitutional-ize the theory of moral relativism, which is the antithesis of natural law' (Feminist Majority Foundation 2001–2005b). An anti-abortion activist, he has served as an officer on the 'Unborn Child Amendment Committee,' a group hoping to pass an amendment to the Arkansas State Constitution that would outlaw *all* abortions except those necessary to save the life of the pregnant woman. The group's proposed amendment provides no exceptions for such circumstances as pregnancy caused by rape or incest or to protect the woman's health. In addition, of course, there is no exception if the fetus is severely deformed, if the mother-to-be is very young, in very early stages of pregnancy, or in any other circumstance (Feminist Majority Foundation 2001–2005a). Holmes's opposition to feminism has been open, as he once wrote that 'the feminist movement brought with it artificial contraception and abortion on demand, with recognition of homosexual liaisons soon to follow' (IWHC 2005c), accomplishments which the judge found abhorrent. Leon Holmes was confirmed to a lifetime seat on the US District Court in Eastern Arkansas on 6 July 2004, by a 51:46 vote.

Charles Pickering

Nominated in February 2002 to the Fifth Circuit Court of Appeals, Judge Pickering is another strong opponent of abortion, having stated that he believes *Roe* v. *Wade* should be overturned. In the past, Pickering has supported amending the United States Constitution so as to make abortion illegal. Pickering also had a record of repeatedly ruling against litigants with claims of employment discrimination, holding that most of these cases were without merit. Based on this record, Pickering's nomination was opposed by a coalition of women's rights, civil rights, and labor organizations (NWLC 2002a).

Judge Pickering's nomination was rejected in committee on 14 February 2002, but Bush renominated him in 2003. This second nomination reached the Senate floor but Democrats succeeded in blocking the nomination by filibuster. On 16 January 2004, President Bush bypassed the Senate confirmation process, granting a recess appointment to Pickering on the Fifth Circuit bench. This appointment was effective until the beginning of the next Senate session, January 2005. Pickering announced in December 2004 that he would retire at the end of his interim appointment (IWHC 2005c).

William Pryor

Pryor was nominated for the Eleventh Circuit Court, which hears federal appeals from Alabama, Georgia, and Florida. Pryor's nomination failed confirmation by the Senate, but Bush gave Pryor a recess appointment in February 2004, allowing him to fill out the term without Senate approval. Bush then renominated Pryor in February 2005, along with several other previously rejected candidates.

Pryor is a former Attorney General of the State of Alabama, probably best known for his vocal support for the display of the Ten Commandments in public buildings (Feminist Majority Foundation 2001–2005c). A vehement and consistent opponent of abortion, he once referred to *Roe* v. *Wade* as 'the worst abomination of constitutional law in our history,' a position he reaffirmed in his confirmation hearings. Pryor has supported states' rights over the rights of individuals in cases of discrimination, as when he questioned as 'political correctness' the Supreme Court's 7–1 decision that the all-male Virginia Military Institute, a state institution, could not legally exclude women (NWLC 2003).

Pryor opposed elements of the Violence Against Women Act, the Civil Rights Act of 1964, and some of the protections of the Family and Medical Leave Act. He signed a 'friend of the court' brief that urged the Supreme Court to vacate an injunction against anti-abortion activists who had tried to close down clinics (NWLC 2005e: 5).

The NWLC also describes Pryor's 'troubling record' on issues involving race, especially where voting rights are concerned. He is opposed to affirmative action and is on record as supporting a ban on the consideration of race and gender in state hiring and school admissions policies. As Attorney General of Alabama, Pryor 'vigorously' investigated and prosecuted suspected voter fraud in a rural mostly-black area of Alabama, a move that civil rights leaders charged was 'racially motivated and intended to intimidate African American voters and discredit leadership in the Black community.' Because of Pryor's actions, many local residents were later afraid to vote; absentee ballots in one targeted county declined from 14,000 to 199 as a result (NWLC 2005e: 6).

After Bush gave Pryor a recess appointment to the court, the NWLC released a statement calling the action 'an insult to the Constitution' and to the American people. The fact that this took place after the widely criticized Pickering recess appointment was seen as further evidence of Bush's refusal to compromise or to listen to advocates of women or racial minorities. Marcia Greenburger, co-president of the NWLC, commented, 'The President has demonstrated the extreme lengths to which he will go to appoint judges with the most extreme judicial philosophies' (NWLC 2004a).

Bush renominated Pryor for a regular appointment in February 2005, a move that was held up by threat of filibuster. On 9 June 2005, William Pryor was confirmed to a lifetime seat on the Eleventh Circuit Court by a vote of 53:45, one of the beneficiaries of the compromise of the Gang of 14 to stave off the 'nuclear option.'

Priscilla Owen

A member of the Texas Supreme Court, Owen was nominated three times by Bush to the Fifth Circuit Court of Appeals. She had been elected to the Texas Supreme Court in 1994 with the help of Karl Rove and was re-elected in 2000. By the time Bush nominated her to the Appeals Court, Owen had a long record of judicial activism in the interest of limiting women's reproductive rights and opposing claims of workplace discrimination, a record that led to her rejection by the Senate Judiciary Committee in 2002. Her nomination was blocked by Senate filibuster in 2003. Rather than attempting to work in a bipartisan manner to find another nominee who would be less controversial, Bush nominated Owen for the third time in 2005. She was another of the 'compromise' judges seated after the 'Gang of 14' agreed to accept a few controversial nominees in return for a Republican pledge not to change Senate rules on filibuster.

Priscilla Owen was opposed primarily because of her record of conservative judicial activism in cases of reproductive rights and her support for corporate interests and rejection of discrimination suits (NWLC 2002b, 2005e). Owen was considered the most right-wing member of a very hard-right court, the Texas Supreme Court, her interpretations of the law having been stricter and narrower than those of her peers on that court (all of whom were conservative Republicans). Especially in cases involving Texas's parental notification statute for minors seeking abortion, Owen almost never sided with a minor seeking a court bypass of parental notification, even in cases where the minor feared parental abuse if they found out about the pregnancy, and even where her conservative peers approved the bypass. Alberto Gonzalez, now the US Attorney General, accused Owen at one point of an 'unconscionable act of judicial activism' for her dissent on one such case, as she relied on personal opinion and rhetoric rather than the intent of the law. The Alliance for Justice called Owen 'an extreme conservative activist' who 'routinely backs corporations' against worker protections, applying more stringent tests than the law itself called for, and than other justices applied. Owen's refusal to recuse herself in cases involving corporations (such as Halliburton and Enron) that had made contributions to her election campaigns was also raised as an issue by her opponents. Rejected twice by the Senate, Owen was confirmed in a compromise on 25 May 2005 by a 55:43 vote (White House 2005a).

Michael McConnell

Nominated to the US Court of Appeals for the Tenth Circuit, McConnell was confirmed 15 November 2002. The NWLC found McConnell to have 'the worst record on reproductive rights of any Bush administration judicial nominee to come before the Senate so far.' McConnell had argued that *Roe* v. *Wade* was wrongly decided and questioned whether a right to privacy is guaranteed by the Constitution. He also has supported the right to life of embryos and fetuses at every stage of development, even arguing for a constitutional amendment that would protect such a right. McConnell had also been critical of the Freedom of Access to Clinic Entrances Act, a law that protects women's clinics from harassment and obstruction of access. Upon O'Connell's confirmation, NWLC released a statement quoting its co-president as saying:

> Those who cherish the legal rights of women, including the right to reproductive freedom, must sit up and take notice that these rights are in grave danger.... If the Senate's confirmation of Michael McConnell to the 10th Circuit is a sign of things to come, our courts will soon be filled with judges who cannot be counted on to protect our fundamental rights and freedoms. (NWLC 2002c)

As is obvious in this brief sampling of court nominees, Bush has named many individuals to the federal courts who are strongly opposed to abortion rights, who consistently favor business or property rights over the rights of workers, consumers or the environment, and who oppose strong civil rights or civil liberties protections. Since the great majority of cases never go beyond these courts, the ideological conservatism of these Bush appointees promises to serve as a barrier to progressive legal change for decades to come.

THE SUPREMES: CHANGING THE COURT OF LAST RESORT

For politically aware supporters of civil rights, women's rights, reproductive choice, and civil liberties, perhaps the most critical issue in the 2004 election was the status of the Supreme Court. For years, the court had been narrowly divided, often deciding cases by the narrowest of margins, 5:4. The court that 'selected' Bush as president in 2000, contrary to the votes of the majority of Americans and contrary to the vote in Florida (if the court had allowed the votes to be counted as legally mandated), was now at risk of becoming completely dominated by right-wing justices. With the aging of its members and Chief Justice Rehnquist's illness, nothing seemed more important. Unfortunately, the fears of women's advocates were fulfilled as Bush narrowly won the election and declared that he had gained 'political capital' which he planned to spend. With the June 2005 announcement of the resignation of the major 'swing voter,' Sandra Day O'Connor, and the soon-to-follow death of Rehnquist, the greatest fears of the progressive left were coming to pass.

Sandra Day O'Connor had been appointed by President Reagan in 1984 and generally was a conservative justice, but her support for *Roe* v. *Wade* had led the conservative movement to oppose her. She did not always stand in the way of limitations on abortion rights, but she had always voted to uphold the basic principles of Roe. Now, with her resignation, Bush was in the position of naming a replacement who would potentially move the majority of the court to the anti-Roe position. In addition to abortion rights, given Bush's other nominations, the situation was ominous for a large array of hard-won rights involving racial justice, women's rights, civil liberties, and gay rights. Bush had stated at one point in his first campaign that his favorite court members were Thomas and Scalia, the two most ideological right-wing justices on the high court.

Both conservatives and liberals dug in for a fight, as Bush and his supporters strategized how to find appointees who could win Senate approval without generating enormous public backlash.

John G. Roberts

Soon after O'Connor announced her resignation, Bush named Judge John Roberts to replace her. Before his confirmation hearings could begin, however, Chief Justice Rehnquist died, and Bush revised his nomination of Roberts from Associate to Chief Justice. As Chief, Roberts would have more authority than as an ordinary member, including the responsibility of assigning the writing of opinions to particular justices and presiding over internal deliberations.

That the White House hoped to present Roberts as a 'moderate' conservative is illustrated by their reaction to the publication in July in several major newspapers that Roberts was a member of the Federalist Society. Roberts denied ever having been a member, and the White House quickly made a series of phone calls demanding retractions, which were quickly printed. Subsequently, the *Washington Post* released a document that showed that Roberts had served on the steering committee of the Washington Chapter of the Federalist Society, contrary to the impression given by Roberts and the White House. In describing this incident, Matthew Bribitzer-Stull wrote:

> This is not an isolated episode. The White House is banking on a strategy of hiding Roberts' right wing views and focusing on his nonconfrontational personality. And so far, most newspapers and networks have bought in, spending a lot more time speculating about how easily Roberts will be confirmed than doing the investigative reporting that the country deserves. (Bribitzer-Stull 2005)

Indeed, in this as with other judicial nominations, the White House under Bush attempted to conceal more than they revealed about the record of the nominee, without allowing the Senate to know exactly where he stood on important issues.

Bribitzer-Stull (2005) details some of what was known about Roberts's record. In his days as a corporate lawyer, Roberts had fought to weaken the Americans With Disabilities Act by denying accommodations for workers who had been injured over time as a result of their job. He had helped an automobile manufacturer avoid a recall even though its safety belts violated federal safety standards. As a judge, Roberts had favored limiting congressional authority to regulate corporate practices, thereby undercutting protections for the environment, workers' rights, and victims of discrimination (Bribitzer-Stull 2005).

Although his current views on abortion were not clear, while working for President Reagan, Roberts had argued before the Supreme Court that *Roe* v. *Wade* should be 'overruled.' In addition, he was a lifelong partisan Republican, having donated thousands of dollars exclusively to Republican candidates (Bribitzer-Stull 2005).

John Roberts's nomination was praised by such ultra-right voices as the anti-abortion group Operation Rescue, James Dobson of Focus on the Family, the infamous Pat Robertson, and Tony Perkins of the Family Research Council. A group of conservative women activists, including representatives of the Independent Women's Forum, held a press conference in late August accusing 'feminists on the left' of unfairly characterizing Roberts's record (VandeHei 2005). The Women for Roberts event was organized by the same public-relations firm that helped the notorious Swift Boat Veterans in their smear campaign against Democratic presidential candidate John F. Kerry in 2004.

A number of black women's groups weighed in against the Roberts nomination. Loraine Cole of the Black Women's Health Imperative released a statement in July 2005 criticizing Bush's missed opportunities to enhance or maintain the gender/racial diversity of the Court. Cole notes that Roberts's record was sparse but highly questionable on women's health, safety, and privacy issues, especially on abortion and clinic access (Cole 2005). In another article written from the perspective of women of color, Roberts's record on women's basic rights was described as 'disturbing' (Chappell, Co, and Horton 2005). Not only had he supported the gag rule that prevented doctors and family-planning clinic personnel receiving federal funding from giving women the full range of advice about their options, but he had co-authored a friend-of-the-court brief in support of the 'military style' tactics of Operation Rescue when it blocked access to women's health clinics. In that case, Roberts argued that Operation Rescue's actions had not constituted discrimination against women and that federal civil rights statutes did not apply.

The authors also questioned Roberts's record on voting rights, civil rights, affirmative action, and religious freedom, noting that these issues have been decided in recent years by very narrow margins that could be reversed should Roberts be confirmed. They made a strong plea for women and men of color to raise their voices against nominees such as Roberts (Chappell, Co, and Horton 2005).

Professor Erwin Chemerinsky of Duke Law School, after reading through Roberts's short recent record as an appeals court judge, opposed the nomination on human-rights and separation-of-powers grounds:

> Roberts' judicial opinions during his short tenure on the Federal Court of Appeals also reveal his staunch conservatism. As an appellate judge, Roberts has expressed great deference to presidential power. He recently joined a decision adopting the Bush administration's position that the protections of human rights found in the Geneva Conventions are not enforceable in U.S. courts, and that detainees designated as 'enemy combatants' may be tried for war crimes before military commissions lacking basic procedural safeguards. (Chemerinsky 2005)

Chemerinsky pointed out that Roberts also dissented from other judges by supporting Bush's presidential order to shut down lawsuits against Iraqi officials brought by American prisoners of war for torture they had undergone during the 1991 Gulf War.

> In virtually every area, all that is known about Roberts shows that he is not a moderate conservative in the mold of O'Connor but likely to move the law far to the right in the years ahead. Roberts has impeccable academic and professional qualifications. But so did Bork. An excellent resume is not enough for the Supreme Court. (Chemerinsky 2005)

During Roberts's confirmation hearings, a number of Democrats expressed frustration that Roberts refused to reveal details of his actual judicial philosophy. Both his supporters and opponents praised his general qualifications, though Democrats were frustrated by the way Roberts dodged questions, appearing to answer them while remaining vague, often appealing to the need not to 'prejudge' questions that might come before the court.

Senator Dianne Feinstein of California was one of five Democrats to oppose Roberts in the committee vote, explaining that she knew little more after the hearings that she had before. She was especially troubled that the nominee was not more forthcoming on issues of reproductive choice, privacy, and women's equity (Lochhead 2005). In spite of many objections, Roberts was confirmed by a 78 : 22 vote in the full Senate and was sworn in as the seventeenth United States Chief Justice of the Supreme Court on 29 September 2005. While many liberals were troubled by Roberts, he did not appear to be as risky as many ideological activists that Bush had sent to other courts, and perhaps the Senators believed he was the best they might get from this administration.

The Miers nomination and withdrawal

The remaining vacancy on the court, after the Roberts confirmation, became critical politically for all sides. The nomination came at a very low point in the Bush presidency, with the war in Iraq going poorly and finally being seen as a mistake by the majority of Americans. In addition, a number of scandals in the Republican leadership and the White House itself, as well as the disastrous response to the devastation of Hurricane Katrina, left Bush wounded and weakened. His first attempt to nominate a 'stealth candidate' whom he trusted (hoping to avoid a fight with the Senate Democrats) led to an enormously hostile reaction by his usually loyal base, the far-right conservatives who had looked forward to this moment for years. When on 4 October Bush nominated his personal friend and White House staff attorney, Harriet Miers, the right wing exploded.[3]

Miers had almost no record, having never been a judge; nor had she received much public attention at all. Indeed, most people had never heard of Harriet Miers when she was nominated. Although Bush implied that he had never discussed abortion with Miers, he sent out many signals that she would oppose *Roe* v. *Wade*, first suggesting her evangelical religion as a qualification, in contrast to his usual statements that religion should not be taken into account in evaluating a nominee. When conservatives objected, Bush tried to make a case for Miers on the basis of qualifications, claiming at one point that she was the most qualified person he could find. Although a few religious conservatives, including Southern Baptist leader Richard Land and Focus on the Family founder James Dobson expressed support for Miers, more traditional conservatives were outraged that Bush had missed an opportunity to put a strong, respected 'strict constructionist' constitutional theorist on the court who would influence legal opinion for decades. For three and a half weeks Bush tried to convince the critics that Miers was the right choice, but he finally acceded to their ever growing demands, accepting Miers's withdrawal of her nomination on 27 October.

Judge Samuel Alito

Conservative critics of Harriet Miers had their fondest hopes fullfilled a few days later, when Bush nominated Judge Samuel Alito to fill O'Connor's seat on the Supreme Court. There were immediate expressions of praise and exhilaration for this nominee from the same people who had attacked the Miers nomination. At the same time, progressive groups sounded the alarm. The Feminist Majority Foundation accused the nominee of demonstrating 'hostility to women's rights, civil rights, workers rights, separation of church and state, and privacy rights' over his career as a judge (Feminist Majority Foundation 2005a).

Alito has a long record as a judge, one that became more troubling to liberals and progressives as it became more familiar. Not only does he oppose abortion, denying that the Constitution provided any protection for such a procedure, he has even questioned the 'one-man, one-vote' principle of reapportionment that had helped to equalize the impact of different voting districts. In a highly critical editorial, the *New York Times* accused Judge Alito of being 'extreme' in his views of law, of lacking respect for judicial precedent, and of being an 'ideologue' for Republican causes. 'On the bench, Judge Alito has voted to uphold extreme limits on abortion and on other important rights, like freedom from unreasonable searches and seizures,' the editors wrote (*New York Times* 2005h).

Among the problematic positions taken by the judge are that he:

- voted against the Family and Medical Leave Act, restricting state employees' right to sue for damages under the Act;
- wrote a solo dissenting opinion questioning the right of Congress to prohibit the possession or transfer of machine guns;
- was the lone dissenter in a 1991 abortion case in which he argued for the constitutionality of a requirement that women notify their husbands prior to undergoing abortion;
- was the only dissenter on a sex discrimination case in employment, where his proposed test of proof of discrimination was so extreme as to make it almost impossible to prove discrimination.[4]

Alito's confirmation, in January 2006, marked what is almost certain to be the beginning of a period of retrenchment for women in the United States.

BUSH'S JUSTICE IN THE COURTS: FAILURE TO PROSECUTE DISCRIMINATION

The Civil Rights Division of the Justice Department has the responsibility for enforcing anti-discrimination laws by bringing suits against those who illegally discriminate on the basis of gender, race, or other protected categories. As noted in Chapter 2, the Bush administration has failed to use the courts vigorously to prosecute illegal discrimination against women and minorities, as indicated by a sharp reduction in cases pursued and by a change in the focus of the suits brought.

A study by Syracuse University researchers raised this issue in a 2003 report comparing the Bush Justice Department to that of previous administrations (Feminist Majority Foundation 2004b). In 1999, the number of civil-rights cases filed by federal prosecutors had been 159; by 2003 that number had dropped to 84, while the number of complaints had remained constant. In addition, there was a one-third drop in civil-rights cases recommended for prosecution by the FBI and other federal agencies over the same period. Out of the 1,903 cases recommended for prosecution, only 5 per cent resulted in charges being filed. The civil-rights complaints included violations such as police brutality and racial profiling, race-motivated violence, and blocking of access to women's health clinics. While the Justice Department denied the validity of the study's results, one of its authors, David Burnham, pointed out that the data came from the Justice Department's own Executive Office of United States Attorneys, obtained through the Freedom of Information Act (FOIA)[5] (Feminist Majority Foundation 2004b). Thus, in its failure aggressively to use the resources and legal remedies available when it took office, the Bush administration has shown itself to be lukewarm, if not hostile, to the full equality of women and racial/ethnic minority individuals in the workplace and elsewhere.

The *Washington Post* in November 2005 reinforced and expanded on these early findings in an article describing a serious decline in the pursuit of racial and gender discrimination crimes traditionally handled by the Civil Rights Division of Justice over the first five years of the Bush presidency (Eggen 2005b). The change in focus had led to 'an upheaval that [had] driven away dozens of veteran lawyers and … damaged morale for many of those who remain,' according to the report.

> Nearly 20 percent of the division's lawyers left in fiscal 2005, in part because of a buyout program that some lawyers believe was aimed at pushing out those who did not share the administration's conservative views on civil rights laws. Longtime litigators complain that political appointees have cut them out of hiring and major policy decisions. (Eggen 2005b)

Within the Civil Rights Division, the level of conflict between career and political staff had been especially contentious, as the division failed to file more than a 'handful' of cases dealing with employment discrimination or discrimination based on 'differential impact' on women or minority groups. Although the total number of criminal prosecutions had been similar to that during the Clinton administration, an increasing proportion of cases was targeting human smugglers, while other types of civil-rights prosecutions declined from 83 cases in 2001 to 49 in 2005 (Eggen 2005b).

Moreover, despite widespread irregularities and accusations of voter suppression in African-American areas in recent elections, the Bush administration has filed only three lawsuits based on the Voting Rights Act that prohibits discrimination against minority voters. Incredibly, none of these cases involved discrimination against African Americans, but one of the three involved a claim that a majority-black county in Mississippi had discriminated against *white* voters (Eggen 2005b).

William R. Yeomans, an attorney who left the civil-rights division in 2005 after twenty-four years of service, wrote that 'morale among career attorneys has plummeted, the division's productivity has suffered and the pace of civil rights enforcement has slowed' (Eggen 2005b). As traditional civil rights lawyers have left, they have been replaced by young ideological conservatives with little commitment to opposing discrimination against women or members of other disadvantaged groups. Since the Justice Department, and specifically its Civil Rights Division, has traditionally been a very important advocate for women's equity, these changes are especially troubling, given that complaints of gender-based discrimination have not declined.

The attempt by Bush to pack the courts with right-wing ideological judges has gone a long way toward changing the general philosophy of the legal system. Since the lower courts are the last resort in the majority of cases, Bush's success in placing conservatives on district and appeals courts will have repercussions for decades to come. His nominations to the Supreme Court, of course, are even more significant. Litigants seeking redress for discrimination will have a more difficult time receiving justice in the future. Additionally, it is likely that laws attempting to restrict abortion rights, gay rights, civil liberties, and due process will have an easier time passing constitutional tests under these judges. Likewise, it will be more difficult to establish new laws regulating business practices that are detrimental to consumers, workers, or the environment. Finally, the Justice Department's failure to use its resources to prosecute discrimination vigorously has already resulted in a loss of justice for many who have sought remedies through the courts in the past few years.

9

WEAKENING SUPPORT FOR
WOMEN'S EDUCATION AND HEALTH

George W. Bush's famous claim to be a 'compassionate conservative' revolves mainly around his purported support for education, one of the key points in his campaigns. He not only wanted to improve schools, he said, but he hoped to close the 'achievement gap' between white and minority children. While these are laudable goals, Bush's methods involved untried means such as school vouchers (almost universally criticized by educators who care about public schools) and achievement testing to evaluate the progress of children in schools, tying resources to measured progress. This latter program was part of his famous No Child Left Behind (NCLB) program, one of his major achievements early in his first term.

The NCLB program had the purported aim of improving and equalizing education in public schools, but its program of rigid annual tests and mandatory defunding of 'underperforming' schools led to serious problems in the educational experience of administrators, teachers, and students. The schools most likely to lose funding were those in low-income areas, although educators at all levels resent the inflexibility of the testing program that takes precious time away from learning. Even so, the administration failed to fund it adequately, while making it mandatory for states, causing great confusion and resentment among governors as well.

Bush refused to fully fund programs to provide the extra support and teacher quality that low-income children, who are disproportionately of color, need to succeed. In the program's first three years, the administration fell short of fully funding NCLB by a shocking $27 billion. (Sen 2005)

Over time, tales of schools subverting the rules of the tests so as to receive the rewards of successful schools began to be heard. Overall, the program never had much support among teachers or educational experts, and its implementation made it even less popular. A recent study by the Civil Rights Project at Harvard University (Orfield et al. 2004) found that lower graduation rates persist in those districts with higher concentrations of minority students, as compared to mostly white districts, in every state. Yet, instead of dealing with the problems of NCLB, Bush and his representatives rely on public-relations campaigns to promote the idea that his programs are successful. They even went so far as to hire African-American talk-show host Armstrong Williams (at a fee of $200,000) to promote NCLB on his television program, in what was presented as objective reporting when in fact it was government-supplied, tax-funded propaganda (Sen 2005).

Although NCLB is still in effect, it seems to have lost much of its support as its weaknesses have become known. But the administration became involved in other programs and initiatives in the field of education, less visibly but probably more importantly for women. In the following section I discuss two different areas in which Bush's Education Department has challenged gender-equity policies: Title IX and Affirmative Action.

CHALLENGING TITLE IX PROTECTIONS

One of the most important achievements of the 1970s' legal reforms for women was the passage of Title IX, legislation enacted in 1972 that outlawed sex discrimination in educational institutions receiving federal funding. Because of Title IX, the number of high-school girls who participate in sports has increased from 294,000 in 1971 to over 2.7 million today, and women's athletics at university level has likewise rapidly expanded. Often associated only with increasing women's participation in college athletics, the law reaches far beyond sports and has helped to equalize women's access to science, graduate school, scholarships, and many other male-dominated areas within schools and universities (Tobias 1997: ch. 8).

Threatening women's athletics

Early in 2003, there were indications that the Bush administration was considering changes to Title IX regulations that would weaken its impact. A Commission on Opportunity in Athletics had been handpicked and given the task of reviewing Title IX and its effects. The commission made several recommendations, which, if enacted, would have significantly weakened protections for women in college athletics. These recommendations alarmed Title IX supporters, who feared a return to the days of limitations on women's programs in favor of men's sports, and a reversal of the growth of women's athletics. At the time, because of a strong public outcry, Bush rejected the proposed changes. Nevertheless, the fact that he commissioned the review was seen by many as a sign of lack of full support for Title IX by Bush (Fletcher 2003).

In March 2005, these suspicions were confirmed. The Office for Civil Rights (OCR) in the Department of Education released a new ruling on how intercollegiate athletics should be evaluated for the purposes of Title IX funding. Without public debate or announcement, the OCR issued a new 'clarification' to the three-part test of university compliance with Title IX. Under the rules, a university can meet the test if it passes any one of three parts:

1. the percent of male and female athletes is substantially proportionate to the percent of male and female students enrolled in the school;
2. the school has a history and continuing practice of expanding participation opportunities for the underrepresented sex; or
3. the school is fully and effectively accommodating the interests and abilities of the underrepresented sex. (US Department of Education 2005)

The 2005 document provides 'further guidance' on meeting the third compliance option, effectively relaxing the requirements in ways that could bring a halt to the gains women's sports have made in the past few years. In order to be judged in noncompliance with the third rule, an institution must meet all three further conditions, including demonstration that a sport exists for which there is 'unmet interest sufficient to sustain a varsity team in the sport' (US Department of Education 2005).

In order to determine if this 'unmet interest' exists, the guidance suggests that web-based questionnaires or surveys be used to measure student athletic interest. OCR provides a 'web-based prototype survey' to be used as a model in these interest assessments. However, there are no rules specifying how to make sure all students possibly interested in the sport would be reached by such a survey, nor any guidelines as to how to deal with results in which there are substantial numbers of students who say they are *not* interested. The strength of Title IX in the past was that it encouraged institutions to create interest in women's sports where little existed before, due to the inertia of habitual thinking. Once teams were organized, scholarships offered, and resources provided, the popularity of women's sports began to increase.

The new OCR guidelines are so vague that almost any 'survey' result could be used to justify no further development of women's sports. A low response rate (very common in online surveys no matter what the topic) could be used as evidence of lack of interest by women students. The *New York Times* editorialized on 12 April 2005: 'The Bush administration has mounted a surreptitious new attack on Title IX, the 33-year-old law that has exponentially expanded the participation of girls and women in sports' (*New York Times* 2005a). The editors argue that the clarification 'amounts to a major weakening of the criteria used to determine compliance' with Title IX. They point out that the previous practice allowed such surveys as one part of an assessment of interest, in combination with more accurate measures such as rates of participation in the sport at 'feeder' high schools or leagues and judgments by coaches and administrators. No similar burden of proof of interest is demanded for male sports. The *Times* editorial concludes:

> This harmful change, made without public notice or debate, marks a dismaying turnaround. Two years ago, the administration rejected a set of hobbling proposals to alter the criteria for Title IX compliance, including a change similar to the one it has now

quietly instituted.... A public outcry may yet persuade the administration to withdraw the new regulation. (*New York Times* 2005a)

Unfortunately for women who are potential college athletes, no such public outcry reached the ears of the administration, and the ruling stands.

In discussing this action, the National Organization for Women (NOW) online news pointed out that while women constitute over half of college students in the United States today, they still receive only 41 per cent of athletic opportunities and an even lower percentage of athletic and sports recruitment budgets. 'The Bush administration is bent on making it easier for schools to discriminate on the basis of sex, rather than trying to strengthen Title IX,' commented NOW officer Terri O'Niell (Litwak 2005).

Single-sex classrooms dispute

In another Title IX dispute, OCR in 2004 proposed allowing single-sex classrooms in federally funded elementary and secondary schools, without mandating the means to ensure that such segregated classes would provide fair and equivalent opportunities for boys and girls, a move viewed with suspicion by many supporters of women's educational equity (AACU 2004). According to the American Association of Colleges and Universities, current law already allowed single-sex programs when appropriate (e.g. for choirs, physical education, human sexuality education), but there were strong protections to ensure that stereotypes were not promoted, nor discrimination allowed – protections that might be dropped if the revisions were instituted (AACU 2004). The changes were also strongly opposed by the American Association of University Women (AAUW), who objected to the lack of accountability in the new regulations and the fact that such changes would take away attention from critical educational needs (AAUW 2004b), among other problems. Nevertheless, the new regulations were released in March 2004.

OPPOSING DIVERSITY IN HIGHER EDUCATION

Bush's record on women is similar to his record on race: he publicly promotes himself as a friend of all groups, placing women and minority individuals in highly visible places, while at the same time opposing and dismantling policies that are proven to help promote equality and fairness. The University of Michigan affirmative-action cases (*Gratz* v. *Bollinger* and *Grutter* v. *Bollinger*, after the two women who filed suit) illustrate this. In the Grutter case, the Michigan Law School had an admissions policy that included numerous criteria on which candidates were evaluated, including various academic measures and other data. One of many items was race, which gave nonwhite students extra 'plus-points' in the desire to create a diverse student body. No nonwhite student was admitted who did not meet other criteria for qualified admission. The Michigan policy was similar to that of many universities that value diversity in the educational process, for the advantage of white as well as minority students who will live and work in a diverse world. In addition, educators tend to believe that diversity in the classroom makes for better educational experiences, as students can learn from each other in ways not always possible when the students are too uniform. However, two white women who had not been admitted to Michigan sued the university, claiming that the school had unfairly discriminated against them on the basis of race. A lower court upheld Michigan's policy, but the case was appealed all the way to the Supreme Court.

In January 2003, the Bush administration entered the case by filing two *amicus curia* briefs, asking the Court to overrule the Michigan policy, calling the extra application points given to minority applicants and underrepresented groups equivalent to 'quotas' that were 'plainly unconstitutional.' The administration's action was strongly criticized by many educators and university groups as well as civil rights and women's organizations. The American Council on Education, representing thirty-eight higher education associations, sent a letter to Bush before the action urging him to support the Michigan admissions policy; ACE filed a counter-brief with the Court in support of the university (American Council on Education 2003). In June of 2003, the high court upheld the lower court ruling, allowing the consideration of race as one of a number of criteria in law school admissions.[1]

The AAUW also supported the decision and gives a detailed discussion of its reasons for supporting affirmative action on its website. In its introduction, the AAUW writes of the continuing need for affirmative action to ensure access to higher achievement:

> Despite the progress that has been made over the last 30 years, ensuring equal opportunity for women in education and the paid workforce remains an elusive goal, in part because women continue to face discrimination. AAUW believes that affirmative action programs have begun to break down the barriers that confront women and minorities in education and employment, and these programs remain essential to ensure equal access to all professions at all levels through recruitment, outreach, and training. (AAUW 2005a)

In spite of the Bush administration's failure to convince the Supreme Court to overrule Michigan Law's admissions policy, anti-affirmative action officials within the US Department of Education have moved in a number of ways to eliminate policies and programs that help economically disadvantaged women and students of color gain access to higher education. The NAACP Legal Defense Fund released a report in June 2005 entitled *Closing the Gap: Moving from Rhetoric to Reality in Opening Doors to Higher Education for African-American Students* (NAACP 2005), which outlined the continuing problems African Americans face in educational access and achievement and the ways in which Bush's Education Department has been an obstacle to advancement. One chapter of the report refers to 'the relentless assault on affirmative action and efforts to close the black–white achievement gap,' in spite of the highly touted 'No Child Left Behind' program. According to the report, a number of vocal groups have been actively resisting the national consensus that the educational gap between black and white students needs to be closed, threatening various attempts by universities to increase their diversity. The report further accuses the Office of Civil Rights of quietly aiding and supporting these groups, contrary to the stated purpose of the office. Their aim seems to be eventually to reverse the Supreme Court ruling. In keeping with that goal, many of Bush's conservative judicial nominees have in common an antipathy to civil-rights protections as well as to remedies against gender discrimination.

Across the nation, anti-affirmative-action groups have increased pressure on colleges and universities to discontinue race-conscious policies, even though those policies are legal and have had some success. Over one hundred educational institutions since the Grutter decision have received letters threatening that (anti-white) discrimination complaints would be filed with OCR if the institution did not dismantle its race-conscious programs (in admissions, scholarships, recruitment, etc.). These groups have also engaged in harassment by making Freedom of Information Act requests for extensive paperwork on admissions, recruitment, financial aid, and retention programs, aiming to 'expose' race-based policies. Similar tactics have been used against gender-based university programs, implying that the institutions are acting illegally or improperly. The threat of an OCR complaint, which must by law be investigated by the agency, is often enough to make the university or college weaken its policies.

According to the NAACP report, the OCR is involved as an active supporter of these efforts, having even hired some of the opponents of race-conscious policies who participated in the Michigan case. The report claims

> Anti-affirmative action groups have an inside track at OCR. OCR has recently hired staff who previously worked for the anti-affirmative action group that represented the plaintiffs in *Gratz* and *Grutter* [the University of Michigan case].... Moreover, OCR has focused its energies on encouraging educational institutions to pursue race-neutral alternatives, even though such policies are insufficient by themselves to close the gaps in African American college enrollment and graduation. (NAACP 2005: 10)

Even though the federal government has promoted race-neutral policies while discouraging legitimate race-conscious policies, in fact even some of the programs it commends for increasing diversity (e.g. Talent Search) were targeted for elimination in the 2006 White House budget proposal. Thus the Bush commitment to 'closing the gap' has been weak at best, hypocritical at worst.

CUTTING PROGRAMS THAT WORK

The 2006 Bush budget proposal contained cuts in the budget of the Department of Education for the first time in ten years, including cuts in student loan programs. The budget also proposed to eliminate other programs that have helped low income students attain higher education, including Talent Search and Upward Bound. These proposed changes affect educational access and have a heavier impact on women than men, since women make up the majority of low-income students and about 61 per cent of those who participate in Upward Bound and Talent Search (Alaima 2005). While women are now about 56 per cent of college students nationally, the female percentages are even higher among low-income and minority populations: women make up 58 per cent of undergraduates from families earning under $30,000 per year, and 60 per cent of African-American undergraduates (Alaima 2005). These and the other actions described in this section call into question the sincerity of the 'compassionate' aims of the so-called 'education president.'

BUSH AND WOMEN'S HEALTH

In Chapters 5 and 6 we looked in detail at some of the important reproductive health policies of the Bush administration, many of which raise serious problems for women. Not surprisingly, the administration has failed to support other aspects of women's health. In the remainder of this chapter I discuss a few ways in which Bush's policies are hazardous to women's health.

Eliminating ergonomics protections

In March 2001, Bush signed the first major policy bill of his presidency. Just as one of his very first public acts had been an anti-woman order (reinstating the global gag rule), his first major bill also had negative implications for women. The bill repealed ergonomic workplace standards that had been signed into law the previous November by President Clinton. These new regulations would have established workplace ergonomic rules to help prevent repetitive stress injuries, injuries that are especially common among women clerical and assembly workers. The rules would have required employers to provide safe working spaces and to compensate employees who were injured from performing their jobs. According to CNN, the Occupational Safety and Health Administration (OSHA) had estimated that the Clinton standards would have prevented over

450,000 musculoskeletal disorders a year and would have 'generated benefits of $9.1 billion a year' every year for the first ten years of implementation (CNN.com 2001).

Announcing the repeal at a gathering of women business leaders, Bush expressed his pleasure at the legislation, which he said would diminish the Clinton legacy of regulating business activity. He cited the costs to employers of the rules as the basis of the repeal, calling the regulations 'unduly burdensome and overly broad.' In a prepared statement, Bush wrote (or someone wrote and he signed): 'The safety and health of our nation's workforce is a priority for my administration. Together we will pursue a comprehensive approach to ergonomics that addresses the concerns surrounding the ergonomics rule repealed today' (*Washington Post* 2001). This statement is all too typical of the Bush approach: supporting in words a laudable and helpful goal for workers, while acting in contradiction to that goal in the interests of business and making an empty promise to revisit the problem in the future with a better solution. As of now, no new rules have been issued. Instead, OSHA has developed some suggestions that are 'voluntary' for businesses to follow, with no enforcement or reporting mechanism whatever.

Martha Burk of the National Council of Women's Organizations (a network of over a hundred organizations representing some 6 million members) called Bush's quashing of the new ergonomics regulations 'a slap in the face of women,' since women suffer many ergonomic injuries from keyboard and assembly work (*Washington Post* 2001). A press release from the NCWO pointed out,

> There are more than 106 million women in the labor force, and women workers are particularly affected by these injuries. While women make up 46 per cent of the overall workforce, in 1998, women accounted for 64 per cent of repetitive motion injuries (42,347 out of 65,866 reported cases) and 71 per cent of reported carpal tunnel syndrome cases (18,719 out of 26,266 reported cases). (NCWO 2001)

The failure of Bush to issue new mandatory rules for worker protection 'delighted many in the business community, embittered organized labor, and further polarized an already deeply divided workplace health and safety community,' according to analyst James

L. Nash, writing for *Occupational Hazards* in October 2004 (Nash 2004). Here, then, is another example of Bush's favoritism to narrow business interests in opposition to the health and safety needs of women workers at risk of injury and subsequent disability.

To illustrate the problems with Bush's voluntary approach, consider the situation of nursing-home workers, who suffer perhaps the highest rates of workplace injury of any occupation, because of the requirements to lift, move, and manipulate patients and equipment. The great majority of these workers are women, often women of color. In March 2005, OSHA issued new voluntary guidelines for nursing homes, to which the United Food and Commercial Workers Union objected in a published statement. The UFCW points out that the OSHA guidelines for nursing home *employers* offer tips to pass on to workers about lifting and moving patients so as to avoid strain and repetitive stress injuries. But the guidelines provide workers with no mechanism to force employers to follow them, and they carry no penalties for employers who ignore the suggestions. The statement points out that the National Advisory Committee on Ergonomics in the Department of Labor comprises seven employer representatives, 'including the lawyer who represented the US Chamber of Commerce in its opposition to the ergonomics standard,' and only two union representatives (United Food and Commercial Workers 2005). In addition, unions that have had long-term involvement with ergonomics issues are not even represented on the committee. The statement goes on to indicate that 'another 3.6 million workers have suffered crippling and sometimes career-ending ergonomic injuries' since Bush signed the law repealing the Clinton standards in March 2003; but workers have no recourse to the federal government for assistance in preventing or reducing these continuing injuries.

Cutting diabetes research

The American Diabetic Association (ADA) reports that over 9 million American women, almost 9 per cent of the population over age 20, have diabetes. The prevalence is at least two to four times as high among women of color, and the number of women at high risk of developing the disease is increasing. A disease without cure, diabetes is the 'fifth deadliest' disease in the US and also one of the costliest (American Diabetes Association 2002). The case of diabetes provides an illustration of how federal health policies can have an impact on women, even though diabetes is not specifically a 'woman's disease.'

Cardiovascular disease is one of the dangerous complications of diabetes, and the risks are greater for women than for men. The death rate from cardiovascular disease for women with diabetes has increased by 23 per cent over the past 30 years, while it declined for other women. The risk of diabetic ketoacidosis (diabetic coma), caused by a lack of insulin, is twice as high for women as for men. Other complications for women with diabetes include peripheral vascular disease, birth defects and pregnancy complications, various infections, and low birthweight babies (American Diabetes Association 2002).

In February 2005 the American Diabetes Association published a statement harshly condemning President Bush's proposed 2006 budget because of its 'cuts to agencies responsible for responding to the diabetes epidemic facing this country.' They express their serious concern that the Centers for Disease Control and Prevention (CDC) are 'slated for a 6.11% funding cut and areas within the CDC responsible for responding to the diabetes epidemic are slated for a 6.5 per cent funding cut' (Medical Technology Business Europe 2005). The statement includes the following comment:

> Make no mistake, the president's budget cuts to CDC amount to America disengaging from the fight against diabetes. Pairing a decrease in CDC funding with a near flat funding for the National Institutes of Health is short sighted. As a nation, we simply cannot afford to turn our backs on Americans living with diabetes and call on the president and Congress to reconsider these proposed cuts. (Medical Technology Business Europe 2005)

Coming on top of Bush's severe restriction of funding for embryonic stem-cell research (which many scientists believe holds out hope for discovering a cure for diabetes and many other chronic diseases), the cut to CDC was even more distressing to the medical research community. Diabetes is only one type of disease that will receive less funding for research, care, and prevention efforts because of Bush budget priorities, and one that is especially important for women, most importantly women of color. As the ADA pointed out, diabetes is rapidly increasing in the US, and is already at 'epidemic' level according to the organization. But the federal budget to deal with the epidemic is declining, in order to sustain tax cuts for the richest Americans, tax breaks for giant corporations, military ventures around the globe, and other Bush priorities.

The FDA moves closer to approval of dangerous breast implants

As we saw in a previous chapter, the Food and Drug Administration (FDA) in 2005 overrode the recommendations of its Reproductive Drugs Advisory Committee and other experts, failing to approve emergency contraception for over-the-counter sales. Shortly after that decision, the same agency overrode another committee recommendation, this time by issuing an 'approvable' letter for silicone breast implants. The FDA has now granted preliminary approval to two different companies for the marketing of risky silicone-gel-filled breast implants, in spite of insufficient data on their safety. Although the letter is not the final stage of approval for marketing, it is a positive step in that direction. The FDA's scientific staff believed that the implants had not been shown to be safe in long-term use. Even if the breast-implant makers are required to monitor women who receive the devices by frequent MRI exams, the companies in question have failed to do so in the past, and there is some evidence that women who reported complications were ignored (NOW 2005).

Kim Gandy of the National Organization for Women pointed out that implants frequently rupture after ten to twelve years of wear, sometimes causing long-term health problems. Silicone gel contains toxic substances that have been associated with increased rates of brain and lung cancer among women with implants. There are some indications that implants might be implicated as well in autoimmune diseases such as lupus, rheumatoid arthritis, and fibromyalgia. Further surgery is also sometimes required due to infection, changes in the tissue around the implants, migration of the implant, and rupture. In one Canadian study, more than half of the women with implants required further surgery. Insurance does not always cover these secondary operation costs. More independent research on the health effects of breast implants is needed, but the industry-friendly Bush FDA administrators seem ready to accept them and leave the risk to women, in spite of their own scientific advisors' cautions (NOW 2005).

POLITICIZING WOMEN'S HEALTH NEEDS IN AFGHANISTAN

Many of Bush's publicized initiatives about women concern those in other countries, especially in Afghanistan and Iraq, where he claims to have engaged in wars in part so as to bring them 'freedom.' That women's rights in these places were not concerns of the president in his decisions to invade is abundantly clear, as I attempt to document in Chapter 12. However, 'women's rights' is a term often used in a propagandistic way to persuade the American public (especially its women) that Bush is a supporter of policies to improve the situation of women in poor countries. This ploy is very convenient, since the administration can make exaggerated claims about its support for foreign women, claims that are not easily verified by American constituents, nor able to be challenged by investigative journalists.

One such claim involved the rebuilding of the Rabia Balkhi women's hospital in Kabul. The public-relations purpose of this effort is indicated by the huge publicity given to the rebuilding and opening. Judith Miller of the *New York Times* (known for her pro-Bush war-related stories that later came into question during the White House CIA-leak scandals) in January 2003 published an uncritical and laudatory article about the renovation, describing the administration's commitment as 'the latest effort to address the health needs of Afghanistan's 25 million people, particularly Afghan women and children' (Miller 2003). Miller goes on to inform her readers about the involvement of the highest-level US officials – Secretary of Health and Human Services Tommy Thompson, Secretary of Defense Donald Rumsfeld, and Secretary of State Colin Powell – who worked together to promote this 'special women's initiative.' After a six-month rebuilding effort, Rabia Balkhi hospital was reopened in April 2003 with elaborate publicity, the ribbon-cutting ceremony attended by Thompson, Rumsfeld and Afghan President Karzai. Although one cannot question the importance of helping Afghan women with their health needs, the high-profile nature of the event and the attendance of such high-ranking US officials raises suspicions of a primary propaganda purpose. Thompson's official description of the event is very self-congratulatory:

> Six months ago, we made a promise to the people of Afghanistan to help rebuild their nation's public health infrastructure. Today is a new day in Afghanistan, where we now have a new hospital for women to receive topnotch health care and a new training program that will provide the best of medical instruction to Afghanistan's health care providers. (US Department of Health and Human Services 2003)

Later description of the hospital raises questions about the quality of the 'topnotch health care' promised by Thompson (and the sincerity of the US effort). In a January 2004 article published in the journal *Acumen*, Christopher Scott tells the hospital renovation story differently. He notes the 'great fanfare' with which the hospital was reopened, which was also attended by Dr Nafisa Abdulla, an Afghan-born Los Angeles-based OB/GYN physician, who remained there for a month to train medical staff. Scott then notes Abdulla's shock at the highly inadequate condition of the hospital:

> Once the ribbon cutting was over, [Abdulla] was stunned by what she saw. Rabia Balkhi delivers between 60 and 80 babies per day, and many women presented with complications.... The obstetrics unit had only three birthing tables, so many mothers delivered on the floor.... 'To say that Rabia Balkhi is a model of postwar reconstruction is wrong – in fact it's the worst model imaginable,' [Dr Abdulla] says, her frustration apparent. (Scott 2004)

After returning to the United States, Dr Abdulla wrote her own description of her experiences in Rabia Balkhi and of the contrast between official promises and the realities on the ground.

> What I saw in the hospital, where I was to begin work within two days, however, showed me that ribbon cuttings and visits by dignitaries are not the solution to the health care problems of the Afghan people. A spruced up facility for one day does not make the cut in the long run. The quality of the medicine that I was a part of 35 years ago had deteriorated significantly. (Abdulla 2003)

Dr Abdulla described working in the hospital where 55 to 80 births were occurring daily, where 20 to 30 women in active labor at once were 'giving birth with very little care, some on cold and naked steel delivery room tables' and others on the bare cement floor. She continues:

> What I saw in the operating room was equally disturbing. It was not unusual during a major operation for my scrub nurse to tell me 'I'm sorry, there are no more sutures.' Patients coming to this hospital often had to bring sutures, blood and antibiotics for their own surgeries. If the supply of sutures was depleted in the middle of an operation, the patient's relatives would be sent out to buy more, if they had the money.... Electric power was also a frequent problem. This 'model' hospital did not even have a back up generator, so surgery sometimes had to be performed by candlelight when the antiquated power grid in Kabul would collapse. (Abdulla 2003)

Abdulla accuses the international community of 'lack of integrity' for allowing this neglect of basic needs to continue, noting that Afghanistan was promised much assistance as part of the war on terrorism, promises that have gone largely unfulfilled because of the turning of attention to the Iraq war. Eloquently and simply, she laments: 'It seems as though this country was lost in the wake of the war in Iraq' (Abdulla 2003).

In addition to the problems detailed in this chapter, Bush budgets have cut back on various educational and health-related programs important to women. These include adult literacy programs, Head Start, the Women's Educational Equity Program, and student loan programs. Medicaid, the primary health-care resource for poor women and their children, has been cut at a time when health costs are rising. And the new prescription drugs plan for Medicare patients has been strongly criticized as confusing to patients and beneficial mainly to insurance companies. Overall, attention to the vital needs of education and health care has declined under this administration, while environmental policies have allowed more unhealthy substances to infiltrate our air, water, and food supplies. Unfortunately, it will take a complete change of direction and leadership in the US to reverse these trends.

10

HOW BUSH'S ECONOMIC AND BUDGET
PRIORITIES HURT WOMEN

For about three decades, American business and political conservatives had been working to push back the gains made in response to
the social movements of the 1970s, gains in worker rights, women's
rights, civil rights, and various social protections such as Medicare
and Medicaid. The further goal was to overturn the New Deal
programs of the 1930s, including Social Security, unemployment,
and welfare (Piven 2004: ch. 3). The theory was that by spending
huge amounts on military ventures and private contracts for various
privatized functions, the national government would be 'starved' and
social programs would eventually have to be abandoned. At the same
time, these conservatives pushed for tax cuts for the wealthy and
deregulation of business practices, a neo-Social Darwinist dream.

DISMANTLING THE GREAT SOCIETY

Instituting increased military spending and giving out huge private
contracts, conservatives hoped, would eventually force the government to cut back on its services, thus creating a 'pure' capital-
ist dream-state. Of course, this would not benefit the vulnerable
members of society, but the theory of these privileged few was that
the poor were not 'deserving' or else they would have succeeded

through hard work and ingenuity. This type of thinking is not helpful for women, especially women who are not safely ensconced in middle-class or higher marriages. For women who need childcare, family leave, educational loans, health care for themselves and their children, and who need a government that aggressively prosecutes gender-based discriminators, the neo-con dream is a nightmare. As Piven wrote,

> The main planks of [the post-1970s big-business] agenda were cutting taxes on business and the affluent, reducing government regulation of business, weakening unions, and slashing the public programs that shored up the power of workers, largely by reducing the pain of unemployment. The agenda gained considerable traction under Ronald Reagan, another president who enjoyed the overwhelming support of big corporations, as well as the support of a right-wing populist base of Christian fundamentalists, gun advocates, tax cutters, and libertarians first activated in reaction to the civil rights and women's movements of the 1960s and 1970s. (Piven 2004: 39)

The advocates of this philosophy are fond of referring to the 'failed programs' of the Great Society, but in fact those programs helped to move women and minority men into the middle class and out of poverty with greater success than any program in US history. It was the Reagan 'revolution' (read 'backlash') of the 1980s that caused these programs to fail by reducing their funding and chipping away at their reach. Poverty rates rose dramatically during the Reagan years, as they have again during the George W. Bush years. Since the 1960s, women have come to comprise the majority of poor adults, so that cutting programs that assist the poor hurts women disproportionately. Indeed, because they forced cuts in state services and infrastructure maintenance, the Bush tax cuts for the wealthy hurt everyone except those who have the means to pay for private education and other services and who hope to exploit the cheap labor left out of the benefits of the Bush 'recovery.'

Although the Reagan administration supported the same goals as Bush – increased military spending, cutting taxes, cutting back of environmental protections and social programs – Reagan had not been as successful because his party did not control the Congress and because of scandals that weakened him politically. Bush has benefited from a whittling away at liberal philosophy over the past two decades, the increasing power of the Christian right as a voting bloc, and the very conservative Republican-controlled Congress, from which moderates have all but disappeared. Bush further took advantage of widespread public support generated by the terrorist attacks on the World Trade Center and the Pentagon and the subsequent foreign invasions to move vigorously on his pro-business agenda (Piven 2004: 41).

The war in Iraq provided cover for a huge government giveaway to corporations with close ties to the Republicans and gave an excuse for cutting the social programs the conservatives had hoped to cut for decades. In Iraq, a number of US multinationals were 'invited to bid' on contracts for restoring oil-producing apparatus, building roads, providing food for soldiers, rebuilding the destroyed infrastructure, and performing many other tasks necessary in the invasion and continuing occupation. Bush incurred huge deficits for American taxpayers, with the expectation that soon the Iraqi oil revenues would be available to help foot the bills. Some companies with close ties to the Bush administration were great beneficiaries of this new revenue-generating opportunity.

> The big winner in the competition to rebuild Iraq is Dick Cheney's old firm, the giant Texas oil services business Halliburton, and its subsidiary, Kellogg, Brown & Root. Halliburton received its first contract for logistical services for American troops in 2001. In September 2002, a secret task force, formed to plan for Iraq's oil industry in the event of war, granted Kellogg, Brown & Root the noncompetitive contract for up to $7 billion to rebuild Iraq's oil operations. (Piven 2004: 17)

Halliburton has garnered at least $11 billion in contracts for work in Iraq, in spite of the fact that it was found in a Pentagon audit to have overcharged the American military by over $60 million for gasoline and was accused by an Army Corps of Engineers auditor in 2005 of overcharges in Iraq of over $1 billion (McIntyre 2003; Witte 2005). Other winners of lucrative contracts from the US occupation of Iraq were the Bechtel Group, which has picked up over $2 billion in reconstruction contracts, even though reconstruction is very difficult in the midst of violence and war. According to Piven (2004: 17), over seventy American companies have benefited from billions of dollars in contracts related to Iraq support and reconstruction.

The 'war on terror' provided the excuse Bush needed to push his conservative domestic agenda further, including massive tax cuts and proposals to slash spending on a wide variety of social programs, some of which are of special importance to women. Many of the Bush proposals and legislative priorities do not directly address women but have a disproportionate impact on them. His budget proposals for federal year 2006 call for increases in military and weapons spending and homeland security and for maintaining or extending tax cuts that primarily benefit those who least need them. This budget proposed drastic cuts in domestic spending for many social programs that disproportionately help women (Medicaid, Food Stamps, job training programs, childcare, youth development, domestic violence, family planning, and housing) while increasing his marriage promotion and abstinence education budgets. These latter programs, as we have seen, tend to promote stereotypes about women and gender and are of little help in addressing women's real problems.

Even though the proposed budget is far from balanced, the cost of the wars in Iraq and Afghanistan, plus any cost of the proposed Social Security changes, were completely left out of the estimates. Moreover, the devastation caused by Hurricane Katrina was likewise not anticipated; nor was there anything set aside for such events. Soon after Katrina, Bush promised to spend billions to rebuild, while 'ruling out' tax increases, stating blithely that the funds would come from cuts in other 'unnecessary' spending, although most would be borrowed from other nations and the debt passed on to future generations. It is clear that Bush's budgetary mismanagement portends serious financial crises for the United States sometime in the future, completely in line with the radical conservative agenda to which he adheres.

THREATENING SOCIAL SECURITY

Early in his first term, beginning with his first Inaugural Address, President Bush proposed significant changes to Social Security involving the partial privatization of this important government retirement and insurance program. The attacks of 11 September 2001 pushed this issue from the top of the agenda, and it did not re-emerge as a priority until safely after Bush's re-election, early in the second term. At that time Bush made the reform of Social Security his top priority. By then, however, the economic situation of the country was very different and many people were much more skeptical of Bush's promises. So in spite of his major cross-country campaign to build public support for his proposed changes, the public generally did not go along, partly because Social Security had been one of the most successful and reliable programs of the New Deal, one that most people had come to take for granted.

Social Security was established by Franklin D. Roosevelt in 1935 as part of his response to the widespread poverty of the Depression, especially among the older population. Based on the European model of 'social insurance' rather than the welfare-type pension plans that existed in some states, the program was perceived as less radical than many of the alternatives that had been proposed at the time.[1] Roosevelt signed the Social Security Act into law in August 1935, creating a program that would pay retired workers a continuing income after age 65 from a fund into which workers would pay through taxes on their wages. The original Act provided retirement benefits only to the worker, but in 1939 beneficiaries were expanded to include dependent family members of the retired worker and survivor's benefits to the surviving spouse and minor children of workers who died prematurely. Later amendments increased the payments for retirees, adding an automatic cost-of-living increase to benefits and disability insurance for workers and their dependents. Social Security benefits are 'progressive' in that workers with lower lifetime incomes receive a relatively larger proportion of benefits (relative to their contributions) than those with higher incomes. However, only the first $90,000 of annual income is taxed for Social Security, so that the highest-income groups pay a much lower proportion of their earnings into the system than do middle- and lower-income workers. Until the Reagan years, every change made to Social Security generally expanded its benefits. During his term, this progressive trend was reversed: benefits were taxed as income for the first time, and the retirement age was increased for future beneficiaries.

With the approaching retirement of the baby-boom generation in the early twenty-first century, concern grew that the income to Social Security (from current workers' payroll taxes) would not be sufficient to cover completely the needs of this large group of retirees. Within this context, George W. Bush made his proposals to 'reform' Social Security by partially privatizing it. Consistent with his usual approach, Bush's rhetoric is misleading and inconsistent. In his 2005 State of the Union address, he claimed that by 2042 the entire Social Security system would be 'exhausted and bankrupt,' a claim that is not supported by even the Social Security Administration's own figures. Contrary to Bush's claims, the Congressional Budget Office and the Social Security Administration both estimated that by 2050, if no changes were made, there would only be enough funds to pay 70 per cent of promised benefits, but it would not be 'bankrupt.' Nevertheless, traveling around the country to drum up public support for his plan, Bush referred to a 'crisis' of Social Security and promoted private accounts as a way to solve the crisis and to ensure greater retirement savings than in the current system. He even directed Social Security Administration employees to promote his message that the system's financial problems need to be solved soon or the program might not exist for coming generations (Weisbrot 2005).

Soon economists were challenging Bush's claims, however, and the public was not buying his plan to change a system that had worked well and reliably for seventy years. Critics pointed out that, while there are some funding problems down the road for the plan, the government's own estimates were that, even if *no* changes were made, the system would be able to pay full benefits at least through 2042 or 2052, depending on the estimating formula. Objective analysts also point out that private accounts would do nothing to solve the funding issue, but would actually make it worse. The transition costs of continuing to pay current beneficiaries while diverting funds at the same time to pay for private accounts would run to trillions of dollars, money that would have to be borrowed from foreign governments, adding significantly to the already-burgeoning national debt. In addition, the plan would certainly result in lower guaranteed benefits and the loss of 'security' for future generations, since with private accounts one's eventual benefits would no longer be guaranteed but would depend on the luck of the market. In addition, higher administrative costs would eat into the savings. As Princeton economist Paul Krugman (2005a) wrote in the *New York Times*, Bush's plan is not to 'reform' Social Security, but 'in essence, to dismantle it.'[2]

Various critics proposed alternatives to shore up the current system. Among the simpler and more effective 'fixes' would be to raise the income cap for payroll taxes from $90,000 to a higher figure, so that higher-income people would have to pay a bit more into the system; or to raise slightly the retirement age. But these were not solutions that fit with Bush's preference for policies that benefit those at the top of the income pyramid and the private sector. In fact, as already noted, right-wing libertarian conservatives have had Social Security in their sights for years as one of the New Deal programs they most dislike. Bush's plan and his approach to selling it appear to be taken straight out of a 1983 manifesto published by the ultraconservative Cato Institute that showed how one might undermine public confidence in the current system and eventually at least partially replace it with private-sector savings accounts (Thomma 2005).

The fact that Social Security is chiefly a women's issue has been largely ignored by the president and most press discussions. However, a number of women's organizations and research groups have raised this issue forcefully in the recent debate. Early in February 2005, the National Council of Women's Organizations, a network of over 200 women's organizations, held a press conference strongly criticizing the Bush plan for its potential harm to women (NCWO 2005). That Social Security should be of concern to women is due partly to population realities: women make up the majority of the primary beneficiary group, the population over 65; moreover, the female percentage increases with each year of age. For example, in the year 2000, 66.7 per cent of the US population aged 80 or above was female; that figure increases to 70 per cent of those aged 85 or older (US Census Bureau 2004). For this and other reasons, women comprise 60 per cent of Social Security recipients.

Although Social Security is the primary source of income for both men and women over 65, women rely on the program for a larger portion of their income than do men (IWPR 2005b). The Institute for Women's Policy Research (IWPR) points out that without their Social Security income, half the women in the US aged 65 and older would be poor (IWPR 2000). Unlike private savings accounts, Social Security provides a safe, reliable, and guaranteed income for life, and it includes some protection against inflation with cost-of-living increases. Women also benefit from the fact that Social Security provides proportionally more to lower-earning groups, since their lifetime earnings are likely to be lower than men's, something that would not continue in a privatized system (IWPR 2005b). The differential racial impact of the Bush proposal is also seldom noted: senior African Americans depend on Social Security even more than whites: fully 60 per cent of African-American and 55 per cent of Latino seniors would be poor without Social Security (Sen 2005).

Older women need a reliable Social Security income more than men because they have fewer resources, on average, than older men. This is because women earn less than men to begin with (even where they work full-time year-round), and they are more likely to work part-time and to drop out of the labor force for some period of their adult lives, so their total contributions to the system are lower. Since benefits are tied to lifetime contributions, women's Social Security earnings and private savings are less than men's in their retirement; with private accounts this gender difference would be enlarged. In addition, women are less likely than men to have pensions associated with their employment, so their Social Security income is more central to their older years than it is to men.

Unlike men, who benefit from Social Security primarily as retirees, women are also more likely to receive benefits as widows, as in the current system widows are entitled to their deceased husbands' retired-worker benefit if their own benefit is smaller, as it usually is. Also, women whose husbands die before the age of retirement receive survivors' benefits, as do their minor children. In fact, women comprise 98 per cent of beneficiaries as surviving spouses, and widows are the largest group of poor elderly women (NWLC 2005d). Thus, Social Security for women is more often a family insurance program, guaranteeing an income after the death of the major breadwinner. Bush and his supporters were silent on this aspect of Social Security reform at first, until, in an interview with the Associated Press on 11 May 2005, administration officials finally admitted that their plan would cut benefits for surviving widows and children (NWLC 2005d). Joan Entmacher, vice-president for Family Economic Security at the National Women's Law Center, had the following comment about the plan:

> President Bush's plan to privatize Social Security presents a triple whammy for women and their families. The President's plan cuts benefits for women workers, and for spouses, surviving spouses and children. The plan ignores the fact that – especially for women – Social Security is a family insurance program [that] ... reduces child poverty more than any other federal programs.[3] (NWLC 2005c)

Social Security also provides disability insurance to covered workers, granting financial support if they become disabled and unable to work. Because women are more likely than men to be responsible for the care of disabled spouses, parents, or children, this loss of disability income also tends to have a heavier impact on women. Again, this aspect of Social Security is often left out of the debate about the Bush plan. This type of benefit is especially important to African-American women, who make up 18 per cent of those drawing disability payments, even though they are only 9 per cent of the labor force. Finally, given women's longer lifespan, under a private accounts system women would either pay more for their annuities or they would risk outliving their assets (IWPR 2000: 2).

It is no wonder that the public was very skeptical of the Bush proposal to 'reform' Social Security, not only because of its enormous transition costs in a time of record deficits, but also due to the uncertainty of its benefits. There was growing awareness that under the Bush plan, the amount and kind of guaranteed benefits to current workers would be cut (NWLC 2005c), and the transition costs would force reductions in other federal programs that benefit women, children, the sick, the young, the poor, and others – programs such as Medicare, educational assistance, and Medicaid. Moreover, the plan would seemingly benefit banks and investment institutions while further weakening the US economy and the social 'safety net' for the majority of citizens, especially its most vulnerable citizens – widows, orphans, and the elderly. These and other problems led to a widespread distrust in the Bush proposals, even among many Republicans. However, the president continued to lobby for his plan through the spring and summer of 2005, until the Katrina disaster and declining approval ratings led him to abandon his efforts, at least temporarily.

BANKRUPTCY LEGISLATION: WOMEN AS ECONOMIC VICTIMS

In the spring of 2005, Congress passed new legislation concerning bankruptcy, legislation supported and signed by the Bush administration. The revisions to previous law made it more difficult for individuals in financial straits to restructure their debt obligations through bankruptcy. This was promoted as reducing fraud and irresponsible consumption, but the major beneficiaries of the bill were credit-card companies, whose debt-encouraging tactics have become more and more predatory.

As with Social Security, bankruptcy is not, on the face of it, a women's issue; but when we look beneath the surface we find a significant gendered aspect to the problem. According to Harvard law professor Elizabeth Warren, bankruptcy *is* a women's issue because 'women are now the largest demographic group in bankruptcy, outnumbering men by about 150,000 per year' (Warren 2005; see also Sullivan et al. 1999). Over a million American women annually in recent years have filed for bankruptcy, most of them middle-class women who have found themselves in financial distress not because of irresponsible consumption, but due to unexpected medical problems or other family crises. Prior to the new legislation, bankruptcy law allowed debtors to discharge certain debts (mainly credit-card debts, which are often the first resort when a person faces financial crises), giving priority to such necessities as rent, car payments, utility bills, tuition, and grocery bills. Debts related to these essentials were not dismissed, but it was possible to restructure them so as to permit lower monthly payments. Under the old system, a bankruptcy order protected the debtor from harassment by bill collectors and gave her time to get her finances in order, even though her credit rating would be ruined for several years.

The new legislation increased the cost of bankruptcy, increased payback requirements, and reduced debt relief from consumer loans (principally credit-card debt). In addition, it is feared that women whose ex-husbands have been ordered to pay child support may find themselves competing with credit-card companies for funds if the man declares bankruptcy, as the priority given to such responsibilities is no longer in place. Warren wrote, prior to the passage of the legislation,

> Some women will be forced out of the system, unable to right themselves financially, living in a permanent state of past due notices, evictions and repossessions. Other women will [pay] ... more in legal fees and [be] forced into more negotiations with creditors. ... In place of the carefully protected access to her ex-husband's post-bankruptcy income she now has, under the proposed legislation a woman trying to collect child support or alimony will find herself more often competing with MasterCard and Visa. (Warren 2005: 1–2)

Bush and his congressional supporters framed this bill in terms of the irresponsibility of consumers, rather than recognizing the more common causes of bankruptcies in medical and other life crises. There was little discussion of the specific effects on women, even though women make up the majority of persons affected by the new legislation. The law went into effect in October 2005, soon after the Katrina hurricane. A group of Democratic House members raised the possibility of waiving some of the more stringent requirements of the new law for Katrina victims, many of whom had lost everything, including the paperwork necessary to make their claims. The Republican chair of the Judiciary Committee, John Sensenbrenner (R–WI), refused even to hold hearings on the suggestion. Sensenbrenner had also been one of eleven Republicans in the House to vote against the aid package for Katrina victims (Bosworth 2005). Women who have the misfortune of expensive family illness, hurricane devastation, or income loss from divorce will receive little help from this new legislation.

TAX POLICY: SHIFTING THE BURDEN, REWARDING THE RICH

Once in office, the Bush team set about quickly to change the tax system, in one of its most perilous policy changes due to its negative impact on revenues. The 2001 tax cut amounts to a $1 trillion loss in revenue over ten years; the 2003 tax cut added another $800 billion to that amount. The 2003 tax cut was billed as an economic stimulus, and any suggestion that it was fiscally irresponsible was denounced by Republicans as unpatriotic and divisive. Senator Kay Bailey Hutchinson, Republican from Texas, charged: 'When our troops are over there fighting, we don't want partisan bickering to be what they see on television back home' (Piven 2004: 45). Again and again, regressive policies were pushed through the Republican-dominated Congress that reduced revenue to the government and benefited the very wealthiest Americans, while undermining the programs and protections for students, women, minorities, the disabled, the poor, and the aged.

The tax cuts drastically shifted the tax burden from the rich and corporations to the middle and lower classes. In addition to giving a huge bonus to the wealthy, these changes also advanced the right's other major agenda, increasing pressures to cut spending on social programs, including welfare, education, health care, and Social Security (the latter without success). At the other end of the balance sheet, Bush's policies have added tremendously to the American deficit, increasing US indebtedness to foreign governments and passing the bill along to future generations.

The administration was fond of saying that the average taxpayer in 2003 would receive a tax reduction of $1,126; a deceptive statistic that masks the fact that the average millionaire would receive a cut of $93,000, compared to the average of $217 for the lower-income half of the population. The Center for Budget and Policy Priorities estimated that over half of black and Hispanic families would receive *no* tax reduction from the 2001 cut. The skewed benefits and the proposed phasing out of the estate tax would hurt poor families even more by reducing the incentive of the wealthy to contribute to charitable organizations in order to reduce their tax liability (Holste 2001). As various resources and services became 'privatized' because of lack of government revenues, fewer and fewer resources and services were available to help people lift themselves out of poverty or overcome traditional barriers (Piven 2004; Morgen and Basch 2005).

Since more than half of women are in low-paying sales, clerical, and care-giving jobs, they fall into the income brackets that received little or no tax benefits from the Bush tax cuts. Because of their lower average income, women's tax reductions were lower on average than those of men. Women are more likely as well to be raising children as single parents, struggling on lower incomes with all the economic burdens of family support. Many of these women need the assistance of tax-supported child care, health care, and other support that the revenue reductions threaten.

INCREASING POVERTY AND THE BUSH RESPONSE

In September 2005, the US Census Bureau reported that the poverty rate had risen for the fourth straight year, corresponding to the Bush years (under Clinton poverty rates had declined each year) (US Census Bureau 2005). Thus, in contrast to his trickle-down rhetoric, Bush's economic policies have greatly increased the level of economic inequality, benefiting those at the top while slowly pushing down those in the middle and lower classes. Bush is fond of claiming responsibility for economic growth, greater productivity, and a recovering stock market, but he fails to mention the darker side of his economic 'recovery': growing poverty, high unemployment, slow job production, trade deficits, and accelerated outsourcing of jobs to foreign locations where labor is cheap.

The income gap between men and women widened in 2003, as women's real earnings fell while men's remained virtually unchanged. The wage gap went from 77 cents to 76 cents earned by full-time working women for every dollar earned by corresponding men. The overall poverty rate that year among adult women was 12 per cent, compared to just under 9 per cent for men (Erickson 2004). Poverty rates for all *families* grew between 2000 and 2004, from 9.3 to 10.1 per cent, with increments each year. Poverty rates for female-headed households are several times higher than those for married-couple households, due to women's lower average income to begin with, and their inability to find adequate child care that might allow them to seek better employment or the education that would improve their prospects. Child poverty rates increased as well, to over 20 per cent (Vallely 2005).

In 2004, the average poverty rate for married-couple families with related children under 18 was 15.5 per cent, compared to 37.6 per cent of corresponding female-headed households. For those with children only under age 5, the difference was even greater: the poverty rate for married couple households in this category was 6.5 per cent, compared to 46 per cent for female-headed households. Thus, for unmarried women with young children, the incidence of poverty is greater than for those with older children, but this is not the case for households of married couples. The rates of poverty for these very vulnerable single-mother households have increased each year of the Bush administration, from 43.4 per cent in 2000 to 46.2 per cent in 2004. Female-headed households, those hurt most by the economic problems of these years, comprise over 12 per cent of American households. Not only are more people falling into poverty, but the depth of poverty has also increased, with over 40 per cent of the poor earning less than 50 per cent of the federal poverty level (IWPR 2005d).

The United Nations released a report in September 2005 that revealed that certain parts of the United States are similar to the Third World in terms of poverty and lack of resources. The report accuses the United States of having 'an overdeveloped military strategy and an underdeveloped strategy for human security' (Vallely 2005). The document pointed out that the infant mortality rate in the United States had increased annually over the Bush years, reversing a long-term trend of decline in this basic measure of social well-being. As of 2005, the rate in the United States was equal to that of Malaysia. Even though the US leads the world in health-care spending per capita, the benefits go disproportionately to the well-off and increasingly are denied to the poor.

The hypocrisy of George W. Bush is very apparent here, as he professes support for a 'culture of life' in his anti-abortion rhetoric yet does nothing to target the increasing mortality rate among US infants in their first year of life. More telling are statistics that reveal the consequences of growing inequalities in the US: African-American mothers are twice as likely to give birth to low-weight babies, and their babies are twice as likely as white babies to die in their first year (Vallely 2005).

The United States stands alone as the only wealthy country without universal health insurance, and the percentage of uninsured is increasing. Without health insurance, a family is 1.5 times as likely to have an infant death in the first year. Fully 21 per cent of blacks and 34 per cent of Hispanics in the United States lack basic health coverage, compared to 13 per cent of whites. Studies show that these uninsured persons are less likely to receive routine health care or to have a regular physician or place of care where their histories can be followed. They are also more likely to skip prescribed drugs because of the cost. If the gap in health care were eliminated, an estimated 85,000 lives per year would be saved (Vallely 2005).

In late August 2005, the US Census Bureau released new data showing that the number of Americans without health insurance had increased for the fourth straight year since Bush took office, to 15.7 per cent of the population (Physicians for a National Health Program 2005). As the percentage of Americans covered by private health insurance declined, the number of Americans enrolled in Medicaid increased. Since 2000, Medicaid enrollment has grown by 9.6 million. Census data showed that the fastest growing group of uninsured Americans were middle-class individuals with incomes between $50,000 and $75,000. The high cost of medical insurance has forced many to drop coverage, leaving them vulnerable to medical crises and bankruptcy. The US health-care crisis is just one of many that the Bush administration has not only failed to address, but has exacerbated by its policies.

Contrary to Bush's carefully honed image as a 'compassionate' conservative, he has a long record of disregard for the poor. Columnist E.J. Dionne interviewed Bush in 1999, reporting that Bush insisted that the causes of poverty are found not in social and economic conditions but in personal, individual shortcomings. 'Oftentimes people are poor because of decisions they make ... Oftentimes people are poor because they ... [aren't] making right choices and staying in school and working hard in school,' candidate Bush told Dionne, apparently forgetting his own legacy admission to Yale and his less than stellar record as a student (Conason 2004: 180–81).

In spite of the well-documented increasingly hard times for poor people in the United States, especially poor single mothers, Bush's policies have attempted to roll back assistance that would help lift these people out of poverty – educational programs, childcare support, health-care assistance, job training, and the like. In their place, Bush has attempted to promote marriage as a panacea for women's problems, even though at this level of poverty, marital relationships have always tended to be unstable, largely because of economic distress and other problems not solvable by the counseling programs that Bush has funded. In addition, the real help that poor women need to improve their condition has been consistently opposed or reduced by this administration.

WELFARE CHANGES AND MEDICAID CUTS

Piven describes the ways in which Bush's campaign against social spending has affected programs known as 'welfare' (2004: 68–9). These programs were begun as part of Roosevelt's New Deal, known at one time as Aid to Families with Dependent Children (AFDC). This program provided cash assistance to very-low-income families, primarily families headed by women. During the Clinton era, 'welfare reform' was achieved in cooperation with an overwhelmingly affluent and male Congress, resulting in the new program called Temporary Assistance for Needy Families (TANF). This reduced the total amount of assistance that one person could receive and mandated work or education in order to receive assistance. At that time, a certain amount of childcare assistance and job training were part of the program. (The original AFDC program had been set up under the assumption that children need their mothers at home, so that work was not expected of these women.)

In 2004, Bush signed a set of changes to TANF. The new rules forced states to require most mothers receiving welfare benefits (70 per cent) to work, and the minimum number of work hours per week was increased from 30 to 40. At the same time, no increase was provided for childcare expenses, even though before the change only one in seven of eligible and needy families received childcare help (Piven 2004: 69). In addition, whereas the previous rules had allowed certain educational and vocational training to count as 'work,' the new rules did not do so, effectively making it impossible for these very poor women to improve their status while receiving these meager benefits. Most women on welfare are there due to temporary difficulties, as very young mothers, following divorce, job loss, or other temporary setbacks. But the new rules are harsher, making a very difficult situation even harder. Piven, commenting on the changes as they had been proposed in 2004, writes:

> The technical details of the Republican proposals ... seem to be animated by a crusading harshness. After all, the welfare program had already been effectively eviscerated as a result of the decades-long campaign that culminated in the 1996 welfare reform law that established TANF. ... Only the most vulnerable families with hard-to-employ mothers, whether because of disabilities or substance abuse or dire family problems, remain on the welfare rolls, and it is they who will be affected by the new work requirements. (Piven 2004: 71)

Thus poor women with children have much less support from the programs meant to help them through rough times. At the same time, other social programs that could support them or give them a hand up have likewise been under attack during the Bush years, including unemployment, housing subsidies, and health-related programs.

Medicaid provides health insurance for poor and low-income people in the United States; the majority (71 per cent) of its adult recipients are women. Women are more likely to qualify for Medicaid because they are more likely than men to be poor, more likely to be uninsured by their employers, and more likely to meet other criteria for eligibility. For its recipients, Medicaid is a welcome source of health-care coverage, but millions more low-income women remain uninsured. The National Women's Law Center developed a factsheet on Medicaid's vital contributions to women's health, which included the following points:

- Nearly 10 per cent of US women receive health-care coverage through Medicaid.

- Medicaid covers health care for one-third of poor women.
- Medicaid is the predominant source of health insurance for single mothers, covering nearly 40 per cent of this population.
- Under Medicaid, women are ensured access to a variety of important health services, including preventive care, acute illness care, family planning services, and diagnosis of chronic illness. The program also covers nursing-home care and long-term care services for older women and provides prenatal care for younger pregnant women.
- The costs of almost 40 per cent of US births are covered by Medicaid, and the program provides more family planning funding than any other public agency.
- In spite of the important coverage of health care by Medicaid for women who could not otherwise afford it, over 17 per cent of American women aged 18 to 64 are without health coverage. (NWLC 2005a)

In spite of increasing poverty rates and an increasing percentage of uninsured Americans, the Bush administration has proposed cuts to this important program of health coverage for low-income Americans.

MARRIAGE AS THE ANSWER TO WOMEN'S POVERTY

George W. Bush has developed and funded projects that 'promote marriage' as a way out of poverty (Baucher 2003). The theory behind these programs is based on a misreading of social science data on poverty and divorce. It is true that there is a positive correlation between the likelihood of being married and one's income, but thinking that we can solve poverty by encouraging women to marry is confusing cause and effect and seriously misunderstanding the situation of poor women. Many low-income women would probably like to marry, if they could find a man who would reliably contribute his share to the family income, and who would be kind, faithful, and loving. However, since poor women do not usually have the option of meeting and dating men who are financially secure, they are often cautious about relationships with men who may wind up being a drain on their own energy and resources. In addition, women on welfare are often in that position precisely because they have escaped an abusive partner, or they have been deserted by their partner, who himself may be in dire financial straits. Some poor women refuse to marry in order to be able to reserve scarce resources for the children, since fathers' work may be unsteady or nonexistent. Marriage under these circumstances is likely to have many more problems than marriage in middle-class and affluent settings (Edin 2000).

Supporters of marriage promotion claim that children in homes raised by their own parents are better off than children of divorce or stepfamilies – they especially emphasize the need for fathers to be part of the household in order for the family to succeed. Of course having two loving, satisfied, and economically comfortable parents (not necessarily biological parents) is the ideal situation, as it can be much less stressful for everyone than a single-parent home or a conflict-ridden two-parent home. This is also at least partly a matter of resources. Single parents who have the resources to provide good housing and supervision for their children can be successful parents. And married couples are not necessarily good parents. In fact, most research shows that children are better off with one stable parent than in a conflict-ridden two-parent household. What single parents (usually mothers) need are more resources – quality childcare, help with education, job preparation, employment and housing assistance. George W. Bush and his supporters are opposed to such assistance to those they blame for their own poverty. They have latched on to the idea of marriage promotion as a way to avoid paying for real resources, blaming single parents for their situation and pleasing Christian conservatives at the same time. The Bush marriage promotion programs also discriminate against same-sex couples, limiting participation explicitly to heterosexual couples, in another reward for religious conservative backing (Baucher 2003).

Most of these programs are 'marriage counseling' or 'marriage preparation' courses, not necessarily harmful but not very helpful in solving the practical problems of poor women. And yet the funding for these programs comes from reductions in other forms of assistance, such as childcare for working women. In addition, many of these programs are run by conservative religious groups, which may discriminate in hiring on the basis of religion, sexual orientation, or other 'religious' concerns, and which may promote explicitly antifeminist teachings. It is highly doubtful whether most of these programs will help those in the greatest need, and they do hurt poor women by taking away resources that could have gone to programs that would help them become financially independent.

FUNDING ANTIFEMINIST RELIGIOUS GROUPS

The Bush budgets have increased funding to many 'faith-based' organizations whose goals are frequently contrary to the advancement of women's interests, at least as they are defined by the majority of women's organizations. One aim of Bush in funding these programs is to maintain conservative evangelical support, and another may be to implement conservative policies 'by the back door' by supporting conservative organizations instead of strictly regulated government agencies.

Establishing this program by executive order, not by statute, Bush has extended federal funding to what he calls 'faith-based' organizations that provide various social services. Although it had already been legal to use federal funds to support religious organizations providing social services, in the past these organizations were required to separate their federally funded programs clearly from their religious proselytizing or services. Bush changed the rules to be able to give federal grants to organizations that do *not* separate their religious practice from their social-service-oriented work. This leaves open the door for providing support to groups whose religious ideology is antifeminist, very conservative on sexual issues, anti-abortion, and so forth. Bush couched his justification for such support (despite the constitutional separation of church and state) in terms of religious rights – the freedom of religion. Since many people are intimidated by the thought that they might be displaying religious intolerance or bias, conservatives have been able to get away with actual discrimination against women on the theory that this is mandated by religious belief.

In Bush's faith-based initiatives, there is a strong element of 'family' rhetoric, which often stands for the suppression of women's rights, especially reproductive rights. One issue that received some media attention was the question of whether these organizations receiving government funds could maintain their hiring practices that discriminate on the basis of religion, sexual orientation, and beliefs. Such discrimination was outlawed under Title VII rulings, but Bush was able to circumvent these protections by appealing to religious rights. He presents his rationale in a White House position paper (White House 2003), in which he claims that federal rules about hiring employees for religious organizations are 'confusing' and need to be clarified. Although the policy presented in this paper disallows discrimination in dealing with clientele of services, the federally funded religious organizations 'retain their right to hire those individuals who are best able to further their organizations' goals and mission' (White House 2003). This last 'principle' allows organizations to discriminate in hiring personnel to carry out their tax-supported mission. In particular, non-Christians, gay or lesbian persons, or, in some situations, women, might be excluded from consideration for employment, completely legally and without accountability. These so-called 'Charitable Choice' rules specifically exempt religious organizations from Title VII mandates, so that they 'can continue to take their faith into account in making employment decisions' (White House 2003: 4).

These programs can now be found in several locations of the federal government, including the Department of Education, Department of Labor, and Health and Human Services. Many abstinence-only programs are funded under this initiative, and many of these have been found to promote gender stereotypes as well as inaccurate medical information, in addition to being largely ineffective (Waxman 2004). The federal guidelines for these programs go completely against previous efforts to ensure equal treatment in hiring, and they do so, ironically, in the name of civil rights and religious liberty. To quote the White House publication,

> President Bush will continue to work to make clear that faith-based organizations that receive Federal funds retain their civil rights to base employment decisions on their beliefs and vision. At the Federal level, this means that the Administration will support changes to laws, like the Workforce Investment Act and the Head Start statute, that currently prevent religious organizations that participate in these programs from taking religion into account when hiring. (White House 2003: 8)

Interestingly, a former White House aide to these programs said in February 2005 that Bush had failed to keep his promise to serve the homeless, the poor, and others in need through these programs (Boston 2005). In a revealing opinion piece, evangelical Christian Jim Wallis condemned the Bush faith-based program for channeling money only to a narrow range of conservative organizations while ignoring what Wallis considers broader issues of social need. Writing specifically of the Bush 2006 budget proposals, Wallis states:

> Billions of dollars are cut from programs that most directly impact America's poorest families – in education, nutrition, child care, health care, affordable housing, job training, heating and cooling assistance, and in community and rural development. At the same time, mere millions of dollars are added as increases to a number of faith-based programs focusing on marriage, fatherhood, and abstinence.... Worst of all is the politicization of the faith-based initiative, with the bulk of support going to the most conservative evangelical groups that politically support the administration rather than to the most effective faith-based initiatives regardless of political affiliation. (Wallis 2005)

Thus, if Wallis is correct, faith-based initiatives appear to be one more ploy to push through a conservative agenda masked by positive language about faith, family, and civil rights. While not all of these funds go to fundamentalist organizations, a fairly large percentage of them do. Beneath the propaganda, many of these organizations may be restricting women's opportunities; squandering funds that could be used to support poor women, childcare, and education; promoting sexist, stereotyped attitudes; and gaining support for Republican political candidates in the future. The resources given to these organizations that regularly coordinate voter drives for conservative candidates, abortion opponents, anti-gay politicians, and their political relatives have important political payback. The most serious problem in all of this may be the lack of accountability of the organizations to any direct oversight, which is undoubtedly part of the plan. Much of Bush's faith-based funding comes back to the Republican Party in terms of votes gained by church-based activism for right-wing causes and other efforts contrary to the basic constitutional principles on which the US was founded.

Bush's 2006 budget proposals contained many cuts or freezes in federal programs that directly affect the lives of women, including childcare; food stamps; the Head Start early childhood education program; the Women, Infant, and Children nutrition program (WIC; Women's Policy 2005); housing, domestic violence, and family planning (Stevens 2005). Administration officials tried to justify these cuts by claiming the programs were 'not achieving results' and by pointing to the need to find places in the budget to cut, while increasing military and 'homeland security' spending for the 'war on terror.' The budget-breaking costly tax cuts, of course, were completely off the table, as far as Bush and his Republican Congressional supporters were concerned; indeed, he was pushing to make them permanent. By the time Congress was working on the budget appropriations in late fall 2005, the Katrina devastation provided yet another reason to cut spending. Although Bush may not be able to get all he hoped for in his proposals for 2006 and in the final years of his term, his overall impact on the financial stability and security of the American public has been unprecedented in its irresponsibility, and much of the cost will be borne by women, by the poor, by people of color, by workers, and by the future generations that will have to deal with the burgeoning debt.

THE REAL BUSH REVEALED:

LESSONS FROM KATRINA

On 29 August 2005, Hurricane Katrina hit the Southern Gulf Coast of the United States, resulting in the most serious and costly natural disaster in the history of the country. The destruction was extensive, as whole communities were wiped out along the coast in Mississippi and Louisiana, but the most devastating loss was in New Orleans. In that city, the levees that held back the waters of Lake Pontchartrain burst, causing serious flooding throughout the city. Many people were stranded by the sudden deep floodwaters, and over 1,000 people lost their lives. The story of the devastation of the city and the incompetence of the government response is well known, having been covered live around the clock for several days by all major networks. In this chapter I look at the Bush response to this disaster as a window into his manner of governing and priorities. The Katrina situation can be seen as a microcosm of the way Bush approaches governing in general.

INITIAL SIGNS OF DISARRAY

Soon after the storm was gone, there were reports of looting, a common phenomenon in disasters; but there was some confusion over whether people were merely taking what they needed in order to survive or were engaged in criminal theft. As in most disasters, the great majority of people were cooperative and law-abiding and pulling together to try to help each other to safety, although even law-abiding citizens will take supplies they need for survival in such situations. The press was found later to have the exaggerated the degree of criminal looting, especially in the poor, non-white areas.

The whole world watched in disbelief as thousands of stranded victims waited for days with no water, food, electricity or toilets, with no help in sight. The Federal Emergency Management Agency (FEMA) moved woefully inadequately, and local officials and police were quickly overwhelmed. The local responders seemed paralyzed, unable to communicate so as to mount an organized effort. The stranded victims grew angrier and more desperate by the day. It is clear that many lost their lives unnecessarily because of the delayed and confused response by agencies responsible for disaster management, particularly FEMA.

President Bush seemed particularly oblivious to the extent of the disaster at first. He flew from his vacation home in Texas to California for a fund-raising trip and remained there for an extra day after Katrina hit. On the way back he flew over the devastated area, his distant gaze down on the scene caught on tape and run over and over for the television audience, becoming a symbol of his lack of involvement. Only a few days later did he realize that perhaps he should have taken some action and responsibility for this unfolding disaster (Thomas 2005).

Bush's first impulse was to worry about property damage and economic fallout. In an exclusive ABC interview on 1 September, Diane Sawyer of *Good Morning America* asked him if we shouldn't distinguish between people 'looting' for survival and those who were taking advantage of the situation to steal expensive electronics and non-survival-related items. Revealing his complete lack of empathy with the people in New Orleans who were already trapped with no food or water or electricity, Bush replied that the policy should be 'zero tolerance' for any looting, no matter what the motivation (ABC News 2005). In his mind, even in the midst of the city's devastation and disorder, property protection took precedence over the lives of the mostly black, aged, or poor residents of the city who were waiting in horrific conditions for assistance. In the early days, Bush also openly worried about gasoline prices, but he showed little concern for the situation of those stranded by the floods, optimistically assuming that everything was being taken care of. Later, when it became clear that public opinion was strongly disapproving of the federal response and of the president in particular, Bush made several highly publicized trips to New Orleans and the Gulf Coast, but he never spoke personally to the many victims in the Superdome or the Convention Center. Since he does not like to hear protest or disagreement, his visits were primarily with officials in protected environments. Even though Bush strongly opposed 'looting' by the mostly poor victims of Katrina, he quickly acted to open up government contracts for a different kind of 'looting' by his corporate friends, just as he had done in Iraq.

The aftermath of Katrina revealed in stark terms some of the results of neglect of basic needs, lack of preparedness, and four years of growing poverty in the United States: those with means were able to escape in their SUVs to expensive hotel rooms in distant cities; those with few resources were left to fend for themselves with little concern by the federal government until their media-exposed neglect and suffering became a political embarrassment. Women, children, old people, the sick, the disabled, and the poor, the majority of whom were African American – all suffered unnecessarily in the aftermath of this storm that pulled back the curtain for a brief time on the fruits of Bush tax cuts, budget cuts, and disdain for the public good. The storm also brought attention to the neglect of infrastructure (failure to reinforce the New Orleans levee system, for example, even though predictions of the dire results of inaction proved hauntingly accurate) (Glasser and White 2005). The increasing severity and length of hurricanes similarly raised the issue of global warming to a new level in the public mind, even though Bush continued to deny scientific warnings in favor of short-term corporate gain (McKibben 2005). The corruption, cronyism, and incompetence of the administration suddenly were topics discussed openly by the mainstream press, at least for a time.

Yet, in spite of growing public awareness of glaring problems, the first impulse of Republicans in the administration and Congress was not to redress the wrongs, but to save political face and take political advantage. Michael Brown of FEMA was fired, but soon Bush representatives were spinning their talking points, blaming the local and state governments for the disastrous response. In the midst of the chaos, Congress quickly voted billions of dollars of relief and reconstruction funds, and Republican-connected corporations and their lobbyists were already lining up to get the lucrative rebuilding contracts. Republican congressional leaders temporarily postponed some of their plans (e.g. to cut Medicaid and other programs in support of the poor) in order to come up with ways to continue cutting back on social spending and privatizing government functions by repackaging them as necessary savings in the wake of Katrina.

MISMANAGEMENT OF THE REAL CRISIS

Tales of mismanagement of the actual crisis in the Gulf Coast states run from the tragic to the absurd. Thousands of flood victims had to wait for days in horrendous conditions at the Superdome and the Convention Center in New Orleans (where they had been told to go if they could not leave the city). Others were trapped in hospitals, nursing homes, and in water-inundated homes – often clinging to rooftops or languishing for days in attics from which they were unable to escape. The slow response, the lack of concern or communication, and the attempts to blame the victims are well known. I will not reiterate the more well-known stories of the disaster here, but I list a few less publicized incidents that illustrate the abject incompetence and folly of the federal response to these events.

- In the early days of the Katrina disaster, as countries around the world were offering assistance, Bush blithely asserted that he did not expect help from other nations and that he had not asked for it. 'This country is going to rise up and take care of it. You know we'd love help but we're going to take care of our own business as well' (Pickler 2005). At this time the president was still apparently unaware of the enormity of the disaster and saw it as a matter of pride not to accept 'handouts' from other countries. Secretary of State Condoleezza Rice quickly corrected this gaffe just hours later, her spokesman telling the press that 'we will accept all offers of foreign assistance' (Stockman 2005).

- The British government sent several hundred tons of food aid in the form of 400,000 NATO ration packs, the same food that British troops in Iraq eat and that are authorized for American soldiers. According to the *Daily Mirror*, after the food arrived in the US and was on its way to the hungry hurricane victims, the FDA and the US Department of Agriculture recalled the delivery trucks because of import restrictions on meat products from Britain. As of the time of the report, the food packs were sitting in a warehouse, condemned as 'unfit for human consumption' and waiting to be incinerated. Food aid from Spain and Italy and thousands of gallons of Israeli-donated pear juice were also being held up for not meeting FDA standards. Officials of the British Defence Ministry, NATO, and numerous international aid agencies were furious at the waste of food that cost the donors millions of dollars, and that the hurricane victims so desperately needed. One aid worker called it 'the most appalling act of sickening senselessness while people starve.' He went on,

> There will be a cloud of smoke above Little Rock soon – of burned food, of anger and of shame that the world's richest nation couldn't organise a p**s up in a brewery and lets Americans starve while they arrogantly observe petty regulations. Everyone is revolted by the chaotic shambles the US is making of this crisis. (Parry 2005)

- In late September, over 200 trucks from across the nation arrived in Portland, Maine, loaded with ice that had been ordered by FEMA for the post-Katrina effort. Some of the drivers told local news reporters that they had 'waited on the Gulf Coast for as long as nine days before being told to head north' (News8 WMTW 2005).

> One driver said he left his home in Houston for New Orleans with a load of ice a few days after Katrina hit. But before he could reach his destination, he was told to go to Selma, Ala., instead. He sat there with the load of ice for a week before being send [*sic*] more than 1,300 miles to Portland. (News8 WMTW 2005)

FEMA explained that they had ordered more ice than was needed, so drivers were redirected to Maine storage facilities. The drivers were being paid $800 a day for this pointless work.

- Reuters reported that a Canadian search-and-rescue team arrived in the suburban Parish of St Bernard, east of New Orleans, five days ahead of US military responders. The Canadian team of about fifty members arrived on Wednesday, 31 August, traveling by chartered plane over 2,000 miles from Vancouver, BC. Two FEMA officials finally reached the parish the following Sunday and the Army contingent arrived on Monday. At that time, floodwaters were still 8 foot deep in some places. State Senator Walter Boasso praised the Canadians, but asked the question that was on many people's minds, 'Why does it take them seven days to get the Army in?' (Reuters 2005).

- On Monday, the day Katrina hit New Orleans, Governor Bill Richardson of New Mexico quickly authorized his State National Guard to send 400 guardsmen to help the Louisiana forces. The New Mexico Guardsmen did not actually leave their state until *Friday* morning, four days later, due to 'federal paperwork' at the Pentagon (Isikoff and Hosenball 2005).

- The government of Cuba, which has one of the most competent public health systems in the world, was quick to offer aid in the form of 37 tons of medical supplies and more than 1,500 physicians. The offer was made on 2 September, after multiple sources reported the desperate need for medical supplies and personnel in the region. A Florida-based airline offered to fly the doctors and supplies to the disaster area free of charge. After a week of silence, the US State Department officially rejected the offer, stating as a reason the lack of full diplomatic relations with Cuba – although it accepted aid from Taiwan, with whom the US also has no full diplomatic relations (Zunes 2005).

- The evening before Katrina hit, New Orleans police visited hotels and guesthouses in an effort to evacuate American tourists, but British visitors 'were told they would have to fend for themselves' and were denied assistance. 'One family from Liverpool, trapped in a flooded section of the city, told relatives ... of their bewilderment when they realized U.S. citizens would be offered preferential treatment.' Throughout the week these British families were trapped in hotels without electricity or supplies, waiting for several days in atrocious conditions, unable to escape and ignored by the authorities (Townsend 2005).

These examples are not isolated or rare incidents, but typical of the many appalling instances of incompetence, disarray, and bureaucratic delay by federal officials.

CHARGES OF RACISM AND CLASS BIAS

While the enormity of the disaster was multiplied by the incompetence of the response, some wondered whether the sluggish action was class- or race-related. Certainly the initial response of Michael Brown, head of FEMA, was to 'blame the victims' for not heeding the call to evacuate, a callous attitude that showed complete lack of understanding of the situation of the thousands who had no way or ability to do so. These were the poor, the aged, the ill, the confined, the homeless, and those who were caring for family members who could not leave. While most commentators condemned such talk, a majority of African Americans, familiar with the effects of racism, believed that the response would have been quicker and more effective if the disaster had been in a more affluent, whiter, area (Lunscombe 2005). Their suspicions were supported by the recollection of how quickly FEMA had responded to the 2004 Florida hurricanes, when even undeserving residents received reimbursement by Brown's agency (Lipton and Shane 2005).

Columnist Riuku Sen took up the racism charge. The Bush administration's 'indifference to the well-being of African Americans,' she wrote, was unmasked by Katrina (Sen 2005). Bush had subordinated planning for disasters to his priorities of tax cuts, war, and occupation. 'These decisions frame the dynamics of Bush's disregard for people of color,' Sen continued, noting as well the administration's insistence on dismantling programs aimed at helping poor people maintain or improve their standard of living. Programs meant to overcome the effects of racial bias had similarly been cut, including bilingual education, job training, educational assistance, civil rights prosecutions, and affirmative-action measures. These policies have left a large mass of poor people vulnerable to the destructiveness of nature and the indifference of public agencies, according to Sen (2005).

Lynne Duke and Teresa Wiltz, writing in the *Washington Post*, argued that Katrina had helped to open 'Mainstream America's' eyes to the poverty in their midst.

> Katrina blew open the box, putting the urban poor front and center, with images of once-invisible folks pleading from rooftops, wading through flooded streets, starving at the Superdome and requiring a massive federal outlay of resources.... The Other is there, staring us in the face, exposing their issues on an international stage.... How do we stop ignoring the folks in the box, the inner city destitute, and realize that their fate is ours as well? (Duke and Wiltz 2005)

Harvard law professor Lani Guinier drew wider implications:

> This is not just about the poor black people in New Orleans. This is about a social movement, with an administration that is bent on weakening the capacity of the national government to act.... This is another early warning that we are ill-prepared to function as a society. (Duke and Wiltz 2005).

Regardless of whether the response was slowed by the color of the trapped citizens, it is clear that the sight of so many suffering people in Third World-like poverty in the United States shocked many people and led to renewed calls for action by many.

WOMEN THE MAJORITY OF VICTIMS

One issue almost never raised in discussions of Katrina was that of gender. Those victimized by the storm and the government's lack of effectiveness were disproportionately people of color, the aged (the majority of whom are women), the poor (the majority of whom are women and children), the sick, and the disabled. Although there still has been no accounting of those who died, it seems probable that this group includes more women than men, and that most of the adult evacuees were women.

A study by the Institute for Women's Policy Research (IWPR) examined census data to gain insight into the characteristics of the Katrina and Rita hurricane victims. The report found that women living in the areas affected were more likely than men to be in poverty and more likely to head single-parent families. Women's poverty rates in the hurricane-affected areas were also higher than for the nation as a whole, especially in New Orleans, where around 40 per cent of female-headed families were poor. Female-headed families made up fully 56 per cent of the population (IWPR 2005e).

The IWPR report urged that rebuilding efforts should recognize the 'unique circumstances of women in the Gulf Coast region' and take that into account in redevelopment. 'Black women and single mothers in this region need policies that extend emergency assistance for more than a few months, and provide living wages and job training that will allow them to find economic security both during the rebuilding phase and beyond,' said the study director Dr Avis Jones-DeWeever. The study also found that older women had experienced high poverty rates in New Orleans (24 per cent) and other areas affected by the hurricane. IWPR President Heidi Hartmann commented:

> Katrina and Rita should inspire us to begin a new national dialogue on poverty and its disproportionate impact on women, especially women of color ... [R]esearch tells us a great deal about the solutions that work such as access to training and work and family supports. We must face the persistent poverty that is growing around our nation and work together to advance policies addressing its root causes. (IWPR 2005e: 2)

Unfortunately, these kinds of policies are unlikely to occur as long as George W. Bush is in the White House.

TAKING POLITICAL ADVANTAGE

As with the 9/11 disaster, Bush quickly took advantage of the disorder and chaos produced by the storm to implement some of his favored policies through emergency executive orders, bypassing the need for congressional action. These orders promoted his anti-labor, pro-business, pro-evangelical agenda. As one of the first of these actions, Bush ordered a suspension of the Davis–Bacon Act for the recovery efforts, so that companies would no longer be required to pay the area's 'prevailing wage' to their workers in recovery-related projects (Dreier 2005). This action increased even more the potential profits for the developers who would rebuild the cities along the Gulf Coast, using taxpayer funds allocated by Congress. Familiar names such as Kellogg, Brown & Root, Fluor Corporation, and Bechtel were the first to receive reconstruction contracts (Dreier 2005). Bush also proposed tax-free zones for businesses in the rebuilding effort (DeParle 2005). The administration was accused of overlooking local businesses and giving contracts to large non-local companies with political connections, even though the cost would be higher, and even though using local contractors would help the region to recover more quickly. During hearings held by House and Senate members in October, 'several members chastised administration officials, citing tales of small businesses in the Gulf states losing work to giants such as Halliburton Co.' Senator Carl Levin of Michigan gave the example of a Mississippi modular classroom manufacturer whose bid to supply 300 classrooms was turned down in favor of that of an Alaska firm charging more than twice as much (Weisman and Witte 2005).

The administration appeared to be using another disaster, this one only partly of its own making, to pursue its neoconservative goals. And although various criticisms appeared in the national press (e.g. *New York Times* 2005e) no one seemed to be able to put a halt to these actions. Republicans controlled the Congress, and Bush and Cheney were single-minded in their pursuit of radical governmental change in the interest of big business and big conservative government. According to Julian Borger (2005), writing in the *Guardian*, the administration and its supporters were eagerly using the Katrina reconstruction as a 'vast laboratory' for right-wing policies it had previously been unable to implement.

In addition to the suspension of Davis–Bacon wage protections, affirmative-action regulations for contract letting were shelved. A *New York Times* editorial of 1 October condemned the action, which was implemented by a brief memo signed by a Labor Department underling (*New York Times* 2005e). 'The memo relieved new federal contractors of the obligation to have a plan for hiring minorities, women, Vietnam veterans and disabled people on Katrina-related projects,' justified on the basis that this would reduce paperwork and encourage companies to become involved in the rebuilding efforts. The editorial pointed out that this rule change was completely unjustified on the pretexts that the administration used for its issuance. Because of the widespread condemnation of this action, Bush finally reversed the decision a month later (PBS 2005).

Plans were also in place to allocate $488 million for school vouchers to allow children displaced by the storm to attend private schools – most of which are religiously based – in another scheme to use federal dollars to support religious institutions and defund public education. This would please Bush's religious base but would exacerbate the problem of providing resources to public schools, where the great majority of hurricane evacuees were enrolled. Thus local communities would be further burdened by the diversion of funds from the public schools where displaced students were enrolling, instead of receiving the extra resources they would need (PFAW 2005d).

Undercutting American workers

In addition to the Davis–Bacon and affirmative action exemptions, Bush continued his pro-business, anti-worker bias in the Katrina recovery in various ways, including:

- *Replacing local workers* Senator Carl Levin of Michigan told a hearing that unionized maintenance workers at the Superdome and Convention Center had been replaced by out-of-state workers at lower wages with no benefits (Weisman and Witte 2005).
- *Transporting immigrant workers* The government also brought in Mexican immigrant workers to take the jobs in the clean-up, displacing the evacuated (mostly African-American) victims, many of whom had lost their jobs (PBS 2005).
- *Temporarily suspending documentation requirements for workers* According to a PBS documentary, 'Latino immigrants are forming a large part of the work force laboring to rebuild the Gulf Coast,' causing many to worry that they are displacing the local labor force and

being exploited with very low wages and poor working conditions. The documentation suspension was reversed on 25 October
2005, but already many of the post-Katrina workers were illegal
immigrants; the PBS documentary uncovered evidence of serious
worker exploitation (PBS 2005).

Experimenting with disaster

The enormous Katrina reconstruction project, expected to cost
some $200 billion, provided the country an opportunity to create
something similar to the New Deal that pulled the US out of
the Great Depression. Instead, the Bush administration, following
conservative think-tank theories, planned to take further advantage
of the disaster by enacting such measures as 'lifting environmental
regulations, eliminating capital gains taxes and permitting private
ownership of public school buildings in the disaster area' (Gumbel
2005). As Doug Kreeger, former CEO of *Air America*, wrote,

> [I]t is certain that Bush's administration will use the tragedy to
> their advantage. The result – school vouchers to solve the educa-
> tion problem, faith-based initiatives to rebuild the communities,
> and the Gulf Coast's environment fouled by relaxing the EPA
> rules. As for the rest of the country, we will have nowhere else to
> turn to fix our schools and crumbling infrastructure caused from
> years of neglect brought on by federal and state tax cuts. Once
> again it will be local communities – already plagued by soaring
> property taxes, sales taxes and, in some cases, parking meters
> – that will shoulder the burden. (Kreeger 2005)

By October the dire predictions about the response to Katrina
were being realized – obscured from the public consciousness partly
by media inattention to behind-the-scenes political machinations in
the midst of more sensational news about Tom DeLay's indictments,
Supreme Court nominations, and Hurricane Rita. Paul Krugman,
Princeton economist and *New York Times* columnist, wrote of the
'faltering' of federal aid to Katrina victims in both health care and
housing (Krugman 2005g). Legislation that would have provided
health care through Medicaid to all low-income victims of Katrina
was blocked by conservative senators, under pressure from the White
House. In a letter from Mike Leavitt, Secretary of Health and Human
Services, Senate leaders were warned that such legislation would

amount to a new 'Medicaid entitlement,' and should be opposed. Instead, Leavitt and the Senators supported 'waivers' that would allow evacuees to receive only what they would have been entitled to in their home states. This left out many displaced evacuees, since many poor individuals do not qualify for Medicaid (for example, working-age adults without children). Many states have also been restricting Medicaid eligibility because of budget pressures. Thus, many Katrina victims are destitute, in need of medical care and medications, but still unable to qualify for Medicaid assistance.

Many hospitals and physicians were willing to treat Katrina victims even if they could not afford to pay, but the cost would then be borne by the local communities where the victims had been transported. Although the administration offered vague promises to help reimburse medical personnel, it was slow to come up with a concrete plan for doing so. In other words, local communities and states, already financially strapped by federal budget cuts for social programs and education, soon realized they would bear the cost of medical care for hurricane victims, while millions in contracts went to corporations (Krugman 2005g).

As for the housing situation, the Bush administration very un-wisely began plans to set up publicly funded trailer parks, rather than providing evacuees with less expensive and more satisfactory housing vouchers. With vouchers, displaced persons could pay rent for privately owned apartments in places of their own choosing; trailer parks, by contrast, force people to live in crowded spaces, often distant from transportation or employment opportunities. Krugman surmised that Bush preferred the more expensive trailer solution because he has always opposed housing voucher programs for needy Americans and did not want to 'legitimize' such programs. 'What administration officials fear isn't that housing vouchers would fail, but that they would succeed – and that this success would undermine the administration's ongoing efforts to cut back housing aid,' observes Krugman (2005g).

Conservative 'faith based' organizations receive support

During the Katrina aftermath, the FEMA website listed a number of organizations to which the public could make donations. The first list contained only two secular organizations, the rest being religious organizations. One organization placed prominently on the list was Operation Blessing, one of Pat Robertson's 'charities' (though the list did not identify him as being associated with the organization). Robertson is an extreme right-wing televangelist, a strong supporter of military action, a friend of African dictators, and prominent Republican supporter, who has been in trouble before for misappropriating funds given for charitable purposes (Sizemore 2003). The fact that his organization would be given a prominent place in government suggestions for Katrina-related donations would be unbelievable, except for the fact that the organization has already received a $0.5 million grant from Bush's 'faith-based initiatives' program. Robertson probably influences many people to vote for Republicans, which doubtless explains why Operation Blessing was given the imprimatur of a federal agency (*Democracy Now* 2005c; Sizemore 2003).

Religious organizations were also given the opportunity to apply for grants in recovery work, and school vouchers also supported religious schools. These organizations are exempt from many worker protection mandates, including anti-discrimination requirements in hiring. Although religious organizations have traditionally been eligible for federal funding, under Bush the restrictions and monitoring of their activities have been greatly relaxed, and they have been accused of promoting conservative political agendas in addition to providing social services (Wallis 2005).

Cronyism unmasked and unleashed

Katrina and its aftermath brought into full relief the incompetence of FEMA under the direction of Michael Brown, whose ability to deal with the crisis and absolute lack of understanding for the victims were quickly apparent to a national audience that watched unbelievingly on television. It took President Bush a bit longer, as at his first televised meeting with Brown he was to congratulate him with the now-famous words, 'Brownie, you're doing a heck of a job.' Bush probably quickly came to regret those words, and Brown was relieved of his duties – though not of his salary, as he was retained on the federal payroll for some months afterwards as a 'consultant.' The appointment of Brown to the important FEMA position was problematic in itself, showing Bush's lack of concern with providing for real protection and security and his promotion of political supporters with little regard to their qualifications.

Disaster management is a highly complex field, one that requires a wide range of expertise and skill. Under President Clinton, FEMA's record of response to disaster had become much more professional and competent, due in large part to his appointment of James Lee Witt to direct the agency. When Bush replaced Witt with his former campaign manager, Joe Allbaugh, and then replaced Allbaugh with the latter's old college roommate Brown, disaster was waiting to happen. Brown's primary experience prior to his FEMA appointment had been with the International Arabian Horse Association, where his job was to make sure judges knew and followed the rules of competition. In appointing Brown, Bush set the stage for the extreme mishandling of the crisis of Hurricane Katrina. It also became apparent that many career experts at FEMA had been very dissatisfied with the appointment of unqualified senior leaders, more than just Brown, and they were very angry at the deterioration of the agency with its reorganization under Bush (Glasser and White 2005).

The many lucrative contracts given out for Katrina clean-up and rebuilding were, not surprisingly, often given to large corporations with Republican political connections. In an editorial appropriately entitled 'Cronies at the till,' the *New York Times* editors wrote:

> Congressional investigators are already looking into AshBritt, a Pompano Beach, Fla., company with ties to Mississippi's governor, Haley Barbour – the former chairman of the Republican National Committee. AshBritt has nabbed $568 million in contracts for trash removal. Questions have also been raised about the political connections of two other major contractors: Shaw group, and Kellogg, Brown & Root, a subsidiary of Halliburton. Both companies have been represented by Joe Allbaugh, President Bush's former campaign manager and former head of the Federal Emergency Management Agency. (*New York Times* 2005d)

The editorial goes on to point out that over 80 per cent of the $1.5 billion dollar contracts had been awarded with no bidding or under limited competition. Thus Bush's 'crony capitalism' was alive and well in the response to Katrina.

PROPOUNDING DISINFORMATION AND PASSING BLAME

As has been standard procedure for Bush and his appointees, false impressions were fed to the media to try to absolve the administration of responsibility for the hurricane devastation and response. This involved excuses for their own ineptitude, overly positive assessments of rescue efforts, and attempts to blame others for the problems in the rescue and recovery efforts. Of particular note are the following instances.

- On ABC's *Good Morning America*, Bush stated: 'I don't think anybody anticipated the breach of the levees,' speaking of the New Orleans flooding. In fact there been numerous publicized warnings by engineers, government officials, and the press that the levees would not withstand a major hurricane and that devastating flooding of New Orleans could result (Schulman and Schweber-Koren 2005). Rather than following experts' advice in previous years, Bush budgets had seriously cut funding for flood-prevention projects (Lipton and Shane 2005).

- Bush's FEMA appointee Michael Brown told Katie Couric of NBC's *Today* on 2 September: 'We've provided food to the people at the convention center so that they've gotten at least one, if not two meals, every single day.' Jeremy Schulman and Shweber-Koren of Media Matters for America point out that on the previous day, NBC News reporter Tony Zumbado reported the following on-site information that completely disputed Brown's claim:

  I can't put into words the amount of destruction that is in the city and how these people are coping. They are just left behind. There is nothing offered to them. No water, no ice, no C-rations, nothing, for the last four days ... somebody needs to come down with a lot of food and a lot of water. (Schulman and Schweber-Koren 2005)

- In the days and weeks following the hurricane, attempts were made by Bush and his supporters to blame everyone but the administration. The first such effort by Michael Brown was to blame the victims themselves for not evacuating, revealing his lack of awareness of the inabilities of people to pick up and leave when they have no transportation, are disabled or ill, or need to stay with dependent or ill family members (CNN.com 2005a). Next, Bush officials and Republicans began to blame local and state officials, claiming that they had not taken responsibility for the crisis and that they had not even asked for help (Roig-Franzia and Hsu 2005). This excuse also was shown to be false. In the following weeks, attempts were made to blame the disaster on 'environmentalists' (Byrne 2005; Mitchell 2005), single mothers (Bonavoglia 2005), and anyone other than the federal government and President Bush. Fortunately, the press did not go along and continued to inform the public about the shortcomings of the federal government in both preparedness and response.

- In order to quell widespread criticism of the government's response to Katrina, Bush and the Republicans in Congress promised to 'investigate' what went wrong, at the same time blocking efforts to set up truly independent investigations (Ivins 2005).

Paul Krugman predicted in October that Bush's promises of full recovery might not materialize once public attention moved elsewhere, just as happened with his promises for aid to New York after 9/11 (Krugman 2005h). The *Los Angeles Times* had a similar analysis of the slow response of the Bush White House due to conservative protests (Gosselin 2005), and an article in the *New York Times* similarly reported that the Katrina response was being undermined by conservatives (DeParle 2005). DeParle quotes Robert Greenstein of the Center on Budget and Policy priorities:

> We've had a stunning reversal in just a few weeks … we've gone from a situation in which we might have a long overdue debate on poverty to the possibility, perhaps even the likelihood, that low-income people will be asked to bear the cost. I would find it unbelievable if it wasn't actually happening. (DeParle 2005)

THE LESSONS OF KATRINA

In the response to Katrina we see all the shortcomings of the Bush–Cheney White House writ large: the Bush presidency is characterized by a relentless support for cronies, whether corporations or individuals, regardless of their qualifications or appropriateness; a disregard for problems of the poor, racial minorities, and women; a preference for privatization and the support of conservative religious organizations; a willingness to undercut workers' rights and a disdain for affirmative measures to prevent discrimination; and a pattern of putting politics above expert advice, even when it comes to maintaining critical infrastructure. In all of these, there is a reluctance to accept responsibility for any problems, constant attempts to blame others for anything that goes wrong, and misinformation and false promises to cover actual policies.

How does all this affect women? In many ways Bush's policies have a disproportionate advantage for men, at least well-heeled men in large corporations. His crony capitalism supports corporations dominated by white men, while his failure to support small businesses unfairly disadvantages women, since most women business owners are in small enterprises. Bush's support for faith-based organizations often means that federal dollars are going to schools and social agencies that discriminate against women and non-heterosexuals. His racial and class bias disproportionately affects women of color and white women, since those groups have higher rates of poverty than corresponding groups of men. His relaxation of worker protections such as affirmative action and wage protections likewise affect women as well as people of color, for whom discrimination and low wages are still problems. Bush's political appointments usually come from an 'old boy' network, or else he draws from women who oppose feminist goals. And finally, Bush's anti-government policies and preference for private solutions with little regulation or oversight fail to provide the kind of resources and change that women need in order to become full and equal members of the political and economic life of the country. In the long run, of course, many groups lose from Bush's policies, but the effects are felt first and hardest by women, the poor people, and other disadvantaged groups.

BUSH WARS AND MILITARISM:

HEAVY BURDENS FOR WOMEN

LOSING THE PEACE IN AFGHANISTAN

Although the war in Afghanistan was partially promoted in terms of support for women's rights (the Taliban's brutal treatment of women was highlighted repeatedly in justifying the invasion), women's groups were aware that this emphasis was somewhat disingenuous. For several years women's organizations and human rights activists had been protesting the Taliban's treatment of women, urging the US government to take action to promote change. Not only did the early Bush administration ignore these pleas, but as late as May of 2001 (just over three months before the September 11 attacks), Bush provided the Taliban government with a $43 million grant as one of our allies in the 'war against drugs' – despite strong protests from women's groups about the horrific treatment of women there (Women's eNews 2001). Furthermore, it is questionable how seriously the administration takes women's rights in either Afghanistan or Iraq, as many women's advocates have noted.

Since the war, are women in Afghanistan better off? In some ways and in some regions they certainly are, but US support for warlords in the regions outside of Kabul is support for a system that is still oppressive of women. A better question might be: Are women as well off as they should be, or as the US government claims? The answer to this is 'No' on both counts. Human Rights Watch (2005b) reported in August of 2005 that women candidates were courageously stepping up and campaigning for public office in the fall election campaign, comprising 10 per cent of candidates for office. But the report documented many obstacles and threats faced by women who dared defy the conservative elements in their society. Women in Afghanistan still live in an atmosphere of fear and intimidation, threatened by warlords who hope to dominate the elections and by the regrouping Taliban, which has gained strength in recent months. Lack of security, unequal access to information, and meager financial resources limit women's ability to compete with men politically.

In Chapter 9, I described the highly touted but woefully inadequate rebuilding of the Rabia Bahkti women's hospital in Kabul, and it would be easy to find many similar examples of inadequate attention to rebuilding Afghanistan as US attention turned to Iraq. Amnesty International reports that in many parts of the country insecurity has been a continuing problem since the fall of the Taliban in November 2001. 'Armed groups have abducted and raped women and girls with impunity. In some cases, individual members of the police or the newly established Afghan national army appear to have colluded in these crimes,' according to the organization (Amnesty International 2004: 5).

In a January 2005 article, Ramita Navai describes some of the challenges women face, three years after George Bush announced that 'the mothers and daughters of Afghanistan were captives in their own home, forbidden from working or going to school – today women are free.' Navai points out that most Afghan women are still afraid to go out without wearing the head-to-toe burqa, and even many women in Kabul are forbidden to leave their homes by the male members of their families (Navai 2005). Navai claims that very few women have returned to work since the fall of the Taliban, and, after years of being denied education, most Afghan women are illiterate. Today only about a third of Afghan girls are in school, and many are subject to forced marriages at an early age, which cuts short their education (Navai 2005; Badkhen 2004). A problem mentioned by many observers is that conservative warlords have been allowed to control rural provinces, and their treatment of women is little different from that of the Taliban (Badkhen 2004; Walter 2004). Between fifty and eighty women committed suicide by setting themselves on fire in 2003, most of them trying to escape abusive or forced marriages; one case involved a 13-year-old bride (Badkhen 2004).

Afghan women are calling for more support in terms of development funds, disarmament, and expanded peacekeeping forces to help create a situation that is safe for women to go to work, to school, and out of the house (Walter 2004). As it is, warlords and religious leaders target women who participate in political or development work. Things have not changed much since Amnesty International found in 2004 that domestic violence, forced marriages, rape by armed militias, and blatant discrimination were the norm across much of the country (Walter 2004).

The continuing problems for women were revealed forcefully by the arrest in October 2005 of the male editor of a women's rights magazine on charges of blasphemy. The editor, Ali Mohaqiq Nasab, had published articles critical of execution and other severe punishments under Shari'a law for such crimes as adultery, thieving, and murder. The order to arrest Nasab was apparently given at the request of Mohaiuddin Baluch, religious advisor to US-supported President Hamid Karzai. Religious conservatives in Afghanistan were calling for a ten- to fifteen-year sentence for Nasab for his 'crime' of speaking out against harsh Taliban-like punishments. Ann Cooper, executive director of the Committee to Protect Journalists, called Nasab's arrest and trial 'a giant step backward for press freedom in Afghanistan' (Feminist Majority Foundation 2005b). Thus, in spite of legal advances for women in Afghanistan since the demise of the Taliban government, their basic human rights are under constant threat, and in many areas their security actually deteriorated during the first half of 2005 (Human Rights Watch 2005b). When Bush turned away from Afghanistan to pursue the war in Iraq, he left behind an unfinished project and has failed to follow through in establishing and maintaining security, especially for Afghanistan's still suffering women.

WOMEN AND WAR IN IRAQ: LOSING GROUND

The Bush war in Iraq was based on manipulated information and severe miscalculations, in a misguided maneuver that has cost the United States dearly in lives, money, and worldwide influence and respect, to say nothing of the cost to Iraq. Nevertheless, in spite of abundant evidence, most Americans did not seem to realize this until it was too late to turn Bush out of office in 2004. I will not reiterate the many false warnings Bush raised to justify his decision to invade Iraq, as these decisions and the continuing military errors have received ample attention from the press. Instead, I will focus on the impact of the war on women and on Bush's use of 'women's freedom' as one pretext for his invasion, topics that have received relatively less attention in media discussions.

Loss of rights after the invasion

As in Afghanistan, Bush occasionally tries to justify the Iraq war on the basis of improving the status of women; but in the case of Iraq, this argument is even more problematic than in Afghanistan. Bush is either unaware or cynically unconcerned about the true status of women in Iraq before and after his invasion. In this regard as in other ways, American news media are largely silent about the many problems women face because of the war and in the proposed constitutional Iraq of the future. Most Americans, encouraged by administration statements, seem to conflate the condition of women in Afghanistan under the Taliban with that of women in Iraq under Saddam. In fact, the tragic truth is that many serious observers, including UN officials and major human rights organizations, find that life was better for women under Saddam, especially before the sanctions imposed after the first Gulf war (Badkhen and Haas 2003; Pleming 2003; Lovell 2005).

Iraqi women in the past few decades were more secularized and freer to take part in public activities than their sisters in many Arab countries, but the war brought about a serious deterioration of their situation due to lack of security and increases in rape, kidnapping, and domestic violence. Because of this, many girls and women after the invasion are still unable to attend school, to go to work, to shop, or to receive medical care – activities that were safe before. In addition, a number of Iraqi women have been imprisoned, some in the infamous Abu Ghraib prison, where their most basic rights have been violated. In view of estimates of over 100,000 civilian deaths attributable to the invasion, the majority of these of women and children, one might wonder if another method of dealing with Saddam Hussein might have been more helpful (Bhattacharya 2004; Bueckert 2003).[1]

Bush's hailing of 'freedom for women' in Iraq is not matched by the realities on the ground, although most American media ignore these problems. To quote a Human Rights Watch report from July 2003:

> Many of the problems in addressing sexual violence and abduction against women and girls derive from the U.S.-led coalition forces and civilian administration's failure to provide public security in Baghdad. The public security vacuum in Baghdad has heightened the vulnerability of women and girls to sexual violence and abduction. The police force is considerably smaller and more poorly managed when compared to prior to the war. There is limited police street presence; fewer resources available to police to investigate; little if any record keeping; and many complaints are lost. (Human Rights Watch 2003: 1)

Women threatened by the constitution

As the constitutional process proceeded in the midst of ongoing violence, Iraqi women began to raise the alarm about the heavy influence of conservative religious elements who wanted to enshrine Islamic Shari'a law in the new constitution (Carroll 2005). Women under Saddam Hussein's regime had benefited from the fact that his government was secular and interested in economic growth, and from the courageous struggles of the Iraqi women's movements over the years. Political scientist Cynthia Enloe describes it this way:

> The regime headed by Saddam Hussein was built on the strength of the Baathist party[, which]... was a secular, nationalist political party. Iraqi women first voted in 1980. Women's education, women's paid work, women's votes, all were encouraged by the Baathist-run government, not for the sake of democratization but for the sake of economic growth, to earn Iraq the status of being a 'modern' nation and to maximize the regime's wartime

mobilization. By 2000, 78 per cent of school-age Iraqi girls were enrolled in primary schools. (Enloe 2004b: 296)

Enloe points out that after the 1991 defeat in the first Gulf war and during the following decade of sanctions, Saddam began to court support from his Islamic neighbors, with the result that many young women adopted a more conservative femininity, 'to the dismay of many older urban Iraqi women, who had fought in earlier decades for women's right to live their lives as autonomous individuals' (Enloe 2004b: 297).

According to Yana Mohamed, a contemporary Iraqi women's rights leader, the US-dominated Coalition government set up the election of the Constitutional Authority (which had the task of writing the constitution) in such a way as to represent selected religious and ethnic groups, but left out the extensive secular groups, which generally supported women's equality. In an interview with BBC News on 4 August 2005, Mohamed said women were afraid that the new constitution would bring about an 'Islamic Republic,' with support for women's equality 'only as consistent with Islamic law,' wording written into the document. She believed the wording would mean, at best, that men would be able to marry up to four women, that women's testimony in court would be equal to only half of men's, that men would have more rights in divorce than women. The fear was that women would lose very significant rights and would be forced back into a very secondary status far worse than their situation under Saddam Hussein.

Women's political participation has been constrained by the ongoing violence. In 2003, one of the three women members of the Governing Council was abducted and executed, casting a fearful pall over women's public activism. The rapid rise and growth of religious extremism in response to the power vacuum caused by the sudden removal of the entire governing structure is also a serious threat to women's rights. According to historian Anissa Helie, 'fundamentalist armed groups specifically target women in order to induce fear and helplessness among ordinary citizens,' as a prelude to establishing an authoritarian Islamist state. These groups threaten not only women, but sexual minorities, Christians, union leaders, hairdressers (who are viewed as promoting non-Islamic lifestyles), and various ethnic minorities as well. One such group, the Mujahideen Shura (Council of Fighters), issued a warning that it would kill any unveiled woman on the streets. Another group (Jamaat al Tawhid wa'l Jihad) actually carried out such an execution, when women's rights activist Zeena Al Qushtaini was kidnapped and murdered. Zeena chose to wear 'Western' clothing, but when her body was found it was wrapped in a traditional abaya (a robe-like garment that covers the woman from shoulder to foot) with a note accusing her of being 'a collaborator against Islam' (Helie 2005).

Today, Iraqi women still worry about the possibility that Islamic Shari'a law will become the law of the land and set back their rights to a pre-Saddam level, overturning their rights to marry whom they will, rights to their children if divorced, rights to divorce an abusive husband, and perhaps even their right to leave the house without a husband's or father's permission (National Public Radio 2005). In addition, the continuing, and escalating, violence and civil war threaten women's very survival, as well as any hope for life in a civil society.

Early Bush supporters are changing their minds. Some Iraqi women who at first supported the US invasion have come to oppose it after seeing the chaos and deteriorating situation in the continuing occupation. In early 2005, soon after the election of the Interim Governing Council, anti-Saddam activist and newly appointed am- bassador to Egypt Safia Taleb al-Souhail was invited to sit with Laura Bush at President Bush's State of the Union address. Wearing blue ink on her finger to symbolize her first vote in the 'new Iraq,' Souhail symbolized women's hopes for a free future (Buncombe 2005a; Walker 2005). As she sat next to the mother of a soldier who had been killed in Iraq, the symbolic value of her support for Bush was powerful, and the photo of her hugging the bereft mother was quickly dispatched around the Internet.

Most US media outlets failed to publish the follow-up story a few months later of how Souhail came to recant her support for Bush. After seeing the disarray involved in the constitutional negotiations and the failure to guarantee women's rights, Souhail lamented in August,

When we came back from exile, we thought we were going to improve rights and the position of women. But look what has happened: we have lost all the gains we made over the past 30 years. It's a big disappointment. (Buncombe 2005a)

Ms Souhail expressed the concern of many Iraqis that the draft constitution allows religious leaders to control family courts, leaving decisions about divorce, child custody, inheritance, and similar issues of importance to women in the hands of Islamic clerics. Suhail claimed that the United States had 'sold out' Iraq's women in its rush to get a constitution approved, due to political pressures in the United States. 'We have received news that we were not backed by our friends, including the Americans,' she commented. 'They left the Islamists to come to an agreement with the Kurds' (Walker 2005). In contrast to Ms Souhail and other women's activists, Bush (and his ambassador to Iraq) claimed at the same time that women's rights were not threatened by the new constitution (Buncombe 2005a).

By September 2005, after the draft constitution was approved but before the ratification vote, women's rights activists were reporting increasingly dangerous conditions due to religious extremism. Even the quota that mandates 25 per cent of the parliament to be women would be circumvented, according to women's advocates, by conservative groups putting forth their own candidates who would vote to limit women's rights. At the same time, more egalitarian women's advocates were being threatened and intimidated. 'Religious zealots who were curbed under Saddam's secular grip can operate freely now,' according to a women's activist interviewed by Agence France Presse. She pointed to a billboard that had appeared in Baghdad near a Christian church, which warned: 'To all unveiled Muslim sisters and Christian sisters: you should wear a veil because Virgin Mary used to be veiled' (Agence France Presse 2005).

UNDERMINING HUMAN RIGHTS

In May 2005 the highly respected human rights organization Amnesty International released a devastating, well-documented, and appalling report on US violations of international human rights and humanitarian laws in its treatment of detainees. The report documents many cases of extreme mistreatment, abuse, and torture, even to the extent of death, of detainees at the hand of American interrogators and guards, all covered up and supported or allowed by explicit policies of Donald Rumsfeld and, ultimately, President Bush. These cases, when investigated at all (never by independent agencies), have usually resulted in no punishment for the perpetrators or only administrative reprimands. The US continues to hold itself above international law by claiming that the president has the right to authorize any treatment of prisoners he defines as 'enemy combatants' held in foreign countries. One can only shudder at the impacts on the young American military personnel who have learned to accept such actions as a 'normal' and 'legitimate' way to treat people, many of whom were innocent of any wrongdoing (Amnesty International 2005b).

In many detention centers, sexual humiliation and assaults are used as part of the process of interrogation and/or punishment. A Bahraini detainee in Guantanamo, for example, told investigators that he was warned that he would be sent to a prison 'where he would be raped,' and another was told he would be sent to a prison 'where he would be turned into a woman,' if they did not cooperate (Amnesty International 2005b: 12).

In other cases, women were reportedly taken hostage in order to persuade their male family members to surrender. On 2 April 2005, two Iraqi women (a mother and daughter) were reportedly taken hostage by American troops in Baghdad – an act absolutely illegal under international law and treaties to which the United States is a signatory. The women were seized at their home and held for six days at a US detention site (Amnesty International 2005b: 16).

American women soldiers have been used to humiliate Muslim male detainees in Guantanamo, Iraq, and elsewhere. Kayla Williams, a member of the 101st Airborne Division of the US Army, recounts one such incident in a book she wrote about her experiences as a woman in the US Army in Iraq (Williams 2005). Williams tells how she was asked to assist in the interrogation of an Iraqi prisoner at the Abu Ghraib prison before the scandal was made public. In an interview with the BBC, Williams explained that she first assumed she was being asked to help because she was an Arabic speaker, or to help in a culturally sensitive way with a woman prisoner. When she arrived at the scene, however, the person she was to help interrogate was male. Williams reported shock and extreme discomfort with the way the prisoner was treated and with her role in the episode:

> I thought I would maybe be helping with a female prisoner – to be respectful of the culture by having a woman present for that. Unfortunately it was quite the opposite.... They removed his clothes and wanted me to be the first thing he would see when they took off his blindfold. I had to mock his prowess and make fun of him – to try to break his spirit.... When they began flicking lit cigarettes at him, I knew that a line had really been crossed. (Davis 2005)

Williams informed her superiors that she would refuse to take part in such episodes in the future, and she grappled with whether to file a formal complaint, but decided against doing so when she heard that an inquiry was already under way. Williams told BBC that the 'testosterone-filled atmosphere' in the combat zone made it difficult for women (Davis 2005).

When asked about documented reports of horrific, illegal, inhuman practices, administration representatives do not always deny them but attempt to justify them by calling the detainees 'bad people' or 'terrorists,' with the implication that these 'bad people,' as determined by Bush alone, have no rights (Amnesty International 2005b; 13).

The Amnesty International report is justly harsh in its criticism of the Bush administration:

> In this report, illustrated with cases throughout, Amnesty International concludes that hypocrisy, an overarching war mentality, and a disregard for basic human rights principles and international legal obligations continue to mark the USA's 'war on terror.' Serious human rights violations, affecting thousands of detainees and their families, have been the result. The rule of law, and therefore, ultimately, security, is being undermined, as is any moral credibility the USA claims to have in seeking to advance human rights in the world. (Amnesty International 2005b: 5)

KAREN HUGHES'S FAILED DIPLOMACY

The failure of the US government to market its policies successfully to women in Middle Eastern and other Muslim-dominated countries was exposed when Bush's newly appointed Undersecretary of State for Public Diplomacy, Karen Hughes, undertook travel through the region to try to promote the administration's view. Hughes had been Bush's political communications advisor from his Texas campaigning days and later White House Communications Director in his first term. Before her appointment to the high-level State Department position, she had no experience in foreign policy. Nevertheless, during her confirmation process, Hughes had pledged to 'share our country's good heart and our idealism and our values with the world' and to 'always do my best to stand for what President Bush has called the non-negotiable demands of human dignity.' Hughes had been closely involved in the White House planning of the 'strategy for selling the war in Iraq to the public' prior to the actual invasion in March 2003 (Brown 2005). The pre-war 'strategy' used by the White House is now widely considered raw propaganda, far removed from the complete truth. Hughes's appointment to this new State Department position is yet another example of how this administration promotes itself with the right words while failing to live up to them by its actions and policies. For Bush and Hughes, the solution to the US image problem involves public relations rather than policy reconsideration (Amnesty International 2005b).

It turns out that women in foreign countries are often more sophisticated about judging propaganda and policy for what it is than are many American voters, so Hughes's techniques frequently meet with skepticism and anger in the diplomatic arena. Her lack of background and knowledge became obvious in her October international diplomatic visits to Muslim countries in the Middle East and elsewhere.

Hughes's message on her Middle Eastern goodwill trip in the fall of 2005 emphasized the theme of 'freedom' and how women might prosper from US intervention and Western-style reforms and govern-ment. She tried to export her political campaigning style, with little success, by emphasizing to Arab women, for example, that she was 'a mom,' when the Arab women who met with her wanted to talk about the serious failures of American foreign policy, especially its unprovoked invasion of Iraq. Most media observers rated Hughes's trip as a failure, due in large part to her almost complete lack of understanding of the cultures or political conditions in the countries she was visiting, and in part also to her weak knowledge of US history. In speaking to Middle Eastern audiences, she displayed a naivety and ignorance of some very basic facts, erroneously claiming that George W. Bush was the first American president to advocate a Palestinian state (it was Clinton) and that the US Constitution contains the words 'one nation, under God' (that's the Pledge of Allegiance, not an official governing document!) (Brown 2005). That Hughes would be that unfamiliar with the US Constitution after having worked at the highest levels of government for years is appalling, and that she is carrying out a very high State Department role without knowing the history of US–Israeli–Palestinian policy is even more disturbing.

Journalist Glenn Kessler described an interchange between Hughes and a delegation of Turkish women activists, many of whom expressed anger at the US role in Iraq. One woman condemned Hughes's support for the Iraq war, stating that war 'erases' the rights of women and is followed by poverty. The same woman denounced the arrest earlier that week of anti-war protester Cindy Sheehan in front of the White House. Hughes defended the war, claiming it was necessary to 'protect America' and 'preserve the peace.' One of the Turkish women retorted that 'war is not necessary for peace,' and another said she felt 'insulted' and 'wounded' by Hughes's justifications for war. 'In every photograph that comes from Iraq, there is that look of fear in the eyes of women and children. ... This needs to be resolved as soon as possible' (Kessler 2005). The exchanges Hughes had with Middle Eastern women provided strong evidence of the keen opposition to, and deep resentment of, US policies in the region.

The Iraq war has led women around the world to be suspicious and angry toward American leaders. Soon after her Middle Eastern trip, Karen Hughes went to Indonesia, where she met with similar anger and rejection from women students at a gathering in Jakarta (Soetjipto 2005). Ms Hughes doggedly defended the Iraq invasion as part of the US response to the September 11 attacks and Saddam's purported 'threat' to US security.

The Jakarta university students repeatedly and vigorously challenged Hughes on the invasions of Afghanistan and Iraq and US support for Israel in the Israeli–Palestinian conflict, but the Iraq war was the most strongly contested. In the end, Hughes failed to acknowledge that the students' criticisms of US policy were valid, treating them instead as a matter of 'deeply held' opinion counter-balanced by the similarly 'deeply held' opinions of US policymakers in the Bush White House:

> I'm not questioning at all that the views are deeply held. I under-stand they're deeply held … In the case of Iraq, I've both heard people around the world express concern. I've also been in the room and watched as our policymakers made the decision that they felt as a matter of very deep conviction was exactly the right thing that we needed to do. (Sipress 2005)

The arrogance of the assumption that the White House 'knows best,' the failure to grapple with or acknowledge the real-world consequences of the US wars, and the belief that the solution to the low US standing worldwide is a matter of public relations, are truly mind-boggling.

WAR AND MILITARISM: THE HIDDEN COSTS TO WOMEN

In fact, war and militarism are almost always harmful to women's rights and status. In an article in the *Madison Capital Times*, Cole and Farsetta (2003) state: 'By normalizing war, the United States is contributing to the marginalisation of women worldwide.' This theme has been widely recognized by social scientists and activist groups for decades, and was one of the principles asserted by the Beijing Declaration in 1995, affirming that peace, protection of human rights, and the peaceful settlement of disputes are important factors in the advancement of women. When militarism becomes normal, traditional masculine values and dominance tend to prevail. An Amnesty International report on women in war concurs:

> Military culture typically prizes aggression and reinforces male stereotypes, while devaluing attributes traditionally associated with women. Armed forces encourage male bonding and expressions of virility so that soldiers trust each other and resist any display of weakness in front of their peers, which is derided as 'feminine.' Male aggression towards women is often tacitly tolerated, or even

encouraged, as raw recruits are turned into hardened 'warriors' through a brutalizing training regime. (Amnesty International 2004)

Civilians now comprise some 80 to 90 per cent of war casualties, the majority being women and children (Amnesty International 2004; Salt of the Earth 2002). Women and children also make up about 80 per cent of displaced persons and refugees as a result of wars and 'bear the brunt of conflict' in multiple ways, including increased sexual violence, loss of family and community, and disruption of their ability to feed and care for their families. Amnesty International's *Casualties of War* (2004) describes the heavy costs of modern warfare to women; it is a report that should be read by every person who thinks that war might be a good solution to a political problem.

One example comes from London's *Guardian* newspaper, which reported in March 2005 that US troops had been under investigation for raping Iraqi women. Four soldiers were alleged to have raped two women while on guard duty in a Baghdad shopping area. An Army investigator interviewed some of the soldiers in the unit but never spoke to the women, quickly closing the case for lack of evidence. According to the *Guardian*, 'only the most cursory attempts' were made to find out what had happened. The soldiers claimed the women were prostitutes, or that they 'wanted sex' – either scenario highly unlikely. The investigation was initiated after *Playboy* magazine reported that the unit 'had engaged in various war crimes,' including rape. As with almost all war-related internal military investigations, the inquiry found 'insufficient evidence' to substantiate or disprove the allegations (Goldenberg 2005b).

Sexual assaults on US soldiers

It is not only the 'enemy' women or those living in war-torn societies who suffer from military action in a foreign setting. American women will suffer negative consequences of the increased militarization of US culture associated with war. Women soldiers in invading military organizations suffer an increase in harassment and violence. There have been reports of a rise in rapes and harassment of American servicewomen since the Iraq invasion in 2003, and women like Kayla

Williams have been used in unethical and illegal ways to humiliate enemy prisoners. A recent survey found that 30 per cent of women who used the Department of Veterans' Affairs health services reported that they had been the victims of rape or attempted rape while on active duty. Stop Family Violence claims that in one recent eighteen-month period there were more than a hundred incidents of rape, sexual assault, or other forms of sexual misconduct reported by United States women soldiers serving in Iraq and Afghanistan, the offending attackers being fellow US soldiers (NCRW 2004b).

According to a Pentagon report, the military's response to these victims has been grossly inadequate.

> Many victims did not receive even the most basic medical care – emergency contraception, rape evidence kits, testing for sexually transmitted infections, prophylactic treatment or testing for HIV, and rape crisis counseling are not consistently available. Military personnel lack even common sense sensitivity as to how to respond to rape; one mental-health counselor cleared an Army sergeant who had just been raped to go on missions again, feeling it would be good for her to 'keep busy'. Prosecution of these crimes is delayed indefinitely, and service women must often continue to serve in the same unit with their assailant. (Weiser 2004)

The Pentagon admits that the US military has a widespread problem of sexual assault, with over 1,000 incidents reported in 2003 alone. A further investigation into the matter was promised, but women's advocates called for action, not more studies (Weiser 2004).

Effects at home

Wives, girlfriends, family members, co-workers, neighbors, and others may well suffer problems from soldiers coming home wounded in body and spirit from their experiences in the combat zones and prisons of Iraq and Afghanistan. One report published in July 2005 found that 30 per cent of returning American soldiers suffered some stress-related mental health problems three to four months after returning from the Iraq war, higher than the 13 per cent of those still in the combat zone and the less than 5 per cent when they first return. Soldiers suffered such symptoms as 'anxiety, depression, nightmares, anger, and an inability to concentrate'; a smaller percentage had full-blown post-traumatic stress disorder, a more serious illness. Such problems are the result of the horrors-of-warfare experience and can lead to later problems with the spouses and children of returning soldiers, including increased domestic violence. Thus the harm caused by war is far-reaching (Lumpkin 2005).

Undermining women's equality

In addition to the problems for women in the military or those associated with returning troops, norms promoting women's equality are often undermined by strong emphasis on militarism and war, and women's voices are often not taken into account in such an environment. A general mood promoting traditional masculinist domination seems to have grown stronger with the accession of the Bush administration and its emphasis on military values, with his frequent appearance at military camps or schools with uni-formed soldiers behind him. Civil liberties have been limited in the name of security (the 'Patriot Act'); women firefighters, emergency workers, and soldiers are hardly ever recognized; and, at home, women's needs for childcare, reproductive services, family leave, and health care are not given high priority. In such a world, men are the main actors, women are those acted for, and violence and force are legitimized as the means for reaching goals. Hierarchical power relations, dominance, and force are viewed as necessary and good organizational principles. Women's rights are devalued in this scheme, and the image of the strong, dominant, military male returns as the cultural hero. When these values prevail, women are the losers. These values reverberate from the war theater into the home culture, and women's gains are halted, pushed back, and activism for equality is discredited.

Stephen Ducat, in *The Wimp Factor* (2004), argues persuasively that such seemingly unrelated issues as welfare assistance, health care, environmental protection, gay and lesbian rights, military intervention abroad, separation of church and state, and government regulation of business have become gendered, the more liberal side of these issues being supported more by women than men, and identified more with women. For Bush and his supporters, governmental protections for the environment and the well-being of vulnerable groups are rejected partly (according to Ducat) because they are seen as 'soft' and not 'manly.' Liberals and Democrats (and women) are portrayed by right-wing advocates as weak and 'feminine' because they support these functions of government.

Following 9/11, anyone who publicly opposed Bush's harsh policies, either domestically or abroad, was likely to meet with attacks that questioned their masculinity (as well as their patriotism). Even so reliable a conservative as *New York Times* columnist William Safire was verbally assaulted when he dared oppose Bush's proposed secret military tribunals in favor of some semblance of due process for those arrested on suspicion of terrorism. The response by 'administration sources' was to compare Safire's 'hysterics' to 'antebellum Southern belles suffering the vapors' (Ducat 2004: 284). Obviously, those who worry about due process are 'feminine' and 'weak' and not to be trusted with national security matters. And who can forget California Governor Schwarzenegger's dismissal of opposing Democratic state legislators as 'girly men'? All of this gendered rhetoric subtly (sometimes not so subtly) reinforces the notion that the feminine is weak, misguided, and dangerous to the strength of masculinist culture.

One can only imagine the depth of the impact on the unconscious assumptions of the many young soldiers who are forced to participate in violent and abusive actions in Iraq, Afghanistan, Guantanamo, and elsewhere. Will the official use of women's sexuality by the Army reinforce the notion that women's sexuality is to be manipulated to serve male interests and needs? When 'female' imagery is used to justify the vilification of 'the enemy' and thus to legitimate violence, intimidation, dehumanization, sexual humiliation, and torture of defenseless prisoners, what impact will that have on (male) participants' attitude toward women and violence when they return to the US? These questions cannot be definitively answered, but they raise troubling thoughts about the future of gender relations in the US and elsewhere.

When sexist (and heterosexist) attitudes are associated with the legitimation of degradation, violence, and abuse, do these experiences not portend danger and trouble for women (including wives, lovers, daughters, employees, co-workers) and for women's issues and leadership? Psychologist Stephen Ducat (2004), among others, shows evidence of a close association between misogyny/antifeminism and pro-militarism, anti-environmentalism, opposition to civil liberties, support for cutting social welfare and health programs, and other 'conservative' values. Thus, training young men in militaristic values (and promoting such values across the entire society as part of 'anti-terrorism' hysteria) is dangerous to many progressive hopes for a more equal, peaceful, cooperative, tolerant, and environmentally responsible society.

RHETORIC AND REALITY: USING FEMINIST LANGUAGE TO UNDERMINE FEMINISM

Bush and his spokespersons issue many claims about 'respect for women' while promoting policies that undermine women's rights and status. That this is simply a political ploy should be apparent, given his dismal record with regard to women's real lives. This use of feminist rhetoric to gain support for imperialist policies is an old strategy, not new to Bush. The British occupation of Egypt in the late nineteenth and early twentieth centuries was justified in part by Islam's 'degradation of women,' by the same Consul General who returned to England and founded the Men's League for Opposing Women's Suffrage (Viner 2002). In that case, as in our time, the language of equal rights and women's freedom functions cynically to legitimate an attack on another country in pursuit of international dominance and resources.

The women's 'liberator' George W. Bush soon abandoned the women of Afghanistan, leaving most of the country to 'marauding *mojehadin* who now run the country and are in many ways as repressive as the Taliban' (Viner 2002). It seems likely that Iraqi women will suffer a similar fate. The growing Islamicization of Arab societies in response to US-led invasions and the 'war on terror' has undercut global feminist goals, especially in the Arab world, where feminism is now demonized as 'Western.'

Back in the United States, women's advocates feel abused by leaders who use feminist-sounding rhetoric as a cover for restricting women's rights and pursuing militarist policies. Although many have recognized the hypocrisy of Bush's actions and words, his control of the American political apparatus, with its enormously destructive military power, is as threatening to the future as it is difficult to successfully oppose.

13

CONCLUSIONS:

WHERE DO WE GO FROM HERE?

Progressive and informed voters, aware of the dangerous and devastating record of the Bush–Cheney first term, launched an all-out effort in 2004 to defeat this team. Unfortunately, because of the success of Bush's government by secrecy, manipulation of information, dirty campaign tactics, and the ability to divide the country along what columnist Maureen Dowd called 'fault lines of fear, intolerance, ignorance and religious rule' (Dean 2005: 202), Bush was re-elected by the narrowest of margins in November 2004. There were serious questions about the validity of the vote in Ohio and Florida (Democracy Now 2005d), both states dominated by Republican election officials, but Democratic candidate John Kerry conceded quickly and his supporters across the country sank into a period of deep depression, disbelief, and anxiety for the future. I have voted in every presidential election since 1968, and, although I have been disappointed many times, I have never witnessed the extent of sheer mourning and dread over the loss of an election as I saw in November 2004. Characteristically, Bush didn't help matters with his arrogant talk about the 'political capital' he had earned and his intention to 'spend it' by further devastating the financial stability of the country and pursuing his military aims.

In his post-election revision of the book *Worse than Watergate*, former Nixon counsel John Dean points out that at least part of the reason for Bush's victory was the ignorance of his supporters about his true policies and character, thanks to the successful packaging efforts of Karl Rove and his other managers. Clear evidence for this claim comes from a national survey conducted in October 2004, not long before the election, by the University of Maryland's Program on International Policy Attitudes and the California polling firm Knowledge Networks. The researchers found that Bush and Kerry supporters occupied 'separate realities,' with the Bush supporters much more likely to hold false beliefs about his policies and the war. They believed, for example, that Saddam Hussein was behind the attacks of 9/11, that weapons of mass destruction were actually found in Iraq, and that Bush supported international treaties such as the Kyoto accords.[1] So they supported Bush, who had convinced them that he was on their side. The survey showed that both Kerry and Bush supporters 'agreed that the United States should *not* have gone to war if there were no weapons of mass destructions in Iraq' (Dean 2005: 204) or if Saddam had not supported al-Qaeda. Most significantly, many Bush supporters reported that they would not vote for him if they believed these things to be true (which in fact they were).

The survey showed that Bush supporters believed his actions and policies on a wide range of issues to be much more moderate than they actually were. Tragically, these misinformed beliefs made the difference in a critical election for the American future, including women's prospects for expanded opportunity and control over their lives. The high level of voter misinformation was the result of deliberate misrepresentations on the part of the Bush campaign apparatus and his White House pattern of secrecy, misleading pronouncements, and false statements – aided, of course, by a tame and corporate-controlled media. 'Anyone who believes that Bush and Cheney did not lie their way back into a second term' is mistaken, argues Dean (2005: 205).

Even though the second term saw a precipitate decline in Bush support and a growing epidemic of voter remorse, Bush was still in a position of incredible power to maintain his military program practically unchecked, to appoint extremist judges who would roll back women's rights, and to fail to address the increasing economic, social, and security-related problems of the country. With the 2004 increase in the tightly controlled Republican majority in the Congress, the prospects for meaningful solutions seemed even dimmer. The main source of hope was that, by the end of 2005, revelations of incompetence, cronyism, and scandal had seriously eroded public support for the Bush regime and congressional Republicans, making it much more difficult for them to push through regressive policies. And yet the degree of damage to the nation is hard to overestimate. The only hope is that the public will see through the message-spin of the right-wing Republican propaganda machine and reverse the course of the country over the past few years by electing leaders who will support a more egalitarian and democratic vision for our future. The recent defection of a few congressional Republicans from the hard-line Bush policies is reason for hope, but it will take many years to undo the damage caused by this one administration. In the meantime, grassroots organization and community- and state-level action can counter some of the worst effects of Bush's policies.

I could easily expand the list of ways in which Bush has been a disappointment for women. But hopefully enough has been said to make the point. So the important questions now are, what can be done to survive this difficult time, and how can we go about the process of stopping the erosion of rights and moving forward again? Clearly, I believe, it will involve vigilance and political change. Control of the US government must be taken back from the neoconservatives and religious fundamentalists if the problems described in this book are to be resolved. The issues for women per se are just a small piece of what is dangerous about the changes the Bush presidency has wrought, not least the growing militarism, anti-environmentalism, fiscal irresponsibility, diminishing civil liberties, and growing inequality. But the standing of women in a society is a good indicator of its general social health. Those societies marked by great inequalities and injustice, militarism, and lack of liberty are also those with the worst records on women's rights. So working for women's rights, in the US and abroad, is a goal that perhaps will bring with it positive change in other ways as well.

There are a number of signs for hope. Women's research organizations are picking up the ball where others have dropped it, publishing information on the situation of women and the threats coming from the right. Advocacy groups are keeping close watch and organizing campaigns to enlighten the public and pressure the Congress for more oversight and stronger opposition to right-wing plans. There is some evidence that public pressure can succeed. We have seen several instances in this book in which questionable actions by Bush officials were halted or turned back by widespread exposure and protest. This would include successful reversals of the attempted closing of the Women's Bureau offices, the repealing of Davis–Bacon rules for Katrina reconstruction, attempts to change Title IX, posting of misleading information to government websites, and even the nominations of some individuals (Thacker, for example) who were clearly unqualified. Vigilance and public outcry can still have an effect in correcting some types of action. Although the Bush administration has done much damage to women's progress, we should keep in mind that it might have been much worse without the constant efforts of activist groups and organizations, working to pull back the veil of secrecy, inform the public, and organize counter-responses.

Unfortunately, there are so many issues at stake that it is difficult to identify them all, much less to find the energy to act on them. And the opposition is very sophisticated in its efforts to maintain political dominance and control. The groups least able to resist such efforts are those that stand to suffer the most: stretched-out workers, the poor, the disabled, members of various disadvantaged constituencies. And so it is up to those who have more resources to become engaged in this serious struggle to move the United States back into the community of nations and into a trajectory toward greater respect for such fundamental democratic ideals as individual rights, minority rights, human rights, civil liberties, and women's rights.

THOUGHTS ON MOVING FORWARD

My suggestions are few, but I think they have to be part of any solution to these enormous problems for women and all citizens now and in the future:

1. *Pay attention*

Learn to distrust words and look at actions. I've seen a bumper sticker that insists, 'If you're not angry, you're not paying attention.' Absolutely true. We need accurate and extensive information, information that is not being provided by the mainstream media, which too often allow the president to set the agenda for news. And we know that Bush and his people are very adept at presenting his goals in words that sound reasonable and beneficial to unwary listeners, while promoting policies 'under the radar' that belie his words. Fortunately, there are some very good research institutes that are working tirelessly to study and publish the stories behind the scenes, uncovering the actual state of reality. US citizens need to stay on top of these resources and educate our families, co-workers, neighbors, community leaders, and other citizens about them. In the Appendix I list some sources that have proven very helpful for me.

2. *Be involved*

Write letters to editors. Write to and phone legislators. Protest. If you disagree with judicial appointments, proposed policies, and so forth, make it known to those in power and to others around you. Vigilance does still matter. There are many good email lists that watch the political scene and alert citizens about upcoming votes or issues, soliciting responses. Supporters of women and progressive policies must make our voices heard, even though it seems that they fall on deaf ears. Register voters. Consider running for office. Encourage others. Informed citizens can support and join efforts to inform others and organize for change.

It is important also that citizens of other countries maintain pressure on their own governments to refuse to go along with US pressures to support undesirable policies. It seems to me that international pressures might prevent further erosion of women's global rights by supporting the Millennium Development Goals and promoting the peaceful diplomatic solution of conflicts. It is clear that international opposition to US proposals at a number of UN conferences forced the US delegation to back down. If countries insist upon adherence to the Geneva Conventions and international law, it is possible that future military aspirations might be reined in and some of the worst abuses might be halted. I believe that most citizens in the United States would be appalled if they were more aware of some of the actions of their government in foreign countries. It is primarily up to US citizens to organize grassroots and official efforts to bring back some sense of sanity and justice to our national government.

3. *Never give up*

I am not at all certain that we will be able readily to reverse the trends I have described. Yet, ironically, I am both heartened and dismayed by the fact that many Bush supporters, surveyed just before his re-election, actually disapproved of the policies and goals he supported but were simply not aware that he advocated them. We have to conclude that our biggest challenge may be inventing new ways to reach the citizens, especially young people, in a world of so much deliberate misinformation and media control that many people are unlikely to know how to obtain and evaluate information. Pulitzer-winning journalist Laurie Garrett, who resigned from a fourteen-year career at New York *Newsday*, wrote in her memo of resignation:

> All across America news organizations have been devoured by massive corporations – and allegiance to stockholders, the drive for higher share prices, and push for larger dividend returns trumps everything that the grunts in the newsrooms consider their missions.... I have been in 47 states of the USA since 9/11, and I can attest to the horrible impact the deterioration of journalism has had on the national psyche. I have found America a place of great and confused fearfulness. (*Democracy Now* 2005b)

Thus the development of alternative sources of information and the reclamation of the press may be the primary keys to recovering from recent losses and moving forward again. This has also been the mantra of such sage American journalists as Bill Moyers and other media critics (Nichols and McChesney 2005).

It is truly a 'brave new world,' and there is no guarantee that we will come out well in the end. Many of the trends seem dark and foreboding. But what choice do we have? If we work hard and remain vigilant, perhaps we can win this battle, slow down its progression, or at least be ready to push forward if the pendulum swings back once more. The struggle for justice in the world is a never-ending one, with positive and negative moments, and we can never be certain of the results of our efforts. I believe this is a precarious moment for American democracy and for the future of women here and around the globe. Yet, as Abraham Lincoln said, 'the probability that we may fail in the struggle ought not to deter us from the support of a cause we believe to be just.'

APPENDIX

RESOURCES ON THE BUSH ADMINISTRATION
AND CURRENT POLITICAL ISSUES

There are many good sources of information, and the Internet has greatly increased access to a wide variety of sources. I will not even attempt a comprehensive list, but here are good starting points for those who want to become more involved and aware.

1. For daily feminist news: Feminist Daily News Wire, www.feminist. org; Women's eNews, www.womensenews.org.

2. For staying informed, here are my favorite web-based 'clearing-houses' for politically important news: www.commondreams.org; www.truthout.org; www.alternet.org. These sites draw on newspapers, magazines, and news services from several countries and repost the best journalism on current issues in one location. It pays to look at one or more of them every day or so – and to let others know about them.

3. Research and advocacy organizations for women's issues: in the US: Institute for Women's Policy Research, www.iwpr.org (focuses mainly on economic policy issues); National Council for Research on Women, www.ncrw.org (has a network of research centers studying many women's issues); National Women's Law Center, www.nwlc. org (policy and legal issues affecting women). For international women's issues: Association for Women's Rights in Development

(AWID), www.awid.org; Amnesty International, www.amnesty.org (human rights, women's rights); Human Rights Watch, www.hrw.org (has important reports on global women's rights and human rights in general); Women Watch, the website of the UN Inter-agency network on Gender Equality, www.un.org/womenwatch (has links to all UN agencies dealing with gender issues).

NOTES

ONE

1. See, for example, the collection of feminist criticisms edited by Laura Flanders, *The W Effect: Bush's War on Women* (2004b), and her *Bushwomen: Tales of a Cynical Species* (2004a). In addition there have been many editorials published about Bush's anti-choice agenda and news stories about other actions that hurt women, but these have seldom been brought together and published as a general analysis of his position with respect to women.

2. See, especially, NWLC 2004b, NCRW 2004a, and various publications of the Institute for Policy Research on Women (IWPR), listed in the References.

3. The most important protections of women's rights have been (1) the Pay Equity Act, passed in 1963 and guaranteeing equal pay for equal work; (2) Title VII of the 1964 Civil Rights Act, which outlawed discrimination in a broad range of employment-related situations; Title IX, passed in 1972, which outlawed sex discrimination in educational institutions that receive federal funds; and *Roe* v. *Wade*, the 1973 Supreme Court decision that struck down most abortion restrictions in the first trimester of pregnancy.

4. A sample of these: Fraser 2000; Teepen 2003; *Emily's List* 2003; Heuval 2003; Enloe 2004a; Charbonneau 2004; Towarnicky 2004.

5. For an excellent overview of the Bush administration's actions on reproductive rights during the first years of his presidency, see *A Planned Parenthood Report on the Bush administration and its Allies: The Assault on Birth Control and Family Planning Programs*,' October 2003; and *The Bush Administration, the Global Gag Rule, and HIV/AIDS Funding*, June 2003. Both reports are available at www.plannedparenthood.org.

THREE

1. See various issue statements and papers on the website of IWF at www. iwf.org.
2. Interestingly, Charles Tiefer in his *Veering Right* (2004: 41) points out that Ashcroft was not Bush's first choice for the position. Bush first nominated Marc Racicot, governor of Montana, who had helped Bush in the contested election in Florida. But Racicot was considered not sufficiently conservative by the standards of Bush's social conservative base, in part because he had supported the extension of hate-crime protections to gays and lesbians after the horrendous murder of gay student Matthew Fox in his state in 1998. Karl Rove persuaded Bush to change the nomination, appointing Racicot to lead the Republican National Committee and substituting the more reliably right-wing Ashcroft for Attorney General.

FOUR

1. See the original revision in NCRW 2004b: 12.
2. The description of the 'better living – flex options' initiative is as follows: 'The specific goal of the 'Flex-Options for Women' project is to help businesses create or enhance workplace flexibility policies and programs for their workforces. The program brings together corporate executives and entrepreneurs who volunteer to mentor business owners interested in developing flexible workplace policies and programs. By encouraging entrepreneurs to focus on work redesign and implementing flexible work options, employees will improve their ability to manage work and life responsibilities. Business owners will realize positive bottom line impacts as well' (www.dol.gov/wb/programs/family2. htm#betterJ).
3. The list of removed documents can be found at www.usccr.gov/pubs/ notvoted.htm. One of the most important of these is a highly critical review of the Bush administration titled *Redefining Rights in America: The Civil Rights Record of the George W. Bush Administration. Draft Report for Commissioners' Review*, September 2004. A copy of the full report can be found at the University of Pittsburgh Law School News & Research site, http://jurist.law.pitt.edu/bushcivilrights.pdf.
4. Abstinence-only programs are not allowed to teach the benefits of contraceptives, nor their proper use. Instead they teach abstinence as the only method for preventing STDs and pregnancy. The only information about contraceptive methods presented in these programs is their failure rates.

FIVE

1. In fact, one of the little-known strategies of the conservative movement was to run candidates for local offices, especially school boards, where public interest is low. By doing so, they were able to gain control in

many places over such policies as sex education and similar conservative causes.

2. The specific curricula reviews are available through the SIECUS website at www.siecus.org.

3. The reviews are found at www.democrats.reform.house.gov/story. asp?ID=888.

SIX

1. US Department of State, 'Office of International Women's Issues,' accessed 18 January 2003. This quotation is no longer on the website, which has been simplified to contain less language about women's empowerment. www.state.gov/g/wi/.

2. The policy is so called because it was first announced by the Reagan administration at the 1984 UN International Conference on Population, held in Mexico City.

3. The Helms Amendment to the US Foreign Assistance Act, passed in 1973, established this policy.

4. See the UNFPA Mission Statement at www.unfpa.org/about/index. htm.

SEVEN

1. Susskind cites Dean 2004 and *New York Times* 2003b for these points.

2. Oliver should not be confused with anti-abortion activist Anna Louise Oliver, who is actually the former's daughter, appointed by Bush as a senior coordinator for International Population policy for the US State Department. Anna Louise Oliver was part of an American delegation to the Asian and Pacific Population Conference in 2004 that unsuccessfully pressured members to remove 'reproductive rights' and 'reproductive health services' from the agreement. Louise V. Oliver's husband is also a Republican activist, having served in the Reagan administration and later holding fellowships at the Heritage Foundation.

EIGHT

1. The so-called 'nuclear option' proposed by Republican leaders would change Senate rules so as to outlaw the use of filibuster to oppose judicial nominations, making possible confirmation with a strict party-line majority vote.

2. Detailed information on many Bush appointments can be found in the National Women's Law Center report, *Slip-Sliding Away: The Erosion of Hard-won Gains for Women under the Bush Administration and an Agenda for Moving Forward*, April 2004, available at www. nwlc.org, and on the Alliance for Justice Independent Judiciary website, www.independent-judiciary.com, or in various other locations on the Internet.

3. Information on the Miers nomination and reactions can be found at the Feminist Majority Foundation website, www.feminist.org.
4. These four examples are from Feminist Majority Foundation, Feminist Court Watch, www.feminist.org/courts.
5. This is another example of the Bush administration's holding back statistics that might portray it in a negative light or that might not support its public-relations projections. Unfortunately, it often takes FOIA requests to get basic information about the social welfare of the country under this administration.

NINE

1. The court did not uphold the undergraduate admissions policy in the Gratz case.

TEN

1. The historical information in this paragraph is based on the website of the Social Security Administration, 'Brief History,' found at www.ssa.gov/history/briefhistory3.html.
2. Further analyses of Social Security reform can be found in Krugman 2005b, 2005c, and 2005d.
3. Entmacher's testimony before the Senate Finance Committee on this issue can be found at www.nwlc.org/pdf/EntmacherNWLCtestimony-ToSenateFinance_April2005.pdf.

TWELVE

1. Figures estimated by a scientific study published in the British medical journal *The Lancet*, October 2004. See online summary by Bhattacharya (2004) at www.newscientist.com/article.ns?id=dn6596.

THIRTEEN

1. See story at www.commondreams.org/headlines04/1022–01.htm. John Dean also refers to these data in his *Worse than Watergate* (2005: 204).

REFERENCES

ABBREVIATIONS

AACU	American Association of Colleges and Universities
AAUW	American Association of University Women
AWID	Association for Women's Rights in Development
DFID	Department of International Development (UK)
IWHC	International Women's Health Coalition
IWPR	Institute for Women's Policy Research
NAACP	National Association for the Advancement of Colored People
NCRW	National Council for Research on Women
NCWO	National Council of Women's Organizations
NOW	National Organization for Women
NWLC	National Women's Law Center
PFAW	People for the American Way
PPFA	Planned Parenthood Federation of America
SIECUS	Sexuality Information and Education Clearinghouse of the United States
UNESCO	United Nations Education, Science and Cultural Organization
WHRNet	Women's Human Rights Network

AACU (2004) 'A new year, a new assault on Title IX,' *On Campus With Women*, 33(2), Winter.

AAUW (2004a) 'Affirmative action,' AAUW Public Policy and Government Relations Department, www.aauw.org/issue_advocacy/actionpages/positionpapers/affirmativeaction.cfm.

AAUW (2004b) 'Single sex education,' www.aauw.org/issue_advocacy/action-pages/positionpapers/singlesex.cfm.

ABC News (2005) 'Bush says focus must be on people,' 16 September. http://abclocal.go.com/kgo/story?section=nation_world&id=3403364&ft=print.

Abdullah, N. (2003) 'Viewpoint,' *LA Daily News*, 22 June. www.afghanmed.org/forgotten per cent20promises.htm.

ACLU (2005) 'ACLU and broad coalition probe government on removal of information on pregnancy prevention in national protocol for treating rape survivors,' press release, 30 August. Washington DC: American Civil Liberties Union.

Agence France Presse (2005) 'Iraqi women say freedoms are slipping away,' 24 September.

Alaima, K. (2005) 'Budget may cut college dreams short,' *Women's eNews*, 29 May. www.womensenews.org.

Alan Guttmacher Institute (1997) 'Title X and the US family planning effort,' Facts in Brief. www.guttmacher.org/pubs/ib16.html.

Alliance for Justice (2004) 'Alliance for Justice condemns Senate vote on Holmes,' press release, 6 July. www.independentjudiciary.com/news_release.cfm?ReleaseID=143.

Alliance for Justice (2005) 'Owen: a record of judicial activism and questionable ethics,' 23 May. www.allianceforjustice.org/hot_topic/collection/owennomination.html.

Alterman, E. (2004) *When Presidents Lie: A History of Official Deception and its Consequences.* New York: Viking.

American Council on Education (2003) 'Bush administration files brief against University of Michigan with the Supreme Court,' 21 January. www.acenet.edu/AM/Template.cfm?Section=Home&template=/cm/ContentDisplay.cfm&contenid=9038.

American Diabetes Association (2002) 'Women and diabetes,' fda.gov.womens/taketimetocare/diabetes/fswomen.html.

Americans for Prosperity Foundation (2003) 'Nancy Pfotenhauer to Head Grassroots Advocacy Group,' news release, 1 December. www.americansforprosperity.org/news/nr_0031201.html.

Amnesty International (2004) *Casualties of War: Women's Bodies, Women's Lives.* London: Amnesty International.

Amnesty International (2005a) 'USA: Attorney General Ashcroft declines to act on domestic abuse asylum claim,' 27 January. New York: Amnesty International USA.

Amnesty International (2005b) 'USA: Guantanamo and beyond: the continuing pursuit of unchecked executive power,' 10 May. London: Amnesty International.

Apple, L. (2002) 'An abstinence of judgment,' *Austin Chronicle* 21(23), 8 February.

ARHP (2005a) 'Examples of political interference with science,' Association of Reproductive Health Professionals. www.arph.org/corevalues/examples.cfm#hhshandselect.

ARHP (2005b) 'Appointee to influential FDA committee criticized as "scantily credentialed",' Association of Reproductive Health Professionals. www. arhp.org/corevalues/examples.cfm#hhshandselect.

Aron, N. (2004) 'Judicial disappointments,' *In These Times*, posted on Alternet. org, 18 February 2004. www.alternet.org/story/17879.

AWID (2000) 'An interview with Ritu Sharma from Women's EDGE,' Resource Net: Friday File Issue 6 (email newsletter), 22 December. New York: Association for Women's Rights in Development.

Badkhen, A. (2004) 'Liberation eludes Afghan women: forced marriages, beatings, suicides persist despite Taliban's fall,' *San Francisco Chronicle*, 16 April.

Badkhen, A., and D. Haas (2003) 'Women losing freedoms in chaos of postwar Iraq,' *San Francisco Chronicle*, 24 May.

Baucher, E. (2003) 'Bush marriage initiative robs billions from needy,' *Women's eNews*, 10 September. http://womensenews.org.

BBC News (2005a) 'Brazil turns down US Aids funds,' 4 May. www.bbc. co.uk/2/hi/Americas/4513805.

BBC News (2005b) 'US "harming" Uganda's Aids battle,' 30 August. www. bbc.co.uk/2/hi/Africa/4195968.stm.

Begley, S. (2002) 'Now science panelists are picked for ideology rather than expertise,' Editorial, *Wall Street Journal*, 6 December, p. B1.

Berkowitz, B. (2004) 'Bloch-ing Justice.' *Working for Change*, 12 October. www.workingforchange.com.

Berry, L. (2000) 'Women's groups blast Bush policies,' *Denver Business Journal*, 13 April. http://denver.bizjournals.com/Denver/stories/2001/04/16/ story6.html.

Bhattacharya, S. (2004) 'Civilian death toll in Iraq exceeds 100,000,' *New Scientist*, 2 December. www.newscientist.com/article.ns?id=dn6596.

Bonavoglia, A. (2005) 'Hurricane pundits blow hot air on single mothers,' Commentary, *Women's eNews*, 14 September. www/womensenews.org.

Borger, J. (2005) 'Hurricane aid used to "test out rightwing social policies",' *Guardian*, 22 September.

Boseley, S. (2005) 'US accused of trying to block abortion pills,' *Guardian*, 4 April.

Boston Globe (2005) 'Rove's Role,' 28 August.

Boston, R. (2005) '"Faith-based" flim-flam: Initiative didn't have a prayer, says former White House aide,' 15 February, Wall of Separation. http://blog. au.org/2005/02/faithbased_flim.html.

Bosworth, M.H. (2005) 'No bankruptcy relief for Katrina victims,' *Consumer Affairs*, April. www.consumeraffairs.com/news04/2005/Katrina_bank-ruptcy03.htm.

Bribitzer-Stull, M. (2005) 'Roberts' radicalism needs media scrutiny,' *Minneapolis StarTribune*, 30 July.

Brown, J. (2005) 'What's WHIG All About? An Open Letter to Karen Hughes,' *Common Dreams*, 19 October. www.commondreams.org/views 05/1019–23.htm.

Bueckert, D. (2003) 'Civilian casualties 'horrifying',' Canadian Press, *Common*

Dreams, 4 April. www.commondreams.org/cgi-bin/print.cgi?file=/head-lines03/0404–14.htm.

Buncombe, A. (2005a) 'Iraqi activist taken up by Bush recants her views,' *Independent*, 28 August.

Buncombe, A. (2005b) 'Colombian abortion law campaign is undermined by Washington,' *Independent*, 13 October.

Burke, A.E., and W.C. Shields (2005) 'Millennium Development Goals: Slow movement threatens women's health in developing countries,' *Contraception* 72, pp. 247–9.

Byrne, J. (2005) 'Democrats savage Justice Department over apparent attempt to blame environmentalists for flood,' *Raw Story*, reposted at www.truthout.org/docs_2005/091805C.shtml.

Campbell, C., and B.A. Rockman (eds) (2004) *The George W. Bush Presidency: Appraisals and Prospects*. Washington DC: CQ Press.

Carroll, R. (2005) 'Women battle for rights in new Iraq,' *Guardian*, 15 August.

Carter, G. (2004) *What We Have Lost*. New York: Farrar, Straus & Giroux.

Cassels, P. (2002) 'White House plays musical chairs in AIDS office,' Bay Windows Online, 25 July. www.baywindows.com/media/paper328/news/2002/07/25/nationalnews/White.House.plays.musical.chairs.in.aids.office-259362.shtml.

Center for Pregnancy Choices (2005) 'Considering abortion,' Jackson, MS. www.mypregnancychoices.org/considering_abortion.htm.

Center for Reproductive Rights (2003) 'The Bush Global Gag Rule: Endangering women's health, free speech, and democracy, July. www.reproductiverights.org/pub_fac_ggrbush.html.

Chappell, C., E. Co, and A. Horton (2005) 'Women of color alarmed by Chief Justice Nominee,' *Women's eNews*, 7 September. www.womensenews.org.

Charbonneau, C.R. (2004) 'Bush steps up attacks on women's rights,' *Seattle Post-Intelligencer*, 22 January.

Chemerinsky, E. (2005) 'Once again, just too conservative,' *Los Angeles Times*, 31 August.

Chibbaro, L. (2003) 'White House denies plans to close AIDS czar's office: McClellan, GOP gay group defend Bush record on AIDS,' *Washington Blade*, 18 July. www.aegis.com/news/wb/2003/WB030706.html.

Chibbaro, L. (2004)'Bush names new czar,' *Washington Blade*, 21 May. www.washingtonblade.com/2004/5–21/news/national/czar.cfm.

Clymer, A. (2002) 'US revises sex information, and a fight goes on,' *New York Times*, 27 December.

CNN.com (2001) 'Bush signs repeal of ergonomic rules into law,' 20 March. www.archives.cnn.com/2001/allpolitics/03/20/bush.ergonomics.

CNN.com (2004) 'Bush calls for ban on same-sex marriage,' 25 February. http://edition.cnn.com/2004/allpolitics/02/24/elec04.prez.bush.marriage/.

CNN.com (2005a) 'FEMA chief: victims bear some responsibility,' 1 September. http://edition.cnn.com/2005/weather/09/01/katrina.fema.brown/.

CNN.com (2005b) 'Second expert resigns over FDA delay,' 6 October. http://us.cnn.com/2005/health/10/06/contraceptive.resignation.reut/index.html.

Cohen, S.A. (2003) 'Bush administration isolates U.S. at international meeting to promote Cairo agenda,' *Guttmacher Report* 6(1), March.

Cole, L. (2005) 'Supreme Court nominee is highly questionable on women's rights,' statement released in behalf of Black Women's Health Imperative, 27 July. www.blackwomenshealth.org.

Cole, M., and D. Farsetta (2003) 'US contributes to the marginalization of women worldwide,' *Madison Capital Times*, 2 December.

Conason, J. (2004) *Big Lies: The Right-wing Propaganda Machine and How It Distorts Truth*. New York: St. Martin's Press.

Coontz, S. (2005) *Marriage, a History: From Obedience to Intimacy, Or How Love Conquered Marriage*. New York: Viking.

Cooper, C.L. (2001) 'Power of Attorney General pervades women's lives,' *Women's eNews*, 1 February. www.womensenews.org.

Cooper, H. (2005) 'What? condoms can prevent AIDS? No way!' *New York Times*, 26 August.

Corn, D. (2004) *The Lies of George W. Bush*. New York: Three Rivers Books.

Davis, M. (2005) 'A woman soldier's war in Iraq,' BBC News online, 25 August.

Dean, J.W. (2004) *Worse than Watergate: The Secret Presidency of George W. Bush*. New York: Little, Brown.

Dean, J.W. (2005) *Worse than Watergate: The Secret Presidency of George W. Bush*, rev. edn. New York: Warner Books.

Democracy Now (2005a) 'Bush appoints arch-conservative Claude Allen as Chief Domestic Policy Adviser,' interview with Doug Ireland by Amy Goodman, 12 January.

Democracy Now (2005b) 'Pulitzer Prize-winning journalist Laurie Garrett: 'When you see news as a product … it's impossible to really serve democracy,' 14 March. www.democracynow.org/article.pl?sid=05/03/14/151255.

Democracy Now (2005c) 'FEMA promotes Pat Robertson charity,' 9 September. www.democracynow.org/article.pl?sid=05/09/09/1411237&mode=thread&tid=25.

Democracy Now (2005d) 'Was the 2004 election stolen? A debate on Ohio one year after Bush's victory,' 4 November. www.democracynow.org/article.pl?sid=05/11/04/1532218.

DeParle, J. (2005) 'Liberal hopes ebb in post-storm poverty debate,' *New York Times*, 11 October.

DFID (2005) 'Millennium Development Goals' and 'Millennium Development Goals: Gender,' London: Department of International Development. www.dfid.gov/uk/mdg; www.dfid.gov/uk/mdg/gender.asp.

Dreier, P. (2005) 'Bush helps disaster profiteers,' *Alternet*, 17 September. www.alternet.org.

Ducat, S. (2004) *The Wimp Factor: Gender Gaps, Holy Wars, and the Politics of Anxious Masculinity*. Boston: Beacon Press.

Duke, L., and T. Wiltz (2005) 'A nation's castaways: Katrina blew in, and tossed up reminders of a tattered racial legacy,' *Washington Post*, 4 September, p. D1.

du Venage, G. (2003) 'U.S. policy blamed for abortion deaths in Ethiopia,' *San Francisco Chronicle*, 12 December.

Economic Opportunity Program (2005) 'What's wrong with the Bankruptcy Bill? Bill Analysis of S.256,' Demos, 24 February. www.demos-usa.org/pub459.cfm.

Edin, K. (2000) 'What do low-income single mothers say about marriage?' *Social Problems* 47(1): 112–33.

Edsall, T.B. (2006) 'Bush appointments avert Senate battles,' *Washington Post*, 6 January, p. A13.

Egelko, B. (2003) 'Dems protest abortion ban enforcement; Overseer of new law would be division that protects clinics,' *San Francisco Chronicle*, 14 November, p. A10.

Eggen, D. (2005a) 'Official in racial profiling study demoted,' *Washington Post*, 25 August, p. A7.

Eggen, D. (2005b) 'Civil rights focus shift roils staff at Justice,' *Washington Post*, 13 November, p. A1.

Emily's List (2003) 'Top ten Bush assaults on women and families,' September. www.emilyslist.org.

EngenderHealth (2005) 'Bush administration withholds funding for UNFPA,' news release, 19 September. www.engenderhealth.org/news/news-releases/050919.html.

Enloe, C. (2004a) 'W stands for women, Dubya does not,' *Stars & Stripes* 1663, p. 20.

Enloe, C. (2004b) *The Curious Feminist: Searching for Women in a New Age of Empire*. Berkeley: University of California Press.

Erbe, B. (2001) 'Singling out contraceptive coverage,' Scripps Howard, *Nando Media*, 17 April.

Erickson, J. (2004) 'Legislative update: Bush administration & 108th Congress damage women's rights, economic status,' *National NOW Times*, Fall. www.now.org/nnt/fall-2004/legupdate.html.

Faludi, S. (1991) *Backlash: The Undeclared War Against American Women*. New York: Crown.

FDA Advisory Committee, 'Stanford's Guidice selected to chair reproductive health drugs committee,' www.fdaadvisorycommittee.com/fdc/Advisory-Committee/Stories/ReproChair.htm, accessed 23 November 2005.

Fears, D. (2005) 'Civil rights commissioner marches in different time; conservative has not been a traditional activist,' *Washington Post*, 17 January, p. A15.

Federalist Society (2005) 'Our purpose,' www.fed-soc.org/ourpurpose.htm.

Feldt, G. (2003) 'Bush's policy hurts vulnerable women,' *Columbia Daily Tribune*, 29 July.

Feminist Majority Foundation (2001–2005a) 'Don't be misled: George W. Bush *is* anti abortion,' Feminist Court Watch. www.feminist.org/courts/gwb.asp, accessed 17 November 2005.

Feminist Majority Foundation (2001–2005b) 'Particularly egregious nominee to Federal District Court: J. Leon Holmes' Feminist Court Watch. www.feminist.org/courts/nominee_info.asp, accessed 17 November 2005.

Feminist Majority Foundation (2001–2005c) 'Worst of Bush's pending nominations,' Feminist Court Watch. www.feminist.org/courts/nominee_info.asp, accessed 17 November 2005.

Feminist Majority Foundation (2002) 'Bush stacks FDA panel: ideology trumps medicine and science again,' *Feminist Daily News Wire*, 26 December. http://feminist.org/news/newsbyte/uswirestory.asp?id=7384.

Feminist Majority Foundation (2003a) 'Nepal: abortion legal but women still imprisoned,' *Feminist Daily News Wire*, 17 April. www.feminist.org/news/newsbyte/uswirestory.asp?id=7720.

Feminist Majority Foundation (2003b) 'Judiciary committee to hold hearing on far right nominee,' *Feminist Daily News Wire*, 22 September. www.feminist.org/news/newsbyte/uswirestory.asp?id=8056.

Feminist Majority Foundation (2004a) 'Study: federal judges appointed by Bush are most conservative,' *Feminist Daily News Wire*, 15 September. http://feminist.org/news/newsbyte/uswirestory.asp?id=8638.

Feminist Majority Foundation (2004b) 'Enforcement of civil rights law declined under Bush administration,' *Feminist Daily News Wire*, 24 November. http://feminist.org/news/newsbyte/uswirestory.asp?id=8763.

Feminist Majority Foundation (2005a) 'Judge Samuel Alito nominated,' Feminist Court Watch, www.feminist.org/courts.

Feminist Majority Foundation (2005b) 'Afghan women's rights editor on trial for blasphemy,' *Feminist Daily News Wire*, 14 October. http://feminist.org/news/newsbyte/uswirestory.asp?id=9329.

Feminist Majority Foundation (2005c) 'Senate foreign relations committee delays vote on Bush nominee Sauerbrey,' *Feminist Daily News Wire*, 2 November. www.feminist.org/news/newsbyte/uswirestory.asp?id=9363.

Flanders, L. (2004a) *Bushwomen: Tales of a Cynical Species*. London: Verso.

Flanders, L. (2004b) *The W Effect: Bush's War on Women*. New York: The Feminist Press.

Fletcher, M.A. (2003) 'Changes to Title IX considered: proposal would allow scholarship limits,' *Washington Post*, 24 January, p. A1.

Fletcher, M.A. (2005) 'What the Federalist Society stands for,' *Washington Post*, 29 July.

Frank, T. (2004) *What's the Matter with Kansas? How Conservatives Won the Heart of America*. New York: H. Holt.

Franken, A. (2003) *Lies and the Lying Liars Who Tell Them*. New York: Penguin.

Fraser, L. (2000) 'Republican war against women,' *Alternet*, 26 April. www.alternet.org.

Gender Monitoring Group of the World Summit (2005) 'International women's groups tell Ambassador Bolton to back off: accuses Bolton of undermining progress and months of work by nations and NGOs to develop global vision,' press release, 26 August. www.commondreams.org/cgi-bin/newsprint.cgi?file=news2005/0826–04.htm.

Glasser, S.B., and J. White (2005) 'Storm exposed disarray at the top,' *Washington Post*, 4 September, p. A1.

Global Policy Forum (2004) 'Foreign Aid Bill to Fund Controversial UN Agencies,' *OneWorldUS*, 27 January. www.globalpolicy.org/finance/docs/2004/0127usagencydues.htm.

Global Virtual University (2005) 'Country indicators,' Globalis. http://globalis.gvu.unu.edu/, accessed 20 November.

Goldenberg, S. (2005a) 'America urges UN to renounce abortion rights,' *Guardian*, 1 March, p. 14.

Goldenberg, S. (2005b) 'US soldiers accused of sex assaults,' *Guardian*, 8 March.

Gosselin, P.G. (2005) 'Bush is in no hurry on Katrina recovery,' *Los Angeles Times*. 17 October.

Groening, C., and J. Brown (2001), 'Christian groups disturbed by Bush's choice of homosexual to head AIDS office,' *AgapePress*, 11 April, http://headlines.agapepress.org/archive/4/112001b.asp.

Grundy, T. (2003) 'Bush "killing women" with pro-life aid,' Scotland on Sunday, *The Scotsman*, 8 June. http://scotlandonsunday.Scotsman.com/archive.cfm?id=635232003.

Guardian (2004) 'Anti-abortion, pro-abstinence: Rights for women in the US remain precarious,' 6 October, p. 9.

Gumbel, A. (2005) 'Outpouring of relief cash raises fear of corruption and cronyism,' *Independent*, 20 September.

Havemann, J., and M. Curtius (2005) 'Bush to propose billions in cuts: farm subsidies and food stamps are among the targets in the 2006 budget plan,' *Los Angeles Times*, 6 February.

Helie, A. (2005) 'The US occupation and rising religious extremism: the double threat to women in Iraq,' *Challenging Fundamentalisms*, June. www.whrnet.org/fundamentalisms/docs/issue-helie_iraq-0506.html.

Hibbitts, B. (2005) 'Civil rights commission yanks report critical of Bush rights record,' *Jurist*, 21 January.

Holland, J. (2003) 'Black Democrats denounce judicial nominee Brown as another "Clarence Thomas",' *San Francisco Chronicle*, 17 October.

Holste, G.C. (2001) 'Bush mega tax cut plan may hurt women, kids,' *Women's eNews*, 3 March. www.womensenews.com.

Human Rights First (2005) 'AG Ashcroft sends domestic violence case back to Appeals Board,' *Asylum Protection News*, 24 January. www.humanrightsfirst.org/asylum/torchlight/newsletter/newslet_35.htm.

Human Rights Watch (2003) 'Climate of fear: sexual violence and abduction of women and girls in Baghdad,' *Human Rights Watch Report* 15 (7), July.

Human Rights Watch (2005a) 'U.S.: restrictive policies undermine anti-AIDS efforts,' 18 May. www.hrw.org/English.docs/2005/05/18/usdom10978.htm.

Human Rights Watch (2005b) 'Campaigning against fear: women's participation in Afghanistan's 2005 elections,' 16 August. http://hrw.org/English/docs/20005/08/16/afghan1633.htm.

Human Rights Watch (2005c) 'Ugandans resist anti-condom agenda,' *Human*

Rights News, September. www.hrw.org/English/docs/2005/09/14/ugan-da11744.htm.

Ipas (2003) 'New report finds and global gag rule contributes to more un-intended pregnancies, unsafe abortion overseas,' Ipas Press Release, 24 September. www.ipas.org/English/press_room/2003/releases/09242003. asp, accessed 23 November 2005.

Ipas (2005) 'World Health Organization approves abortion medication for list of essential medicines,' press release, 7 July. www.ipas.org/English/ press_room/2005/releases/07072005.asp.

Isikoff, M., and M. Hosenball (2005) 'Red tape,' *Newsweek*, MSNBC Web exclusive, 14 September. www.msnbc.msn.com/id/9344582/site/news-week/.

Ivins, M. (2005) 'George Bush investigates!' *Alternet*, 9 September. www. alternet.org/story/25267.

IWHC (2005a) 'The assault on women's sexual and reproductive health and Rights,' *Bush's Other War*. www.bushsotherwar.org.

IWHC (2005b) 'Charlotte "Charlie" Ponticelli,' *Bush's Other War*. www.iwhc. org/resources/bushsotherwar/othernominations.cfm.

IWHC (2005c) 'Judicial Nominations,' *Bush's Other War*. www.iwhc.org.re-sources/bushsotherwar/judicialnominations.cfm.

IWHC (2005d) 'Other nominations,' *Bush's Other War*. www.iwhc.org/re-sources/bushsotherwar/othernominations.cfm.

IWHC (2005e) 'The so-called partial birth abortion ban: criminalizing abor-tion,' *Bush's Other War*. www.iwhc.org/resources/bushsotherwar/domestic. cfm.

IWPR (2000) 'Why privatizating social security would hurt women,' pub-lication D437RB, March. Washington DC: Institute for Women's Policy Research.

IWPR (2004) 'Statement by IWPR on the BLS decision to discontinue data collection on women's employment,' 7 December. Washington DC: In-stitute for Women's Policy Research.

IWPR (2005a) 'Social Security reform and women,' Fact Sheet. Washington DC: Institute for Women's Policy Research.

IWPR (2005b) 'Women and Social Security: important facts.' Washington DC: Institute for Women's Policy Research. http://womenandsocialsecurity. org/women_social_security.

IWPR (2005c) Women and Social Security alert (Women SSA), email alert on women and Social Security 10, 6 June. Washington DC: Institute for Women's Policy Research.

IWPR (2005d) 'Persistent inequalities: poverty, lack of health coverage, and wage gaps plague economic recovery,' 30 August. Washington DC: In-stitute for Women's Policy Research.

IWPR (2005e) 'Women of Gulf Coast key to rebuilding after Katrina and Rita,' news release, 11 October. Washington DC: Institute for Women's Policy Research.

Jackson, C. (2005) 'Ousted civil rights leader speaks out,' Southern Poverty Law Center, 9 February. www.tolerance.org/news/article_tol.jsp?id=1155.

Jackson, D.Z. (2004) 'Deleting the truth on health care,' *Boston Globe*, 25 February.

Jackson, D.Z. (2005) 'A blind eye to gender bias,' *Boston Globe*, 12 October.

James, K. (2005) 'Illinois blocks anti-choice move; Bush doesn't,' *Women's eNews*, 1 October. www.womensenews.org/article.cfm?aid=2472.

Kaufman, M. (2005) 'Decision on Plan B called very unusual,' *Washington Post*, 12 October.

Kessler, G. (2005) 'Turkish women blast US envoy on Iraq war,' *San Francisco Chronicle*, 29 September.

Kreeger, D. (2005) 'Bush's raw deal,' *Alternet*, 20 September. www.alternet. org/.

Kristof, N.D. (2002) 'Women's rights, why not?' *New York Times*, 18 June.

Krugman, P. (2005a) 'Spearing the beast,' *New York Times*, 8 February.

Krugman, P. (2005b) 'Social Security scares,' *New York Times*, 5 March.

Krugman, P. (2005c) 'A gut punch to the middle,' *New York Times*, 2 May.

Krugman, P. (2005d) 'The final insult,' *New York Times*, 9 May.

Krugman, P. (2005e) 'Killed by contempt,' *New York Times*, 5 September.

Krugman, P. (2005f) 'All the president's friends,' *New York Times*, 12 September.

Krugman, P. (2005g) 'Miserable by design,' *New York Times*, 3 October.

Krugman, P. (2005h) 'Will Bush deliver?' *New York Times*, 10 October.

Lamb, C. (2004) 'The Return of the Taliban,' *New Statesman*, 22 March.

Lancet (2004) 'Does Washington really know best?' *Lancet* 34, 10 July, p. 114.

Lane, C. (2005) 'Justices to hear challenge to Oregon assisted suicide law,' *Washington Post*, 23 February, p. A06.

Lederer, E. (2004) 'More than 250 global leaders endorse U.N. population agenda – but Bush administration objects to mention of "sexual rights",' Associated Press, 13 October.

Lederer, E. (2005) 'U.S. under pressure from Europe and many other countries to drop anti-abortion language in women's declaration,' Associated Press, 2 March.

Levine, J. (2004) 'No-sex education: from chastity to abstinence,' in M.S. Kimmel and R.F. Plante, *Sexualities: Identities, Behaviors, and Society*. New York: Oxford University Press, pp. 438–55.

Lewis, A. (2000) 'An unfit nominee,' *New York Times*, 30 December.

Lewis, L. (2005) 'Justice drops emergency contraception guidelines,' National Public Radio, morning edition, 14 February. www.npr.org/templates/ story/story.php?storyID=4497898.

Lipton, E., and S. Shane (2005) 'Leader of federal effort feels heat,' *New York Times*, 3 September.

Litwak, K. (2005) 'Good news and bad news for Title IX,' National Organization for Women, 31 March. www.now.org/issues/title_ix/033105 titleix.html.

Lobe, J. (2003) 'Bush chooses Reagan-era Republican for UNESCO,' oneworld.net, 2 October. http://us.oneworld.net/article/view/69441/1/.

Lobe, J. (2005a) 'Bush jihad against UNFPA enters fourth year,' InterPress

Service, 17 September. www.commondreams.org/headlines05/0917–03.htm.

Lobe, J. (2005b) 'Another Bush disaster nominee assailed,' InterPress, 19 October. www.commondreams.org/headlines05/1019–04.htm.

Lochhead, C. (2005) 'Feinstein refuses to back Roberts in vote,' *San Francisco Chronicle*, 23 September.

Loder, A. (2003) 'Bush's anti-choice policies felt around the world,' *Women's eNews*, 20 January. www.womensenews.org.

Logan, M. (2004) 'Bush ideology hurts women worldwide – groups,' Inter Press Service, 20 April. www.commondreams.org/headlines04/0420–03.htm.

Londoño, E., and M.A. Fletcher (2006) 'Former top Bush aide accused of Md. thefts,' *Washington Post*, 11 March, p. A1.

Lovell, J. (2005) Amnesty: Iraqi women no better off Post-Saddam,' Reuters, 22 February. www.commondreams.org/cgi-bin/print.cgi?file=/headlines05/0222–08.htm.

Lumpkin, J.H. (2005) 'Iraq affecting mental health of troops,' *Washington Post*, 28 July.

Lunscombe, R. (2005) 'Black fury at Bush over rescue delay,' *Observer*, 4 September.

McCaffrey, S. (2001) 'Bush administration denies New York's contraceptive request,' *Salon*, 20 July. www.salon.com/mwt/wire/2001/07/20/contraceptive/index.html.

McCarthy, S. (2005) 'In US world policy, women lose out,' *Newsday* (Long Island NY), 10 March, p. A44.

McGarvey, A. (2005) 'Dr. Hager's family values,' *The Nation*, 12 May.

McIntyre, J. (2003) 'Bush: If Halliburton overcharged the government, it will have to pay,' CNN, 12 December. http://edition.cnn.com/2003/WORLD/meast/12/11/sprj.irq.Halliburton/.

McKibben, B. (2005) 'Katrina havoc reflects the new America,' *Newsday*, 14 September.

Malek, K. (2003) 'The abortion–breast cancer link: how politics trumped science and informed consent,' *Journal of American Physicians and Surgeons*, Summer.

Maloney, C. (2005) 'The clock's still ticking: no answer yet if President opposes contraception,' 18 July. www.house.gov/maloney/press/109th/20050718Contraception.htm.

Medical Institute (2005) 'Executive and board members: Freda McKissic Bush,' www.medinstitute.org/about_us/executive_board.html?executive_board_item=819&db-item=staff, accessed 19 November.

Medical Technology Business Europe (2005) 'American Diabetes Association disappointed with Bush's budget cuts for chronic disease prevention,' http://mtbeurope.info/news/2005/502010.htm.

Miller, B. (2001) 'US resists "comfort women" suit; Japan's war actions are covered by treaties, officials say,' *Washington Post*, 14 May, p. A19.

Miller, B. (2001) 'Comfort women suit against Japan dismissed,' *Washington Post*, 5 October, p. A01.

Miller, J. (2003) 'U.S. expands Afghan aid for maternal and child health,' *New York Times*, 27 January.

Mitchell, J. (2005) 'E-mail suggests government seeking to blame groups,' *Clarion–Ledger*, 16 September.

Moore, J., and W. Slater (2004) *Bush's Brain: How Karl Rove Made George W. Bush Presidential*. New York: John Wiley.

Morgen, S., and L. Basch (2005) 'Guest viewpoint: women bear the brunt of an unfair tax policy,' *Register-Guard* (Eugene OR), 14 April.

Myers, B. (2001) 'A shortsighted president shortchanges women,' *Boston Globe*, 10 April.

NAACP (2005) *Closing the Gap: Moving from Rhetoric to Reality in Opening Doors to Higher Education for African-American Students*. New York: NAACP Legal Defense and Educational Fund. 23 June.

Nakashima, E. (2001) 'Cut in birth control benefit of federal workers sought,' *Washington Post*, 12 April, p. A29.

Nash, J.L. (2004) 'Ergonomics, OSHA rulemaking haunt 2004 election,' *Occupational Hazards*, 7 October. www.occupationalhazards.com/safety_zones/58/article.php?id=12461.

National Leadership Network of Black Conservatives (2005) 'About Project 21,' www.nationalcenter.org/P21Index.html.

National Public Radio (2005) 'All things considered,' 13 March.

Navai, R. (2005) 'Afghan women still in chains under Karzai,' *Sunday Herald*, 23 January.

NCRW (2004a) 'Missing: information about women's lives,' National Council for Research on Women, 6 March. www.ncrw.org.

NCRW (2004b) 'Missing – information about US military abuse of women,' National Council for Research on Women, 21 July. www.ncrw.org/misinfo/misinfo_13.htm.

NCRW (2005) 'Why taxes are a women's issue,' National Council for Research on Women. www.ncrw.org/researchforaction/taxes.htm.

NCWO (2001) 'National Council of Women's Organizations condemns ergonomics vote in Congress,' press release, National Council of Women's Organizations, 7 March. www.commondreams.org/news2001/0307–11.htm.

NCWO (2005) 'NCWO speaks out against privatization of Social Security,' 8 February. www.womensorganizations.org/pages.cfm?ID=192.

New York Times (2003a) 'Abortion and breast cancer,' Editorial, 6 January.

New York Times (2003b) 'The war against women,' Editorial, 12 January.

New York Times (2005a) 'A new attack on women's sports,' Editorial, 12 April.

New York Times (2005b) 'Taking the prostitution pledge,' Editorial, 2 July.

New York Times (2005c) 'Day-after pill decision prompts a resignation,' 31 August.

New York Times (2005d) 'Cronies at the till,' Editorial, 27 September.

New York Times (2005e) 'How not to get the job done,' Editorial, 1 October.

New York Times (2005f) 'M. Brown, redux,' Editorial, 31 October. www. nytimes.com/2005/10/31/opinion/31mon2.html.

New York Times (2005g) 'Strange behavior at the FDA,' Editorial, 15 November.

New York Times (2005h) 'Ignore the man behind that memo,' Editorial, 16 November.

News8 WMTW (2005) 'FEMA ice trucks still stuck in Portland; drivers: 750 more trucks on their way,' 21 September. www.wmtw.com/irresist-ible/4995340/detail.html.

Nichols, J., and R.W. McChesney (2005) 'Bush's war on the press,' *The Nation*, 18 November.

Noah, T. (2001) 'Abolish the White House Office on Race! (Whoops, they already did),' *Slate*, 8 February. www/slate.com/id/1007043.

NOW (2005) 'FDA poised to approve dangerous implants, shows disdain for women's health,' press release, 22 September. Washington DC: National Organization for Women.

NWLC (2002a) 'NWLC applauds committee's decision to reject divisive Pickering nomination,' 14 March. Washington DC: National Women's Law Center. www.nwlc.org/details/cfm?id=1057&section=newsroom.

NWLC (2002b), 'Justice Owen's record shows hostility to reproductive rights and other legal issues of importance to women,' 17 July. Washington DC: National Women's Law Center. www.nwlc.org/pdf/Owenreport2002. pdf.

NWLC (2002c) 'NWLC denounces Senate approval of McConnell Nomina-tion,' 18 November. Washington DC: National Women's Law Center. www.nwlc.org/details.cfm?id=1241&section=newsroom.

NWLC (2003) 'William Pryor's troubling record on issues of critical im-portance to women,' 10 June. Washington DC: National Women's Law Center. www.nwlc.org/pdf/PryorReport2003.pdf.

NWLC (2004a) 'Pryor recess appointment an insult to Constitution, American people,' press release, 20 February. Washington DC: National Women's Law Center. www.nwlc.org/details.cfm?id=1786&section=newsroom.

NWLC (2004b) *Slip-Sliding Away: The Erosion of Hard-won Gains for Women under the Bush administration and an Agenda for Moving Forward*, April. Washington DC: National Women's Law Center. www.nwlc.org/details.cfm?id=184 0&section=newsroom.

NWLC (2005a) 'Women and Medicaid,' January. Washington DC: National Women's Law Center. www.nwlc.org.

NWLC (2005b) 'The Federal Refusal Clause: threatens women's access to reproductive health care, tramples state sovereignty, and should be re-pealed,' factsheet, April. Washington DC: National Women's Law Center. www.nwlc.org.

NWLC (2005c) 'Social Security privatization a triple whammy for women,' news release, 10 May. Washington DC: National Women's Law Center. www.nwlc.org.

NWLC (2005d) 'Administration admits Social Security plan targets widows and children,' news room release, 12 May. Washington DC: National Women's Law Center. www.nwlc.org.

NWLC (2005e) 'The unworthy judicial nominees: wrong for women, wrong for our courts,' 12 May. Washington DC: National Women's Law Center. www.nwlc.org/details.cfm?id=2275&section=newsroom.

Orfield, G., D. Losen, J. Wald, and C. Swanson (2004) *Losing Our Future: How Minority Youth are being Left Behind by the Graduation Rate Crisis.* Cambridge MA: Civil Rights Project at Harvard University, with Advocates for Children of New York and Civil Society Institute.

Parry, R. (2005) 'Up in flames: Tons of British aid donated to help Hurricane Katrina victims to be burned by Americans,' *Daily Mirror*, 20 September.

PBS (2005) 'Katrina: The response,' *NOW*, 28 November. www.pbs.org/now/society/katrinalabor.html.

PFAW (2003) 'Judicial nominee Janice Rogers Brown – to the right of Thomas and Scalia,' press release, 21 October. Washington DC: People for the American Way.

PFAW (2004) Bush's extreme anti-choice nominee gets lifetime judgeship,' press release, 6 July. Washington DC: People for the American Way.

PFAW (2005a) 'Right wing watch, right wing organisations: federalist society for law and public policy studies,' Washington DC: People for the American Way. www.pfaw.org/pfaw/general/default.aspx?oid=3149.

PFAW (2005b) 'Heritage Foundation's principal issues,' Washington DC: People for the American Way. www.pfaw.org/pfaw/general/default.aspx?oid=4287.

PFAW (2005c) 'Right wing watch, right wing organisations: Independent Women's Forum,' Washington DC: People for the American Way. www.pfaw.org/pfaw/general/default.aspx?oid=11625#3.

PFAW (2005d) 'Under cover of Katrina, Bush advances right wing school voucher plan,' press release, 20 September. Washington DC: People for the American Way.

Physicians for a National Health Program (2005) 'Physician group decries 859,000 rise in uninsured; Medicaid ranks swell by 1.9 million as poverty rises and private coverage drops,' press release, 1 September. www.commondreams.org/cgi-bin/newsprint.cgi?file=/news2005/0901–05htm.

Pickler, N. (2005) 'US gov't launches massive relief effort,' ABC News, 1 September. http://abcnews.go.com/Politics/wireStory?id=1086649&page=2.

Piven, F.F. (2004) *The War at Home*. New York: W.W. Norton.

Pleming, S. (2003) 'Iraqi women no better off, U.N. official says,' Reuters, 24 September. www.commondreams.org/cgi-bin/print.cgi?file=headlines 03/0924–03.htm.

Population Action International (2005) 'Fact sheet on how the global gag rule undermines US foreign policy & harms women's health,' 2 August. www.populationinaction.org/resources/factsheets/factsheet_5.htm.

Population Action International (2006) *Access Denied: The Impacts of the Global*

Gag Rule in Zambia. www.globalgagrule.org/pdfs/case_studies/GGRcase_Zambia_2006.pdf.

Population Connection (2003) 'Effects of the Global Gag Rule,' Washington DC. www.populationconnection.org/reports_publications/reports/report368.html.

Power, S. (2002) *A Problem from Hell: America and the Age of Genocide*. New York: Basic Books.

Pozner, J. (2001) 'Bush dupes media with abortion disinformation,' *Alternet*, 29 May. www.alternet.org/story?html?storyID=10939.

PPFA (2003a) 'Bush administration to broaden harmful restrictions on international health programs,' 20 February. New York: Planned Parenthood Federation of America. www.plannedparenthood.org/about/pr/030220_AIDSgag.html.

PPFA (2003b) 'The Bush administration, the global gag rule, and HIV/AIDS Funding,' June. New York: Planned Parenthood Federation of America. www.plannedparenthood.org.

PPFA (2004a) *A Planned Parenthood Report on the Administration and Congress*. New York: Planned Parenthood Federation of America. www.plannedparenthood.org.

PPFA (2004b) 'Re-appointment of Dr. David Hager to FDA committee is bad medicine; anti-choice ideologue compromises FDA's credibility,' *US Newswire*, 28 June.

Rampton, S., and J. Stauber (2004) *Banana Republicans: How the Right Wing is Turning America into a One-Party State*. New York: Tarcher/Penguin.

Reuters (2005) 'Canadians beat U.S. Army to New Orleans suburb,' 8 September.

Revkin, A.K., and K.Q. Seelye (2003) 'Report by the E.P.A. leaves out data on climate change,' *New York Times*, 19 June.

Rockwell, P. (2005) 'New revelations about racism in the military – Army reservist witnesses war crimes,' *The Black Commentator* 133, 7 April.

Rodgers, P. (2001) 'Court gives ex-comfort women symbolical victory,' *Women's eNews*, 7 December. www.womensenews.org.

Roig-Franzia, M., and S. Hsu (2005) 'Many evacuated, but thousands still waiting,' *Washington Post*, 4 September, p. A1.

Salt of the Earth (2002) 'Save the Children looks at the state of the world's mothers,' http://salt.claretianpubs.org/stats/2002/06/sho206.html.

San Francisco Chronicle (2003) 'Gays shocked at Bush choice for AIDS panel; appointee calls homosexuality a 'deathstyle,' 23 January.

Santelli, J. (2005) Letter to Rep. H. Waxman from John Santelli, 1 May. www.democrats.reform.house.giv/Documents/20050713100920–75578.pdf.

Sapiro, V. (2003) *Women in American Society*. New York: McGraw-Hill.

Schulman, J., and R. Schweber-Koren (2005) 'Eight big lies about Katrina,' Media Matters for America, 9 September. www.alternet.org/story/25227/.

Scott, C. (2004) 'Amid death, a model for hope,' *Acumen*, 2(1), summarized in Management Sciences for Health news release, 25 January. www.msh.org/news_room/news_releases/25jan04.html.

Segal, J. (2000) 'Representative decision making on the federal bench: Clinton's District Court appointees,' *Political Research Quarterly* 53(1), March, pp. 137–50.

Sen, R. (2005) 'The inequality president,' *TomPaine.commonsense*, 14 September. www.tompaine.com/articles/2005/09/14/the_inequality_president.php.

Seper, J. (2004) 'Federal employees file rights complaint,' *Washington Times*, 4 March.

Sherman, E. (2003) 'The family-unfriendly administration,' 19 February. www.tompaine.com/Archive/scontent/7267.html.

SIECUS (1996–2005) 'SIECUS reviews fear-based, abstinence-only-until-marriage curricula,' www.SIECUS.org/reviews.html.

SIECUS (2004) 'A brief explanation of federal abstinence-only-until-marriage funding,' www.siecus.org/policy/states/2004/explanation.html.

SIECUS (2005a) 'Claude Allen appointed to serve as Bush's domestic policy advisor in the White House,' policy update, January. www.siecus.org/policy/pupdates/pdate0150.html.

SIECUS (2005b) 'Take action: New HHS website misinforms parents,' Sexual Information and Education Clearinghouse, Families Are Talking, at www.familiesaretalking.org/hhs_letter.htm.

Sipress, A. (2005) 'Hughes misreports Iraqi history,' *Washington Post*, 22 October, p. A15.

Sizemore, B. (2003) 'Pat Robertson's right-wing gold mine,' *Ms. Magazine*, Fall.

Social Security Administration, 'Brief History,' www.ssa.gov/history/briefhistory3.html.

Soetjipto, T. (2005) 'Indonesians challenge US envoy in lively exchange,' Reuters, 21 October.

Sojourners (2004) 'Study finds abortion rising under Bush, linked to economic policies,' press release, *Sojourners*, 13 October. www.sojo.net/index.cfm?action=news.display_archives&mode=press_release&article=PR_041013.

Soraghan, M. (2003) 'Some fear AFA inquiry bias panel leader fought coed training; backers say she supports women,' *Denver Post*, 2 June, p. B01.

SourceWatch (2005) 'Nancy Pfotenhauer,' www.sourcewatch.org/index.php?title=Nancy_Pfotenhauer, accessed 10 September.

Stapp, K. (2005) 'U.S. women under siege, at home and abroad,' Inter Press Service, 10 September. http://commondreams.org/cgi-bin/print.cgi?file=/headlines05/0910–03.htm.

Stearns, M. (2004) 'Controversial pick for civil rights post,' *Seattle Times*, 8 December, p. A6.

Stevens, A. (2003) 'Bush extends global gag rule to AIDS funds,' *Women's eNews*, 25 February. www.womensenews.org.

Stevens, A. (2005a) 'Women's groups ready for budget fight,' *Women's eNews*, 17 February. www.womensenews.org.

Stevens, A. (2005b) 'U.S. engages in a tug-of-war at Beijing Plus 10,' *Women's eNews*, 7 March. http://womensenews.org.

Stockman, F. (2005) 'US sends mixed signals on accepting aid from abroad,' *Boston Globe*, 2 September.

Sullivan, T., T.E. Warren, and J.L. Westbrook (1999) *As We Forgive Our Debtors: Bankruptcy and Consumer Law in America* [1989]. Washington DC: Beard Books.

Susskind, R. (2004) *The Price of Loyalty: George Bush, the White House, and the Education of Paul O'Neill*. New York: Simon & Schuster.

Susskind, Y. (2005a) 'Gutting the World Summit: Bush betrays poor women again,' *Common Dreams*, 10 September. www.commondreams.org/views05/0910–20.htm.

Susskind, Y. (2005b) 'A reality check on Bush's speech to the U.N. World Summit,' *Common Dreams*, 16 September. www.commondreams.org/cgi-bin/print.cgi?file=/views05/0916–29.htm.

Sydney Morning Herald (2005) 'Comfort women miss chance to sue Japan,' 29 June.

Taylor, S.S. (2001) 'Heated debate on welfare may focus on marriage,' *Women's eNews*, 3 May. www.womensenews.org.

Taylor, S.S. (2001) 'Plan to close working women's offices draws fire,' *Women's eNews*, 20 December. www.womensenews.org.

Teepen, T. (2003) 'Bush to women: tough nuggies,' Cox News Service, 17 March.

Tessier, M. (2001) 'Women's appointments plummet under Bush,' *Women's eNews*, 1 July, revised 1 October, www.womensenews.org/article-cfm/dyn/aid/600/context/archive.

Tessier, M. (2002) 'Bush appointments include fewer women,' 11 February. www.womensenews.org.

Thomas, E. (2005) 'How Bush blew it,' *Newsweek*, 19 September. www.msnbc.msn.com/id/9287434.

Thomma, S. (2005) 'Social Security overhaul is long-standing conservative dream,' *Knight-Ridder*, 5 February. www.commondreams.org/headlines05/0205-05.htm.

Tiefer, C. (2004) *Veering Right: How the Bush Administration Subverts the Law for Conservative Causes*. Berkeley: University of California Press.

Tierney, J. (2002) 'Tierney wants funds restored for Equal Pay Initiative, protests elimination of DOL program that bridges wage gap for women,' press release, 22 March. www.house.gov/tierney/press/equalpay032202.shtml.

Tobias, S. (1997) *Faces of Feminism*. Denver CO: Westview.

Towarnicky, C. (2004) 'On women's issues, Bush is going backward,' *Philadelphia Daily News*, 28 October.

Townsend, M. (2005) 'You're on your own, Britain's victims told,' *Observer* (London), 4 September.

Tristam, P. (2005) 'Manipulative math on Social Security,' *Daytona Beach News Journal*, 8 February.

UCS (2004a) 'Scientific integrity in policymaking: an investigation into the Bush administration's misuse of science,' February. www.ucsusa.org/global_environment/rsi/page.cfm?pageID=1355.

UCS (2004b) 'Scientific integrity in policymaking: further investigation of the Bush administration's misuse of science,' July. www.ucsusa.org/global_environment/rsi/page.cfm?pageID=1642.

UCS (2004c), 'Restoring scientific integrity in policymaking,' www.ucsusa.org/global_environment/rsi/page.cfm?pageID=1320.

UN News Centre (2004) 'Countries of the Americas, except U.S., reaffirm reproductive health accord-UN,' 12 March. http://un.org/apps/news/story.asp?Newsid=10054&cr=hiv&crl=aids.

UNESCO (1995) 'Platform for Action,' 15 September. www.unesco.org/education/information/nfsunesco/pdf/beijin_e.pdf.

UNESCO (2006) 'What it is and what it does,' http://portal.unesco.org/en/ev.php-url_id=3328&url_do=do_topic&url_section+201.html, accessed 9 March.

UNIFEM (2004) *CEDAW Made Easy*. Christ Church, Barbados: Caribbean Office, United Nations Development Fund for Women.

United Food and Commercial Workers (2005) 'Bush administration offers unenforceable ergonomics for nursing homes,' *Workplace Connections*. www.ufcw.org/workplace_connections/health_care/workplace_issues/ergo_guidelines.cfm.

USA Today (2005) 'Drapes removed from Justice Department statue,' 24 June.

US Census Bureau (2004) Table 1: 'Annual estimates of the population by sex and five-year age groups for the United States: April 1, 2000 to July 1, 2004', NC-EST2004–01.

US Census Bureau (2005) 'Percentage of families and people whose income in the past 12 months is below poverty level,' 2004 *American Community Survey*, September.

US Commission on Civil Rights (2004) *Redefining Rights in America: The Civil Rights Record of the George W. Bush Administration*, draft report for commissioners' review, September. http://jurist.law.pitt.edu/bushcivilrights.pdf.

US Commission on Civil Rights (2005) 'Gerald A. Reynolds,' Washington DC. www.usccr.gov/cos/bio/reynolds.htm.

US Department of Education (2001) 'Revised sexual harassment guidance: harassment of students by school employees, other students, or third parties, notice of availability,' *Federal Register* 66(14), 19 January.

US Department of Education (2005) 'Additional clarification of intercollegiate athletics policy: three-part test – part three,' 17 March. Washington DC: Office of Civil Rights.

US Department of Health and Human Services (2003) 'Secretary Thompson helps open women's hospital in Kabul,' press release, 21 April. www.usembassy.it/file2003_04/alia/A3041803.htm.

US Department of State (2003) 'International Women's Issues,' www.state.gov/g/wi, accessed 18 June 2003.

US Department of State (2004) 'Grants to support democratization training for women,' statement by Secretary Colin L. Powell, Washington, 27 September. www.state.gov/secretary/former/powell/remarks/36496.htm.

US Department of State (2006) Office of International Women's Issues. www.state.gov/g/wi/, accessed 9 March.

US Newswire (2004) 'PPFA: Reappointment of Dr David Hager to FDA committee is bad medicine; anti-choice ideologue compromises FDA its credibility,' 28 June.

US Office of Special Counsel (2005) 'The Honorable Scott J. Bloch,' www.osc.gov/specialcounsel.htm.

Vallely, P. (2005) 'UN hits back at US in report saying parts of America are poor as Third World,' *Independent*, 8 September.

VandeHei, J. (2004) 'Pipeline to the president for GOP conservatives: give and take flows through Public Liaison,' *Washington Post*, 24 December, p. A15.

VandeHei, J. (2005) 'Group defends Roberts' rights record: conservatives answer critics who point to Reagan-era remarks,' *Washington Post*, 25 August, p. A3.

Vanden Heuval, K. (2003) 'Bush's assaults on women,' *The Nation*, 7 October.

Viner, K. (2002) 'Feminism as imperialism: George Bush is not the first empire-builder to wage war in the name of women,' *Guardian*, 21 September.

Walker, A. (2005) 'Bush abandons Iraqi women,' TomPaine.com, 26 August. www.tompaine.com/articles/20050826/bush_abandons_iraqi_women.php.

Wallis, J. (2005) 'Immorality of the Bush Budget,' 9 March, www.alternet.org.

Walter, N. (2004) 'The winners are warlords, not women,' *Guardian*, 12 October.

Warren, E. (2005) 'Bankruptcy: the new women's issue,' *Around the Kitchen Table*, March. www.demos.org/pub465.cfm.

Washington, W. (2004) 'Bush touts support for women's rights,' *Boston Globe*, 13 March.

Washington Post (2001) 'Bush signs repeal of ergonomic rules,' 21 March.

Washington Post (2005a) 'Memo may have swayed Plan B ruling; FDA received "Minority Report" from conservative doctor on panel,' 12 May, p. A02.

Washington Post (2005b) 'Politicizing the FDA,' Editorial, 30 August, p. A16.

Washington Post (2005c) 'Rice unable to attend N.Y. dinner with female peers,' 18 September, p. A04.

Waxman, H.A. (2004) 'The content of federally funded abstinence-only education programs,' 1 December. www.democrats.reform.house.gov/documents/20041201102153-50247.pdf.

Waxman, H.A. (2005) Reviews of 4Parents website, www.democrats.reform.house.gov/story.asp?ID=888.

Waxman, H.A., and L.M. Slaughter (2005a) 'The administration's distortion of stem cell science,' May. www.democrats.reform.house.gov/investigations.asp?Issue=Politics+and+Science.

Waxman, H.A., and L.M. Slaughter (2005b) 'Fact sheet: the politicization of emergency contraception,' www.democrats.reform.house.gov/investigations.asp?Issue=Politics+and+Science.

Weiburg, S. (2001) 'Bush's pick to enforce Title IX raises concerns,' *USA Today*, 27 September.

Weisbrot, M. (2005) 'Social Security deception funded with tax payers' dollars,' 18 January, www.commondreams.org.

Weiser, I. (2004) 'One hundred twelve women assaulted in Iraq, Afghanistan,' 18 May. www.commondreams.org/cgi-bin/print.cgi?file=/views04/0518-06.htm.

Weisman, J., and G. Witte (2005) 'Katrina contracts will be reopened,' *Washington Post*, 7 October.

Weiss, R. (2002) 'New status for embryos in research,' *Washington Post*, 30 October, p. A1.

Weller, R. (2003) 'Task force opens meeting in to sex scandal at the Air Force Academy,' Associated Press, 23 June.

White House (2003) *Protecting the Civil Rights and Religious Liberty of Faith-Based Organizations: Why Religious Hiring Rights Must be Preserved*. Executive Summary, White House Faith Based and Community Initiatives. Washington. www.whitehouse.gov/government/fbci/booklet.pdf.

White House (2005a) 'Judge Priscilla Owen,' Washington, 25 May. www.whitehouse.gov/infocus/judicialnominees/owen.html.

White House (2005b) 'Press briefing by Scott McClellan,' Washington, 26 May. www.whitehouse.gov/news/releases/2005/05/20050526-1.html.

White House (2005c) 'Press briefing by Scott McClellan,' 18 June. www.whitehouse.gov/news/releases/2005/07/20050718-2.html.

WHRNet (2005) 'Challenging abortion law in Colombia: an interview with Monica Roa,' Association for Women's Rights in Development, July. www.whrnet.org/docs/interview-roa-0507.html.

Williams, K. (2005) *Love My Rifle More Than You*. New York: W.W. Norton.

Witte, G. (2005) 'Halliburton contract critic loses her job: performance review cited in removal,' *Washington Post*, 29 August, p. A11.

Wokusch, H. (2004) 'We just don't talk anymore: Bush's communication problem with women,' 25 June. www.commondreams.org.

WomenWatch (2005) 'State parties,' UN Inter-agency Network on Gender Equality, *Women Watch*, www.un.org/womenwatch/daw/cedaw/states.htm.

Women's eNews (2001) 'Bush gives Taliban $10 million to fight Opium,' 26 May. www.womensenews.org.

Women's eNews (2002) 'Two against gender violence law named to its board,' 14 September. www.womensenews.org.

Women's Policy (2005) 'Budget briefing papers, 2006,' www.womenspolicy.org.

Zunes, S. (2005) 'Arrogance in the face of disaster,' *Common Dreams*, 5 October. www.commondreams.org/views05/1005-24.htm.

INDEX